M000100194

OLD TALES
OF
SAN FRANCISCO

Second Edition

Arthur Chandler

San Francisco State University
San Francisco, California

KENDALL/HUNT PUBLISHING COMPANY
4050 Westmark Drive   Dubuque, Iowa 52002

Dared I but say a prophecy.
As sung the holy men of old.
Of rock-built cities yet to be
Along these shining shores of gold.
Crowding athirst into the sea.
What wondrous marvels might be told!
Enough to know that Empire here
Shall burn her loftiest, brightest star.

—Poet of the Sierras

Copyright © 1977, 1987 by Kendall/Hunt Publishing Company

Library of Congress Catalog Card Number: 87–81249

ISBN 0–8403–4385–X

Printed in the United States of America
20 19 18 17 16 15 14 13

Contents

List of Illustrations   v
Preface   vii
Acknowledgments   ix

PART ONE: From the Founding to the Gold Rush

I. Introduction   3
II. From *The Diary of Father Santa Maria*   5
III. From *A Voyage of Discovery* by Otto von Kotzebue   17
IV. From the Diaries of Chamisso and Choris   25
V. From *Two Years Before the Mast* by Richard Henry Dana   39
VI. From *Reminiscences and Incidents of "The Early Days" of
San Francisco* by John Henry Brown   47
VII. From "Filings from an Old Saw" by Joseph Downey   53
VIII. Selections from the *California Star*   63

**PART TWO: From the Gold Rush to the Completion of the
Transcontinental Railroad**

I. Introduction   73
II. From *The Annals of San Francisco* by Frank Soulé, John
Nesbit and John Gihon   75
III. From *Reminiscences and Incidents of "The Early Days" of
San Francisco* by John Henry Brown   85
IV. From *California Adventure* by Vincente Pérez Rosales   93
V. From *Last Adventure* by Albert Bernard de Russailh   101
VI. From *El Dorado, Or Adventures in the Path of Empire* by
Bayard Taylor   111
VII. From *Pen-Knife Sketches, or Chips of the Old Block* by Alonzo
Delano   131
VIII. From *Prentice Mulford's Story* by Prentice Mulford   139
IX. From *The Dame Shirley Letters* by Louise Clappe   145

X. "The Luck of Roaring Camp," "To the Cliff House," and "San Francisco from the Sea" by Bret Harte   155

XI. Five Sketches by Mark Twain: "The Pioneer's Ball," "The Great Prize Fight," and "Early Rising," "The Great Quake of '65," and "Earthquake Almanac"   169

XII. Six Proclamations by Emperor Norton   185

PART THREE: From the Railroad to the Earthquake

  I. Introduction   197

  II. "California" by Ina Coolbrith   201

  III. "The Man and the Snake" and "Prattle" by Ambrose Bierce   207

  IV. From *American Notes* by Rudyard Kipling, "Rudyard Kipling at the Golden Gate"   215

  V. "A Raid on the Oyster Pirates" by Jack London   221

  VI. From "Polk Street," "The Passing of Little Pete," and "Among Cliff Dwellers" by Frank Norris   231

  VII. From "Lights and Shades of San Francisco" by B. E. Lloyd   243

  VIII. From "Love Sonnets of a Hoodlum" by Wallace Irwin   253

  IX. "The Bohemians," "Ballad of the Hyde Street Grip," and "Architectural Shams" by Gelett Burgess   259

  X. "The Cool, Grey City of Love" and "A Wine of Wizardry" by George Sterling   273

  XI. Earthquake Writing:

"The Damndest Finest Ruins" by Lawrence W. Harris   281

"Barriers Burned" by Charles K. Field   282

"Earthquake and Fire" from *As I Remember* by Arnold Genthe   284

Bibliography   293

List of Illustrations

1. San Francisco in 1846–47 — 46
2. "Perils of the Wilderness" — 70
3. Departure of a Steamship — 81
4. Chinese Miners Panning for Gold — 99
5. A Dive on the Barbary Coast — 110
6. A Water Carrier — 133
7. Portsmouth Plaza in the 1850's — 136
8. Sharpshooters of the Vigilance Committee, 1856 — 141
9. Bret Harte — 153
10. The First Cliff House — 167
11. Sutro's Cliff House — 168
12. Emperor Norton — 191
13. The Hopkins and Stanford Mansions on Nob Hill — 193
14. Union Square — 206
15. The Palace Hotel — 214
16. Jack London — 220
17. Frank Norris — 230
18. Market Street, about 1900 — 258
19. George Sterling — 272
20. Bohemians and Writers — 280
21. Ruins of a Trolley Car — 282
22. Cable Car Tracks — 283
23. Mayor Schmitz Inspecting the Ruins, 1906 — 292

Preface

Old Tales of San Francisco gathers together some of the best writing from and about the City of Saint Francis from the last decades of the 18th through the first years of the 20th century. San Francisco's literary heritage is rich, but elusive and scattered. Much of the highest quality and most revealing writing about San Francisco is out of print, buried in long-forgotten journals and books, or else available only in expensive, limited edition reprints. What this book contains is only a sampling of the abundant treasures that lie buried in books, papers, and microfilms of San Francisco's libraries. If you enjoy what you find here, and are led to search out and read works like Father María's diary, Bayard Taylor's *El Dorado,* or Gelett Burgess' *The Heart Line,* then *Old Tales of San Francisco* has done its job.

The material in this book is divided into three main historical areas: 1775–1848 (founding years to the gold rush), 1849–1869 (gold rush to the completion of the transcontinental railroad), and 1870–1906 (railroad to the fire and earthquake of 1906). To help the reader envision the context of the works, each section begins with a brief historical sketch of San Francisco during the years when the works appeared. Each author's work or works is then introduced by a modest preface that should give each selection a biographical context.

Acknowledgments

I want to thank the Bancroft Library for the use of their inexhaustible resources. I also wish to acknowledge a long overdue debt of gratitude to my colleagues in the Humanities Department of San Francisco State University, and especially to Al Fine, Matt Evans, Stan Andersen, and Roger Birt, Marvin Nathan, and Richard Sammons. It has been our work together on San Francisco that played a decisive role in bringing this book to light. And finally, to my wife Jeanie, who read, criticized, and typed the whole manuscript for this book: love, and many, many thanks.

For permission to reprint the Emperor Norton photo and edict on page 191, I thank the California Historical Society and the Imperial Gallery.

Grateful acknowledgment is also given to the various publishers for permission to reprint from their books.

PART ONE

From the Founding
to the Gold Rush

Introduction

In the beginning the whole earth lay submerged beneath the ocean. Only Mount Diablo reared up over the waters, and on the mountaintop lived the eagle, the hummingbird and the coyote. As the waters subsided, this trinity created all living things. The most holy of their creation were the sun and the redwood tree. This is the legend of the Ohlone Indians who dwelled on the beaches and by the estuaries of the Bay before the manifest destiny of Western European culture overspread San Francisco.

The "Coastanoans" (as the Spanish called the Ohlones) moved in a world alive with spirits—good, evil, and mischievous—and they thrived together for untold centuries before the Spanish penetrated the land and waters of the Bay in 1775. Within a hundred years after the Spanish settled in what was to become San Francisco, the entire culture of the Bay Area Indians was obliterated.

The conquering Spaniards concentrated on securing a firm foothold in Central and South America, while gradually advancing their forces up the west coast of North America. Their approach to settling the San Francisco Bay was an instance of their standard procedure. First, they established a military base (the Presidio) and a mission (Mission Dolores). If these twin outposts survived and thrived, they would become the core of a *pueblo*, which essentially meant a permanent, self-sustaining village outpost under home rule from Spain. Ideally, the military, religious, and economic populations would form a unity that would bind their lives to the new land, and their loyalties to the mother country.

This ingenious imperialism worked with only indifferent success in San Francisco. The land at the tip of the peninsula was quite unsuited to agriculture without extensive preparation. Food-raising immigrants, therefore, naturally gravitated south to the Santa Clara region, or inland east and north. Furthermore, once Mission Dolores and the Presidio were established, the central government, first of Spain and then of Mexico, neglected the insignificant community of Yerba Buena (as San Francisco was called until 1846) and devoted their attention to more pressing problems geographically closer to home. What leadership there was in Alta California centered in Monterey, not Yerba Buena.

So lethargic was the development of the Bay area that it was more than 50 years after the founding of Mission Dolores and the Presidio that Yerba Buena finally achieved *pueblo* status. Spanish and Mexican policy was xenophobic from the very outset, and with good reason: virtually every trading or exploring vessel, whether from the United States, Russia, or England, was a threat to the security and stasis of the Spanish colonies. Eventually, of course, the actions of the United States justified the paranoia of Spanish officials to the fullest. As Governor Pio Pico noted ruefully just before the United States annexed California:

> We find ourselves threatened by hordes of Yankee emigrants . . . whose progress we cannot arrest. Already have the wagons of that perfidious people scaled the almost inaccessible summits of the Sierra Nevada, crossed the entire continent, and penetrated the fruitful valley of the Sacramento. . . . Already they are cultivating farms, establishing vineyards, erecting mills, sawing lumber, and doing a thousand other things which seem natural to them.[1]

As Franklin Walker has aptly summed up the first phase in the European life of San Francisco: "The Spaniards in California had not developed a frontier; they had merely held it for fear someone else would get it."[2]

But in truth, a perceptible change had come over the life of little Yerba Buena a good decade before the Americans took over. The inchoate beginning of commerce drew in ships from the Pacific, and marketable wares from the interior. Poised at the center of this seedling capitalism was William Richardson, jack-of-all-trades from England, who had traded his Protestantism for the Commandante's daughter and the rights to establish San Francisco's first port to interior trading enterprise. Within the decade preceding the American takeover in 1846, the "perfidious people" dominated San Francisco, both in numbers and in the total energy of their enterprises. Fremont's seizure of the city only confirmed the existing state of affairs. From then onwards, San Francisco would benefit and suffer from the tutelage and control of the United States.

This, then, is the historical background to the selections in the first part of *Old Tales of San Francisco*. From the earliest exploits of explorers and missionaries, down to the years just before the Gold Rush, the outward history of San Francisco presents a picture of a quiet, isolated outpost of Spanish-American civilization. But in the writing of those who lived through that history, we can find two very distinct viewpoints towards the City and its inhabitants. There were those men, like Father Maria, Kotzebue, Chamisso, Choris, and Dana, who came to San Francisco as transients. None of them planned to live here; and as a consequence their remarks all have the quality of an observant and even predatory detachment. Their respective attitudes towards the inhabitants of the area—Indian, Spanish, or Mexican—rarely reach beyond the gamut of pity, condescension, and contempt.

The second group of writers—Brown, Downey, and the journalists for the *California Star*—lived in San Francisco. They saw her characters with a more tolerant eye; and even when they discover faults or absurdity, the early local writers rarely descend to the level of malice indulged in by the visitors. It is this quality of *belonging* that makes the first group of writers part of the history of the development of the Bay Area, and the second group integral chapters in the biography of the City of Saint Francis.

---

1. Quoted in Harold Kirker's *California's Architectural Frontier* (Santa Barbara: Peregrine Smith, 1973), p. 25.
2. *San Francisco's Literary Frontier* (New York: Alfred Knopf, 1943), p. 17.

II

From *The Diary of Father Santa María*

The extensive selection from Father Vicente Santa María's account of his visit to San Francisco Bay is here for two reasons: it tells us something of the aboriginal inhabitants of the area, and it reveals even more about the character of the Spanish missionaries who, along with the soldiers at the Presidio, were the germinating seeds of San Francisco's Spanish culture. Father María served for a time at the Mission Dolores, but was soon transferred by Junípero Serra, who intimated that Father María "is not exactly one for being kept in hand." His removal was unfortunate, since Father María was one of the rare few Spaniards who bothered to learn the Indian's language.

The diary gives us a clear look into the heart of Father María. Though he felt a civilized Christian's superiority to the savage heathen, he genuinely liked, and occasionally even admired, the quick intelligence of the Indians. Father María was one of the first, and one of the last, Europeans to feel anything like a kindred humanity with Native Americans.

A Visit I Made to the Indians

Rash, seemingly, was what I did with five sailors and the surgeon on the afternoon of the 9th of August: we decided to go as far as an Indian ranchería that was about a league from the shore and with a poor approach. We were sustained only by our Catholic faith, and were impelled by godly zeal lest our gains be lost. It so happened that the Indians had assembled with their usual daily present, but we could not go over to get it because the dugout, inadequate though it was as a conveyance, was not available, being in immediate need of repair. About midday, twelve Indians appeared with the new supply. Though they called repeatedly to us, it was not feasible for us to respond to them; we lacked the means, since the longboat had not yet returned from its first (extended) expedition. Tired, at last, of pressing us and seeing that we did not comply with their requests, they all began putting on a dance. When they were done, they returned to calling us over to where they were waiting for us; and then, as we could not give them that pleasure for want of a boat, they went away as if with hurt feelings, showing by the

From J. Galvin, ed. *The First Spanish Entry into San Francisco Bay, 1775.* San Francisco: John Howell-Books, 1971.

speed of their departure that they had begun to feel worried at so decided a change in our behaviour.

When we had about given up hope of satisfying our Indians, the longboat returned to the ship with the sailing master, José Cañizares. Day and night he had gone exploring what parts of the harbour he could. This time he had come upon the real circular bay, satisfying himself that it was not the one earlier conjectured; and of this bay, as of what else he had explored, he brought some rough drafts of maps. This would have been about a quarter past 6 o'clock in the evening, and the captain, as a mark of kindness, asked if I should like to take a walk along the shore. The surgeon and I accepted the favour, and setting out in the longboat we went ashore without delay. We were mindful that the Indians might have gone away offended; so, like the hunter fearless of dangers, who leaps over the rough places and forces his way through obstacles until he meets his quarry, we went up the slopes, taking chances, hunting for our Indians until we should find them. In pursuing this venture we did not share our intentions with the captain because, if we had, from that moment he would have had nothing to do with it in view of the risks involved in our desire to visit the ranchería at so unseasonable a time and in so remote a place. Notwithstanding all this, and even though we had no notion of how soon we might reach the Indians, we were nevertheless making our way by their very path. As night was now approaching, we were considering a return to the ship, and were of two minds about it, when we caught sight of the Indians. At the same time seeing us, they began inviting us with repeated gestures and loud cries to their ranchería, which was at the shore of a rather large round cove.

Although we might on that occasion have succumbed to dread, we summoned our courage because we had to, lest fear make cowards of us. We thought that if we turned back and for a second time did not heed the call of the Indians, this might confirm them in their resentment or make them believe that we were very timid—not an agreeable idea, for many reasons. As none of those who came along declined to follow me, ignoring our weariness we went on toward the ranchería. As soon as the Indians saw that we were near their huts, all the men stood forward as if in defense of their women and children, whom undoubtedly they regard as their treasure and their heart's core. They may have thought, though not expressing this openly to us, that we might do their dear ones harm; if so, their action was most praiseworthy.

We were now almost at the ranchería. As we were going to be there a while, an Indian hustled up some clean herbage for us to sit on, made with it a modest carpet, and had us sit on it. The Indians sat on the bare ground, thus giving us to understand in some degree how guests should be received. They then made quite clear to us how astonished they had been that we had not joined them at the shore; but we succeeded in giving them some reassurances. When I saw there was so large a gathering, I began to speak to them for a short time though I knew they could not understand me unless God should work a miracle. All the time that I was speaking, these Indians, silent and attentive, were as if actually comprehending, showing by their faces much satisfaction and joy. When I had finished speaking, I said to those who had come with me that we should sing the "Alabado." When we had got as far as the words "Pura Concepción," there was a great hubbub among the Indians, for some of them had come with two kinds of hot atole and some pinoles, and they gave all their attention to urging our participation in the feast. So our chorus stopped singing and we gave the Indians the pleasure they wished, which was that we should eat. After the sailors had finished with the supper that our hosts had brought, I called to the Indian who seemed to me the head man of the ranchería and, taking his hand, began to move it in the sign of the cross, and he, without resisting, began repeating my words with so great clearness that I stood amazed and so did those who were with me.

One of the sailors had brought a piece of chocolate. He gave some of it to an Indian who, finding it sweet, made signs that he would go get something of similar flavor. He did so, bring back to him a small tamale that has a fairly sweet taste and is made from a seed resembling *polilla*. We gave the Indians, as usual, some glass beads, and received their thanks; and as they saw that the moon was rising they made signs to us to withdraw which we then did.

Because there was not much daylight when we got to the ranchería, we couldn't take note of the appearance and the features of the Indian women, who were at some distance from us; but it was clear that they wore the pelts of otters and deer, which are plentiful in this region. There were a number of small children about. Many of the Indian men we had seen at other times, including some of the leaders, were not present. We headed back for the ship, and as we reached the shore we came upon the usual present, which the disquieted Indians had left in the morning. After having made them this visit, we were without sight of the Indians for four days, that is, until the 13th of August.

On that day the captain, the second sailing master, the surgeon, and I, with some sailors, went ashore. Three Indians who had been sitting for some time at the top of a slope that came down to the shore, as soon as they saw us landed, fled from our presence to the crest of the ridge without pausing in their flight to heed our friendly and repeated calls.

Accompanied by a sailor, I tried to follow them in order to pacify them with the usual gifts and to find out what it was that troubled them. With some effort we got to the top of the ridge and found there three other Indians, making six in all. Three of them were armed with bows and very sharp-tipped flint arrows. Although at first they refused to join us, nevertheless, when we had called to them and made signs of good will and friendly regard, they gradually came near. I desired them to sit down, that I might have the brief pleasure of handing out to them the glass beads and other little gifts I had had the foresight to carry in my sleeves. Throughout this interval they were in a happy frame of mind and made me hang in their ears, which they had pierced, the strings of glass beads that I had divided among them. When I had given them this pleasure, I took it into my head to pull out my snuffbox and take a pinch but the moment the eldest of the Indians saw me open the box he took fright and showed that he was upset. In spite of all my efforts I couldn't calm him. He fled along the trail, and so did his companions, leaving us alone on the ridge; for which reason we went back to the shore. As the place where we were anchored would not in any case be a good one for the ship, on account of the strong currents, today the captain decided to go to an island that we called Santa Maria de los Angeles. This was done, and when the ship was anchored again we went ashore to reconnoiter the island terrain.

With one sailor along, I was foremost in making a diversion of this duty, in hopes of coming upon Indians. All afternoon of the 14th I wore myself out at it. On the pitch of a hill slope I discovered two huts, certainly Indian lodgings though deserted. I went near them, and seeing them unoccupied I was minded to take the path to a spring of fresh water, to quench a burning thirst brought on as much by the great seasonal heat as by the hard work of climbing up and down such rugged high hills. In a short while I came to a large rock with a cleft in the middle of it, in which rested three remarkable droll objects, and I was led to wonder if they were likenesses of some idol that the Indians reverenced.

These were slim round shafts about a yard and half high, ornamented at the top with bunches of white feathers, and ending, to finish them off, in an arrangement of black and red-dyed feathers imitating the appearance of a sun. They even had, as their drollest adornment, pieces of the little nets with which we had seen the Indians cover their hair.

At the foot of this niche were many arrows with their tips stuck in the ground as if symbolizing abasement. This last exhibit gave me the unhappy suspicion that those bunches of feathers representing the image of the sun (which in their language they call *gismen*) must be objects of the Indians' heathenish veneration; and if this was true—as was a not unreasonable conjecture—these objects suffered a merited penalty in being thrown on the fire. After spending several days in going over other parts of the island I came upon two rancherias with no one in them. I inferred that they served as shelters to Indians when they came there to hunt deer, which are the most numerous animals on the island.

On the 15th of August the longboat set out on a reconnaissance of the northern arm (of the Bay) with provisions for eight days. On returning from this expedition, which went to have a look at the rivers, José Cañizares said that in the entranceway by which the arm connects with them (Carquinez Strait) there showed themselves fifty-seven Indians of fine stature who as soon as they saw the longboat began making signs for it to come to the shore, offering with friendly gestures assurance of good will and safety. There was in authority over all these Indians one whose kingly presence marked his eminence above the rest. Our men made a landing, and when they had done so the Indian chief addressed a long speech to them. He would not permit them to sit on the bare earth; some Indians were at once sent by the *themi* (which in our language means "head man") to bring some mats cleanly and carefully woven from rushes, simple ground coverings on which the Spaniards might lie at ease. Meanwhile a supper was brought them; right away came atoles, pinoles, and cooked fishes, refreshment that quieted their pangs of hunger and tickled their palates too. The pinoles were made from a seed that left me with a taste like that of toasted hazelnuts. Two kinds of atole were supplied at this meal, one lead-coloured and the other very white, which one might think to have been made from acorns. Both were well flavoured and in no way disagreeable to a palate little accustomed to atoles. The fishes were of a kind so special that besides having not one bone they were most deliciously tasty; of very considerable size, and ornamented all the way round them by six strips of little shells. The Indians did not content themselves with feasting our men, on that day when they met together, but, when the longboat left, gave more of those fishes and we had the enjoyment of them for several days.

After the feast, and while they were having a pleasant time with the Indians, our men saw a large number of heathen approaching, all armed with bows and arrows. It was a frightening sight to those of the longboat, the Indians' advantage for an attack was so great and the resistance so slight that could be made by no more than ten men, which was all there were in the longboat's party, with barely weapons enough for defending themselves if there should be a fight. This fear obliged the sailing master to make known by signs to the Indian chieftain the misgivings they had in the presence of so many armed tribesmen. The *themi,* understanding what was meant, at once directed the Indians to loosen their bows and put up all their arrows, and they were prompt to obey. The number of Indians who had gathered together was itself alarming enough. There were more than four hundred of them, and all, or most of them, were of good height and well built. All were naked. Their hair was well done up; some wore it on top of the head, and others confined it in a small woven net such as I have already mentioned.

On this occasion, also, the Indians gave the visitors a feather rope, some bunches of feathers such as they use in headdresses, a large quantity of pinoles, and some loaves made from the same substance. Our side made a return of favours, not only giving them many glass beads, but also handing over some handkerchiefs they were wearing.

The Indians of this ranchería, unlike those of the one earlier visited, did not keep their women out of view. No sooner were signs made to the women to approach than many of them ran up, and a large number of their small children, conducting themselves toward all with the diffidence the occasion demanded. Our men stayed longer with the little Indians than with the women, feeling great commiseration for these innocents whom they could not readily help under the many difficulties that would come with the carrying out of a new and far-reaching extension of Spanish authority.

The Indians' Visit Aboard and Their Wonder
on Viewing the Structure of the Ship

Once our ship had been removed from neighbourly contact with the Indians we had first dealt with, we thought our absence might lose us that new friendship. And so it seemed, for several days passed without our seeing them again, hardly even on the hills, where on other occasions they usually appeared. We didn't think their non-appearance very important, for we supposed that the distance to the ship and the Indians' apprehensions about coming on board explained why they did not care to waste time on visits that would not gain them the object of their desires; and furthermore, this was in any case an advantage to us because, the longboat being engaged in its explorations, we were spared the distress of not being able to make visits in return for theirs.

However, their great liking for us from the time of the first visit made them forego their fears and come to see us on board at a time when we were least expecting them. It would be about 10 o'clock in the forenoon of the 23rd of August when, towards the point of the Isla de Santa María de los Angeles near which we stayed, two reed boats were seen approaching, in which were five Indians. As soon as the captain was informed of this, he directed that signs be made inviting them aboard, to which they promptly responded by coming, which was what they wanted to do. Leaving their boats, they climbed aboard quite fearlessly. They were in great delight, marvelling at the structure of the ship, their eyes fixed most of all on the rigging. They wondered no less at the lambs, hens, and pigeons that were providently kept to meet our needs if someone on board should fall sick. But what most captivated and pleased them was the sound of the ship's bell, which was purposely ordered to be struck so we could see what effect it had on ears that had never heard it. It pleased the Indians so much that while they were on board they went up to it from time to time to sound it themselves. They brought us, as on other occasions, gifts of pinoles, and they even remembered men's names that we had made known to them earlier. They brought among their party an Indian we had not seen before. Soon after receiving our greetings he went away alone in his boat, leaving in another direction than the one they had taken. We thought he had been sent by the others to bring us back a present; but when he did not return even after the others had gone away we dismissed this unworthy thought from our minds.

Throughout the time the Indians were on board we tried to attract them to Christian practices, now having them cross themselves or getting them to repeat the "Pater Noster" and "Ave Maria," now chanting the "Alabado," which they followed so distinctly that it was astonishing with what facility they pronounced the Spanish.

The Indian chieftain, less reserved than the others, showed how much pleased he was at our warmth of feeling; more than once he took to dancing and singing on the roundhouse. I paid close attention to their utterances that corresponded with their actions, and found that their language went like this; *pire* means, in our language, "Sit down"; *intomene,* "What is your name?"; *sumite,* "Give me"; and this last is used with respect to various things, as, a man on the ship having given an Indian a cigar, the Indian said, *sumite sot sintonau,* which means, "Give me a light to start it with." They call the sun *gismen,* the sky *carac.* And so on. Close on midday they took to their boats again, bidding farewell to us all and promising to be back on the morrow, and they made good their promise so effectually that at 7 o'clock the next morning they were already aboard. They had no sooner arrived than I went to meet and welcome these guests, although I did not stay with them as long as they wanted me to because I was about to say Matins and to prepare myself for celebrating the Holy Sacrament of the Mass. I made signs to them to wait for me until I should be through and those who occupied the cabin should get up; but they couldn't hold their expectations in suspense so long, for while I was at my prayers in the roundhouse the Indian chieftain, seeing that I was putting them off, began calling the surgeon by his name and saying to me, "Santa María, Vicente, Father, *ilac,*" which means "Come here"; and seeing that the surgeon did not leave his bunk, and that I did not come down, he came up to where I was reciting my prayers and, placing himself at my side on his kneecaps, began to imitate me in my manner of praying, so that I could not keep from laughing; and seeing that if the Indian should continue I would not be getting on with my duty, I made signs to him to go back down and wait for me there. He obeyed at once, but it was to set out in his boat with a chieftain, not known to us before, whom he had brought to the ship, and as if offended he left behind the daily offering of pinoles.

Word of the kindliness with which those on the ship dealt with these heathen was spread so quickly from ranchería to ranchería that it served to dispel the fears of a number of Indians not hitherto seen by us, so that they hastened to come aboard. They came, at the same time, to offer us (perhaps depriving themselves) the food of their daily sustenance. This event, which set before our eyes a new spectacle, took place that same day, the 24th of August, two and a half hours after those Indians I have just told about had gone away. These others came in two balsas and numbered about eight in all. When they were in sight close by, and we made signs to them to come to the ship, one of them, who doubtless came to the bow of his boat for the purpose, began to make a long speech, giving us to understand that it was the head man of the ranchería who came, and that he was at our service. This visit was not a casual one, for all of them appeared to have got themselves up, each as best he could, for a festive occasion. Some had adorned their heads with a tuft of red-dyed feathers, and others with a garland of them mixed with black ones. Their chests were covered with a sort of woven jacket made with ash-coloured feathers; and the rest of their bodies, though bare, was all worked over with various designs in charcoal and red ochre, presenting a droll sight.

As soon as they left their boats, it was made clear to them who it was that commanded the ship, and they endeavoured to point out their leader to us. The chieftain of the ranchería had all his men, one after another, in the order of their importance, salute our captain, and when this ceremony was completed he begged us all to sit down, as the Indians also did, for distribution among us of their offering, which they brought to us in all tidiness. All being in their places in due order, the second chieftain, who was among the company, asked of another Indian a container made of reeds that he carried with him, in which were many pats or small cakes of pinole. It was given him, and having placed it beside him he indicated that he was to be listened to. With no lack of self-composure he spoke for quite a while, and then, opening the container, handed the pinole cakes to the first chieftain, who as soon as he received them handed them to our captain, making signs to him to distribute them among all the men of the ship, insisting, moreover, that he be the first to taste the pinole. The second chieftain was now very watchful to see if by chance anyone of the ship's company had missed partaking of the bread of hospitality, he went up to the roundhouse, and several times stuck his head in the after hold; there was no limit to his painstaking inspection. After this our captain directed the steward to bring some pieces of pilot bread and gave them to the Indian head man, who distributed them with all formality among his party.

We gave them glass beads and other little gifts, which they put in their reed container. This done, I brought out a representation of our holy father St. Francis, most edifying, and upon my presenting it to the Indians to kiss they did so with so much veneration, to all appearances, and willingness, that they stole my heart and the hearts of all others who observed them. Then I had them make the sign of the cross and repeat the "Pater Noster," which they did very clearly and showing in their faces that they took pleasure in such things although lacking comprehension because the Spanish language was beyond them.

They left us about 1 o'clock in the afternoon, taking to their boats and heading toward the island contiguous to us. On it were some casks with which our supply of water aboard was in part replenished, and a board and some tools that had been taken off the ship for making certain repairs to the dugout. The Indians went ashore, and our captain, on seeing them do so, prudently entertained doubts of their trustworthiness, thinking that, if not through self-interest, at any rate from greed, they might take some of the things we had on the island. The Indians, however, were of quite another mind: as soon as they saw the dugout approach land, they all headed for it, bent on catching up with it and helping our men to run it ashore. Next after seeing that it was intended to take aboard ship the things that were on shore, the Indians, supposing that the sailors were going after wood, went to a tree that was lying at the waterside and exerted their strength prodigiously to put it aboard the dugout. Then our men came loaded down with the water casks on their shoulders, and going to meet them two of the Indians took the casks on their own backs, carried them to the dugout, and stowed them in it. They all helped to get the dugout afloat again to return to the ship.

I watched all this from the ship, and as the Indians remained seated on the shore I could not bear to lose the rest of the afternoon when I might be communicating with them; so, setting out in the dugout, I landed and remained alone with the eight Indians, so that I might communicate with them in greater peace. The dugout went back to the ship and at the same time they all crowded around me and, sitting by me, began to sing, with an accompaniment of two rattles that they had brought with them. As they finished the song all of them were shedding tears, which I wondered at for not knowing the reason. When they were through singing they handed me the rattles and by signs asked me also to sing. I took the rattles and, to please them, began to sing to them the "Alabado" (although they would not understand it), to which they were most attentive and indicated that it pleased them. I gave them some glass beads that I had had the forethought to bring with me, and they made me with my own hands hang them in their ears, which most of them had pierced. Thus I had a very pleasant afternoon until, as nightfall neared, our captain sent the dugout for my return to the ship. . . .

Soon after these Indians came to the ship there came eight others of our new friends, and at first it appeared that those of the one and the other rancheria did not look at each other with much friendliness, but our treating them all as equals made them friends and on speaking terms with one another.

We taught all of them how to cross themselves; and although those who came under Sumu's command were better disposed toward these pious observances, the Indians who came under the command of the other rancheria's head man became compliant, and all of them came to me to be instructed. Among all these Indians Mutuc is noticeably clever, so perceptive that he not only grasped at once what we said to him in Spanish, and repeated it exactly, but also, as if well versed in our language, he showed how the Spanish terms we asked about were expressed in his. On this day it came off colder than usual, and of the poor unfortunates on board those who could do so took refuge under my cloak, showing with piteous looks how keenly, being stark naked, they felt the chill. Luck, it seems, offered a sailor's long coat to Supitacse, the oldest and least forward of them all, as soon as he came on board, and he took it at once and kept himself warm in it, huddling in corners. When it was time to leave, he most considerately put the garment back where he had taken possession of it. True, the first day that Sumu's party came aboard, most of his Indians, especially Jausos and one other, were somewhat troublesome because they had a fancy for everything. Everything looked good to them and they all wanted to barter with their feathers and little nets, but once we had given them to understand that this was doing wrong they behaved quite differently thereafter, so that two who had been wandering all over the ship did not now leave my side unless they were called. This was a striking example of how tractable they were.

On the 7th of September we hoisted sail to leave this harbour, but were unable to succeed because when we were near the mouth a very strong head wind supervened so that we had to put into a cove that was very near the outlet. Our rudder hit some rocks near the cove's entrance, and this kept us in a state of anxiety because the rudder and two of its pivots were damaged. Consequently we had to stay in harbour until repairs were completed, which took until the feast of the Stigmata of St. Francis (September 17th).

In these days Indians came from another ranchería, to which on the 11th I went, accompanied by a number of heathen and a sailor and the surgeon. Our reception was such that on our approach all the Indian men and women living there came out and the *themi,* or head man, putting his arms over my shoulders, steered me to a council house in the middle of the ranchería. As soon as we reached the entrance, he made signs for me to go in first, then the surgeon and the sailor who had come with me. On going in by the small entranceway I said, "Ave Maria," whereupon five old Indians who were there said "Piré, piré," which means "Sit down, sit down." We sat down, and then all the Indians came in. After making the customary speech, I began handing out glass beads to all of them, which they received with much pleasure. While I was making this distribution, there came in three old women (who among them would sum up three hundred and fifty years), each with her little basket of pinole for us to eat; later they brought us water, which we drank. After this social affair, I set to inquiring their names and writing them down on paper. This gave them great amusement; for when I had finished, a number of them kept coming up and asking me how the names were spoken, and as I answered according to the paper they gave way to bursts of laughter. Thus we enjoyed ourselves that afternoon until we took our leave. The head man of this ranchería comported himself so politely that he came out with one arm around me and the other around the surgeon and went with us a part of the way until, taking leave of us, he went back to his ranchería and we returned to the ship, which was more than half a league distant. This is the manner in which these unfortunates have behaved toward us. What is certain is that they themselves seem to be asking a start at entering within the fold of our Catholic religion. Not to avail of this opportunity would be a lamentable misfortune. To succeed as planned would be the best fortune for all. This is the news that, for the present, comes to you from Your Reverence's most humble servant,

Fr. Vicente María

III

From *A Voyage of Discovery* by Otto von Kotzebue

Otto von Kotzebue, a shrewd, imperious adventurer, entered San Francisco Bay in 1816 to reconnoiter for Russia, which was sizing up the prospects for colonization and trade in northern California. In his writing we can feel the contempt of the civilized Western adventurer for both the Spanish conquerors (excepting the Presidio horsemen) and the vanquished, converted Indian. Von Kotzebue also describes the *Californios'* notorious bull and bear fights which, according to another early visitor to San Francisco, "were the everlasting topic of conversation with the Californians, who indeed have very little else to talk about."

Port St. Francisco

October the 1st. Favored by a strong wind from N. and N.W., which sometimes blew a storm, we made the voyage from Oonalashka to California in a very short time. At midnight we saw by moonlight the *Cape de los Reyes,* and at four o'clock in the afternoon dropped anchor in Port St. Francisco, opposite the Presidio. Our little Rurick seemed to throw the Presidio into no small alarm, for as we approached the fortress of St. Joaquin, which lies on a tongue of land, consisting of high rocks, and forming the southern entrance, we saw many soldiers on foot and on horseback, and in the fortress itself they were employed in loading the cannon. The entrance of the harbour is so narrow, that you are obliged to pass the fortress within musket-shot. As we drew near, they enquired through a speaking trumpet, to what nation we belonged, the Russian Imperial flag not being known here. Having answered that we were Russians, and friends, I fired a salute of five guns, which were answered by as many from the fort. A full hour elapsed after we had cast anchor before they troubled themselves about us; the soldiers had all left the fort, and posted themselves on the shore opposite our ship. It at last occured to me, that Vancouver had not met with any boats here; I therefore sent Lieutenant Schischmareff, accompanied by M. Chamisso, on shore, to announce our arrival to the commandant, Don Louis d'Arguello, who received the two gentlemen very politely, and promised to supply the Rurick daily with fresh provisions. He immediately sent me a basket of fruit, which was a welcome present, after we had been so long deprived of it. As he had already received from his government orders respecting us, he likewise despatched the same day a courier to Monterey, to acquaint the Governor of California of our arrival.

October the 3d. Early this morning I was visited by an artillery-officer, belonging to the Presidio, sent by the commandant, accompanied by a priest of the Mission. The former offered us, in the name of the commandant, all possible accommodation; the priest did the same in the name of the Mission: gratefully accepting these obliging offers, I merely expressed a wish to be supplied daily with fresh provisions for my whole crew. They found my request extremely moderate, renewed their promise of supplying us with all the refreshments the country produced, and already on the same afternoon sent us a fat ox, two sheep, cabbage, gourds, and a great quantity of fruit. After long abstinence we now enjoyed superfluity, and I congratulated myself on the wholesome diet which would give my crew new vigour for the long voyage they were about to undertake. It is true, that they all appeared to enjoy the most robust health, yet the germ of the scurvy might be already in some of them, because the hardships which they had endured in Beering's Straits, the total want of fresh provision, and the damp weather, were well calculated to lay the foundation of that disorder. To guard as far as possible against this evil, I caused water-melons, and apples, which were here remarkably excellent, to be distributed to them every day in large quantities.

The following day the festival of St. Francisco was to be celebrated in the mission, and the priest invited us all to dinner. This afternoon, accompanied by all our gentlemen, I took a walk into the Presidio, where we were received at the gate by the commandant, Don Louis d'Arguello, and saluted with eight guns, and then conducted to his residence. I found the Presidio as described by Vancouver; the garrison consists of a company of cavalry, of which the commandant is chief, and has only one officer of the artillery under his command.

The 4th, at eight o'clock in the morning, we all rowed to shore, and went into the Presidio to ride to the Mission, according to our promise, in company with the commandant. The horses were already saddled, and we began our journey, accompanied by ten horsemen, all very fine and expert men, who manage their carbines and lances with the dexterity of our Cossacks. They owe their skill to constant practice, for it is well known, that the military in California serve only to protect the Mission against the incursions of the savages; besides, they assist the clergy to make converts among these tribes, and to keep those already converted in the new faith. The weather was extremely fine, and an hour's ride brought us to our journey's end, though above half of the road was sandy and mountainous. Only a few small shrubs here and there diversified the barren hills; and it was not till we arrived in the neighborhood of the Mission, that we met with a pleasant country and recognized the luxuriant scenery of California. After passing through a street inhabited by Indians, which is the name given by the Spaniards here to the savage tribes, we stopped before a large building, adjoining the church, the residence of the missionaries, and were received by five priests, of whom three belonged to this Mission, and the two others had come from St. Clara to be present at the celebration of the festival; they conducted us to a large, dirty room, plainly furnished, where we were received with much respect. Precisely at ten we entered the church, which is spacious, built of stone, and handsomely fitted up, where we already found several hundred half-naked Indians kneeling, who, though they understand neither Spanish nor Latin, are never permitted after their conversion to absent themselves from mass. As the missionaries do not trouble themselves to learn the language of the Indians, I cannot conceive in what manner they have been instructed in the Christian religion; and there is probably but little light in the heads and hearts of these poor creatures, who can do nothing but imitate the external ceremonies which they observe by the eye. The rage for converting savage nations is now spreading over the whole South Sea, and causes much mischief, because the missionaries do not take pains to make men of them before they make them Christians, and thus, what should bring them happiness and tranquility, becomes the source of bloody wars; as for example, in the Friendly Islands, where the Christians and heathens reciprocally try to exterminate each other. I was surprised at observing, that those who were not baptized were not suffered to rise from their knees during the whole ceremony; they were afterwards indemnified for this exertion by the church-music, which seemed to afford them much pleasure, and which was probably the only part they comprehended during the whole service. The orchestra consisted of a violoncello, a violin, and two flutes; these instruments were played by little half-naked Indians, and were very often out of tune. From the church we went to dinner, where there was abundance of dishes, and wine, which is made by the missionaries themselves. After dinner they showed us the habitations of the Indians, consisting of long, low houses, built of bricks, and forming several streets. The uncleanliness in these barracks baffles description, and this is perhaps the cause of the great mortality; for of a 1000 Indians at St. Francisco, 300 die every year. The Indian girls, of whom 400 are in the mission, live separate from the men, likewise in such barracks: both sexes are obliged to labour hard. The men cultivate the ground; the harvest is delivered to the missionaries, and stored in magazines; from which the Indians receive only so much as is necessary for their support. It serves also for the maintenance of the soldiers of the Presidio; but they are obliged to pay a very high price for the flour. The women spin wool, and weave a coarse stuff, which is used partly for their ordinary clothing, and partly exported to Mexico, and exchanged for other necessary goods. The costume of the Indians is faithfully represented in the drawings made by M. Choris. This being a holiday, the Indians did no work, but, divided into groups, amused themselves with various pastimes, one of which requires particular dexterity. Two sit on the ground opposite each other, holding in their hands a number of thin sticks, and these being thrown up at the same time with great rapidity, they immediately guess whether the number is odd or even; at the side of each of the players, a person sits, who scores the gain and loss. As they always play for something, and yet possess nothing but their clothing, which they are not allowed to stake, they employ much pains and skill on little white shells, which serve instead of money.

The coast of California is inhabited by so many tribes, that there are frequently in the Mission, Indians of more than ten different races, each of which has its own language. As we were leaving the Mission, we were surprised by two groups of Indians, which were also composed of different nations. They came in military array; that is, quite naked, and painted with gay colours: the heads of the most were adorned with feathers, and other finery; some of them however had their long disordered hair covered with down, and their faces daubed in the most frightful manner. There is nothing remarkable in their war-dance, and I only regretted that I did not understand the words of their song. . . . The missionaries assured us that it was difficult to instruct them, on account of their stupidity; but I believe that these gentlemen do not give themselves much trouble about it. They also told us, that the Indians came far from the interior of the country, and voluntarily submitted to them, (which we likewise doubted,) that their instruction in religion immediately commenced, and that they were baptized sooner or later, according to their abilities. California is a great expense to the Spanish government, which derives no other advantage from it, than that every year a couple of hundred heathens are converted to Christianity, who however die very soon in their new faith, as they cannot accustom themselves to the different mode of life. Twice in the year they receive permission to return to their native homes. This short time is the happiest period of their existence; and I myself have seen them going home in crowds, with loud rejoicings. The sick, who cannot undertake the journey, at least accompany their happy countrymen to the shore where they embark, and there sit for days, together, mournfully gazing on the distant summits of the mountains which surround their homes; they often sit in this situation for several days, without taking any food, so much does the sight of their lost home affect these new Christians. Every time some of those who have the permission, run away; and they would probably all do it, were they not deterred by their fears of the soldiers, who catch them, and bring them back to the Mission as criminals; this fear is so great, that seven or eight dragoons are sufficient to overpower several hundred Indians.

Two large rivers flow into the bay of St. Francisco, of which the northern is the most considerable, and is called by the Spaniards Rio-grande. This, according to the account of the missionaries, has not its equal in the world, and is navigable for the largest vessels; its banks are fertile, the climate mild, and the population numerous. The missionaries often make excursions on this river, in large and well-armed boats, to procure proselytes to their faith, in which, however, they seldom succeed, as the Indians there are valiant and well-armed. After taking another cup of chocolate, and thanking the missionaries for their kind attention, we rode away, and reached the Rurick in the evening just as a courier had arrived from Monterey, despatched by Don Paulo Vicente de Sola, governor of Old California. He gave me a very polite letter from the Governor, in which he assured me of his joy at my safe arrival, and promised to come himself to Francisco, as soon as his business permitted him, to convince himself that all my wishes were complied with. At the same time the commandant had obtained leave at my request, to despatch a messenger to M. Kuskof, to whom I immediately wrote to procure me some necessary articles, which he could easily do, as he traded with the American ships.

October the 5th. The Rurick was obliged to be caulked, the sails to be repaired, and much rotten rope to be changed: the necessary works were favoured by the fine weather. While Schischmareff superintended these, I employed myself with the instruments, which I caused to be brought into a tent erected on shore, where I observed the daily going of the chronometers. Our naturalists were also employed, as there was much room for new discoveries in this country, so seldom visited by learned men. M. Choris was busily occupied in painting; and when the day had thus quickly passed over in various kinds of employment, we assembled in the evening to enjoy the repose of the beautiful climate, in which we were joined by the officers of the Presidio. The soldiers seem as dissatisfied with the government as with the Mission; and this is not surprising, as it is already seven years since they have received any pay, and are destitute of almost every article of clothing; besides this, the inhabitants are entirely without European goods, as no trading vessel is allowed to enter any harbour in California; and it is to be regretted, that this fine and fruitful country should thus lie entirely useless.

On the 16th, at five o'clock in the evening, seven guns from the fortress announced the approach of the Governor; and soon after, eight guns from the Presidio, his arrival there.

The 17th. To-day, to our great joy, a large baydare arrived from M. Kuskof with all the articles we had asked for. We had the pleasure to entertain the Governor and his suite, at dinner, in our tent. His polite and open behaviour pleased us much and made us very desirous of his acquaintance; and as he also seemed to take pleasure in our company, we saw each other daily either in the Presidio, or with me. He kindly complied with all our wishes, and we were indebted to him, for many agreeable days.

The 18th. . . . I made known to M. Kuskof, the wish of the Governor to see him here, to speak to him respecting his settlements in Bodega. I was astonished on hearing from the Governor, that there were many Russian prisoners in California; a ship belonging to the Company had ventured on the coast for the purpose of trading; and as this is contrary to the Spanish law, a part of the crew, who, not suspecting any evil, had ventured on shore, were seized by the soldiers, and dragged to prison. By the express orders of the Viceroy of Mexico, the Governor was not permitted to deliver them up to M. Kuskof; but he would give them up to me, if I would take them away. Unfortunately I was unable to accept this offer, on account of the smallness of the ship; I could only take three men, and therefore chose three Russians, who had suffered for another's fault, and had long been in the service of the American Company. Besides these, I also took Mr. Elliot on board, to leave him, according to his request, at the Sandwich Islands, from whence he might easily get to M. Baranof, at Sitka, by a North American ship. John Elliot de Castro, a native of Portugal, has come to Sitka, on board an American ship, and was there engaged by M. Baranof, to go as super-cargo with the trading ship, bound for California, where he was made prisoner with the rest of the crew.

October 23d. To-day, the Governor had prepared us an interesting spectacle, in a fight between a bull and a bear; the latter are here so numerous, that you have only to go a mile from the habitations into the woods, to meet them in great numbers. The species is distinguished from ours, by its pointed head, and its ash-grey colour; they are likewise bolder and more lively than ours. Notwithstanding this, the dragoons here are so active, and courageous, that they are sent on horseback into the forests for a bear as we would order a cook to bring a goose from the pen. Three dragoons on horseback, provided only with a noose, are sufficient to overpower a bear; in this kind of chase, they endeavour always to keep him in the middle, and to provoke him. As soon as the furious animal is going to rush on one of the horsemen, the other throws the noose, which is fastened to the saddle by strong thongs, round his fore-leg, and spurs his horse, by which the bear is thrown down; the other takes advantage of this moment, and throws the noose round his hind-leg, and while he lies without being able to move, the third ties all his four feet together, and he is thus carried home without any danger. In this manner, the dragoons had brought a bear to-day, while others had caught a wild bull in the same mode. The cattle, which are left the whole year in the pasture, become wild; and when one is to be killed, it is caught in the same manner, by a couple of horsemen, with nooses. The combat between these two animals was remarkable, and though the bull often tossed his raging antagonist on his horns into the air, he was at last obliged to yield.

The 29th. After the Governor had had a conversation with M. Kuskof, who has come according to his request, had satisfied all our wishes, and saw the Rurick ready to sail, he departed for Monterey, accompanied by our sincerest thanks. Ivan Strogonoff, one of the Russians, whom I had taken here on board, had been so much hurt on the chase by his powder-horn taking fire, that he expired in spite of the skill and careful attention of our surgeon.

November the 1st. The Rurick was not again quite in order; the going of the chronometers had been carefully determined, and all the instruments brought on board. We had been abundantly supplied with provisions by the inhabitants; my crew were all in good health, and, favoured by the tide, and a N.E. wind, we quitted our anchoring-place at nine o'clock, saluted the fortress, and at ten o'clock were out of the bay. When we were two miles out at sea, we could still hear the loud howlings of the sea-lions, which were lying on the shore on the stones. Sea-otters are found in great numbers on the coast of California, and as they had never been seen there in former times, it is probable they have come from the Aleutian islands, and the northern part of America, to escape the pursuit to which they are there exposed.

IV

From the Diaries of Chamisso and Choris

Von Kotzebue was accompanied on his scientific expedition by two men without a country. Louis Charles Adelbert von Chamisso, the naturalist, was an expatriated Frenchman who came to Germany after the loss of the family estate in the French Revolution. Entirely self-educated, he became a serious student of languages and, finally, of botany. He was brought on the voyage to study and classify the flora of the new world; and it is to Chamisso that we owe the cacophanous scientific term for the California poppy, *Eschschloizia California,* named for his friend, the surgeon aboard the *Rurik.*

Louis Choris was a native of Russia, but of German origin. Only twenty years old when he was signed aboard the *Rurik,* his job was to aid future explorers by making sketches of the lands visited by the ship. Some of the earliest sketches of the San Francisco region come from Choris' hand. He returned to America some years after the *Rurik* voyage, and was assassinated by bandits.

Both men kept diaries of their experiences on the trip. Chamisso's diary is especially valuable, for he narrates several incidents passed over in silence by Kotzebue, such as the hassle over the cannonball salute. In the end Chamisso and Kotzebue had a falling out. When they returned from their voyage of exploration, Chamisso published a scathing denunciation of Kotzebue for turning back before the expedition was over. Kotzebue fell sick and ordered the boat back before they had completed their task—the search for the Northwest Passage. "This would never have happened," Chamisso charged indignantly, "on an English ship."

Diary of Adelbert von Chamisso

On the afternoon of the 2d of October, 1816, at four o'clock, we sailed into the harbor of San Francisco. A great deal of movement in the fort at the southern entrance of the channel was apparent. They hoisted their flag; we hoisted ours, which did not seem to be recognized, and saluted the Spanish by firing seven times. This salutation was returned by the same number of shots, less two, according to the Spanish custom. We anchored before the Presidio, but no boat started from the shore to us, since the

Spaniards possess not a single boat in this glorious water- basin. I was immediately commanded to accompany Lieut. Schischmareff to the Presidio. Lieut. Don Luis de Arguello, Commandant *ad interim,* since the death of the Captain, received us in an exceptionally friendly manner, and cared for the most pressing needs of the *Rurik,* by sending fruit and vegetables on board. On the same evening, he dispatched a courier to Monterey to apprise the Governor of New California of our arrival.

The next day, the 3d, I met the artillery-officer, Don Miguel de la Luz Gomez, and a padre of the Mission here, who came on board the ship just as I was going to the Presidio on a commision for the Captain. I accompanied them on board; they brought with them the most friendly offers of aid from the Commandant, and from the wealthier Mission. The reverend father invited us for the next day, which was a feast-day, to the Mission of San Francisco, and promised horses in readiness to carry us thither. According to the expressed wish of the Captain, we were promptly furnished in the greatest abundance with beef and vegetables. In the afternoon, the tent, observatory, and Russian bath were erected on the shore. In the evening, we paid a visit to the Commandant, and eight cannon-shot were fired from the Presidio, by way of reception to the Captain.

Not, however, on these superfluous salutes was the heart of the Captain set, but upon two still lacking to the courtesy due to the Russian flag; and he insisted, with firmness, on these being supplied. This started a long negotiation, and only forced and unwillingly (I do not know if not, first, by express command of the Governor) did Don Luis de Arguello finally condescend to give us the two missing supplementary salutes. One of our sailors had to be detailed to the fort, to put in order the halyards by which the flag was hoisted, since they had been broken when last used, and there was no one among the natives capable of climbing the flagstaff.

The festival of St. Francis gave us the opportunity of observing the missionaries in their ministry, and the people, to whom they were sent, in their more tractable condition. . . . The Captain here, as in Chile, succeeded in making the Commandant and his officers familiar guests at our table. We ate on shore, in the tent, and our friends from the Presidio were always promptly on hand. This condition of things arose spontaneously. The misery in which they languished, forgotten and deserted for six or seven years by Mexico, their mother-land, did not permit them to be hosts; and the need felt to pour out their hearts to some one, drove them to us, with whom they could live so easily and comfortably. They spoke with bitterness of the missionaries, who, with all the lack of provision, yet lived, having abundance of the produce of the earth. Now that their money was spent, the missionaries would deliver to them nothing without a requisition, and even then only that which was absolutely indispensable to their sustenance, this not including bread or meal; so that for years, without seeing bread, they had lived on maize. Even the garrisons, which were in all the missions, for their protection, were provided with necessaries only upon requisition. "*Los Señores* are too good," exclaimed Don Miguel (meaning the commandants); "they should insist on supplies." A soldier went further, and complained to us that the Commandant would not permit them to press men of the vicinity, in order to force them to work for the soldiers, as they do in the missions.

Discontents arose, also, because the new Governor of Monterey, Don Pablo Vicente de Sola, had, since his entry upon the duties of his office, set himself in opposition to smuggling, which alone had provided them with the most indispensable necessaries. . . .

The year was already old, [October] and the country, which in the spring months (as Langsdorf has seen it) blooms like a flower-garden, presented now to the botanist only a dry, arid field. In a swamp, near by our tent, a water-plant had grown, which Eschscholtz asked me about after our departure.

I had not observed it; he, however, had reckoned that a water-plant, my especial love, would not have escaped me, and did not wish to get his feet wet. So much may one expect by relying on one's friends!

On the naked plain, which lies at the foot of the Presidio, stands a solitary oak, further eastward, between low bushes. My young friend, Adolph Erman, has recently seen this tree. If he had more closely examined it, he might have observed my name cut on the bark.

On the 15th of October, the courier from Kuskoff came back; and on the evening of the 16th, artillery salvos from the Presidio announced the arrival of the Governor from Monterey. At the same time, a messenger came to us from the Presidio, announcing that two men had been dangerously injured by the firing of a cannon, and desiring the help of our surgeon. Eschscholtz responded immediately to the call.

On the morning of the 17th, Herr von Kotzebue waited on board for the first visit from the Governor of the province; while, on the other hand, the Governor, an old man, and of higher official rank, waited at the Presidio for the first visit from Lieut. von Kotzebue. The Captain was, by chance, informed that he was expected at the Presidio; whereupon he sent me there with a difficult commission, which I was as gently as possible to impart to the Governor—namely: the Captain had been informed that the Governor would visit him on board ship early in the morning; he therefore awaited the Governor's visit. I found the little man in full regimentals, up to a nightcap, which he still wore on his head, though ready to take it off *a tempo*. I delivered myself, as well as I could, of my message, and saw that his face lengthened itself to three times its natural extent.

He bit his lips, and said that he regretted he could not endure the sea before eating, and he was truly sorry that he must renounce the pleasure, for the present, of becoming acquainted with the Captain. I saw it would turn out, that the old man, with matters all unarranged, would mount his horse, and set out on his courier journey across the desert to Monterey; for I did not allow myself to conceive that Herr von Kotzebue could give way when once the issue was raised.

Reflecting on this, I went slowly down to the beach, just as a good genius placed itself between us, and sealed anew the bond of peace by the tie of friendship, before we had come to a decided difference. The morning was already consumed, and the hour had come when Herr von Kotzebue took the mid-day sun, and when, in order to regulate the chronometer, he must go on shore. The lookout, therefore, at the Presidio announced that the Captain was coming; and as he stepped on shore, the Governor strode down the slope to meet him. The Captain, on his part, ascended the slope in order to receive the Governor; and so Spain and Russia, each going half-way, fell into one another's open arms!

. . . We did not see the Governor on the 18th; perhaps he was waiting for a visit of ceremony from us at the Presidio. On the 19th, we were feasted at the Presidio, and salvos of artillery accompanied the toast to the alliance of the sovereigns, and the friendship of the nations. On the 20th, we were, on our side, the hosts, and in the evening danced at the Presidio. As the clock struck eight, the music ceased for awhile, and in the quiet that ensued, arose the tones of the evening prayer. Herr von Kotzebue was, in conversation, of the most prepossessing amiability, and Don Pablo Vicente de Sola, who thought a great deal of formalities (of which enough had been dispensed with to get along), was consoled in the matter by giving himself up to us entirely. The famous spectacle of a combat between a bear and a bull had been promised to us. On the 21st, ten or twelve soldiers went over to the northern shore, in the shallop of the Mission, in order to capture bears with the lasso. Late in the evening, one could hear distinct loud cries, which came from the bear-hunt on the opposite shore; no bivouac-fires, however, could be seen. The Indians must have had remarkably shrill voices.

On the evening of the 22d, the hunters brought in a small bear. They had also caught a larger one, but so far in the interior, they were unable to bring him to shore. As for the bear which was to fight on the following day, he remained all night in the shallop, having his head and mouth free, according to custom, that he might be fresher for the combat. The Governor remained the whole day, afternoon and evening, in our tent. All night, great fires burned on the land at the back of the harbor; the natives were accustomed to burn the grass, to further its growth.

On the 23d, the bear-baiting took place, on the beach. Unwilling and bound as the animals were, the spectacle had in it nothing great or praiseworthy. One pitied only the poor beasts, who were so shamefully handled.

In the evening I was at the Presidio, with Gleb Simonowitch. The Governor had just received information that the ship from Acapulco, several years out, had once again arrived at Monterey, for the provisioning of California. He had, with this information, the latest news from Mexico; and he shared with me the newspapers, since at every opportunity he showed me the utmost kindness and courtesy. As the papers were edited only by royal authority, they contained but short notices *"de la pacificación de las provincias,"* and a long leading article, the story of Johanna Kruger, subaltern in the Kolberg regiment—which story was not new to me, as I had already had the opportunity of learning about the brave soldier, through an officer of his regiment.

Don Pablo Vicente, as he came to our tent from the Presidio brought a present *á su amigo Don Adelberto*—a flower which he had picked on the way, and which he gave me ceremoniously. It happened to be our wild pansy, or silver leaf *(Potentilla anserina),* and could not bloom more beautifully, even in Berlin.

At this time, in Monterey, were many prisoners, of different nations, whom the smuggling trade and the capture of sea-otters had allured here, that they might seek adventures on this coast, and among them a few individuals suffered for the rest. Here, in Monterey, were two Aleutians, or Kodiakers, with whom an American had carried on the business of sea-otter catching, for seven years, in the Spanish harbors of this coast. The Russians do not alone use these northern people—they hire them to others for their use, in consideration of half profits. I have even met Kodiakers scattered about in the Sandwich Islands.

Among the prisoners in Monterey, was a Señor John Elliot de Castro, of whom we will speak further, by and by. After many adventures, as a supercargo of a ship of the Russian-American Company, sent out by Herr Baranoff, of Sitka, for the smuggling trade on this coast, he fell into the hands of the Spaniards, with a part of the crew. There were also three Russians, besides these; old servants of the Russian-American Company, who had left the settlement at Port Bodega, and now, missing the language and customs of their home, regretted the step they had taken.

Don Pablo Vincente de Sola permitted the Captain to ransom these Russian prisoners—Aleutians and Kodiakers being classed as Russians. It does not appear that the Spaniards had desired any service, or taken any advantage of these men, whom the strange greed of their native land had robbed of their home, that it might flourish by their strength. The King of Spain indemnified, or should indemnify, every prisoner of war by the payment of one and a half reals a day. The Captain, limited by his circumstances, was able to take only the three Russians on board, and offer to Mr. Elliot a passage to the Sandwich Islands, from whence he could easily go to Sitka when he pleased. The Governor sent after these Russians, and when they arrived delivered them to Herr von Kotzebue, from whom he exacted his solemn word of honor, that they, in that they had sought and found protection in Spain, should receive no kind of punishment. I found his conduct in this respect very noble.

Among these Russians was an old man, Ivan Strogonoff, who was overjoyed that he should once more go to his own people. As he was of no use as a sailor, the Captain ordered him to serve us passengers in the gun-room, and notified us of the order. The last day that we remained in the harbor, he was sent out on a hunting expedition. The unfortunate fellow! On the evening before our departure, his powder-horn exploded and he was brought back mortally wounded. He wished to die only among Russians, so the Captain received him on board out of pity; on the third day of our voyage out he expired. He was buried at sea, and with him vanished our last hope that our boots would ever be blacked again on this journey. Peace be to Ivan Strogonoff!

. . . The time for our sojourn in California had ended. On the 26th day of October, on Sunday, after a ride to the Mission, a feast and a parting-dinner were given under our tent. The artillery of the *Rurik* accompanied the toast to the union of the monarchs and the nations, and the health of the Governor. A good missionary dipped his mantle too deep in the juice of the grape, and reeled visibly under the burden. On the 28th, the camp was broken up, and we again embarked. While we sealed the protocol at the Presidio, Herr Kuskoff, with the knowledge of Herr von Kotzebue, sent out two shallops in the rear of the bay, for catching otters!

On the 29th, started, early in the morning, Herr Kuskoff with his shallops to Bodega, and, on the other hand, the good Don Pablo Vicente de Sola for Monterey. This latter gentleman took our letters with him to send them to Europe, the last our friends would receive from us during the journey. With them vanished all traces of us; for, since we did not return to Kantschatka in the year 1817, our friends must have given us up as lost.

On the 30th, the necessary livestock was shipped, and vegetables in the greatest abundance; at this time, the air was thick with an endless swarm of flies which came on board. We had taken fresh water on board, which at other ports in summer is a difficult business, and we had to thank the Governor for a cask of wine from Monterey. Our friends from the Presidio dined with us at noon on the *Rurik,* and now we were ready to sail. On the 31st, we took a last leave of our friends; and some of us rode in the afternoon to the Mission. Late in the evening, John Elliot de Castro arrived, doubtful whether he should make use of the Captain's offers or not. He decided finally that he would. On the first of November, 1816, All Saints' Day, at nine o'clock in the morning, we weighed anchor, while our friends were yet in church. We saw them arrive at the fort, as we sailed away. They hoisted a Spanish flag, and fired a gun; we raised our flag, and did the same. They then saluted us by firing seven times; and we returned the salutation, shot for shot.

The water of the harbor of San Francisco was phosphorescent, through its whole extent, with luminous points of light. The waves rolled up on the beach of the shore beyond the boat, perceptibly shimmering with fire. I examined the water of the harbor under a microscope, and found nothing abundant therein, except certain infusoria, to which I can ascribe no particular connection with the phosphorescence.

We looked daily here upon the play of the fog, which, blown eastward by the strong sea-breeze over the bright, sunshiny land, dissolved and scattered itself everywhere. Singularly beautiful was the spectacle displayed for us at our departure, when the mist would sometimes hide and sometimes unveil the different peaks and valleys of the coast.

. . . Melancholy feelings attend our offering a few words on the Spanish settlements on this coast. With an avaricious thirst for possession, Spain extends her territory here, merely because she envies others the room. She maintains her Presidios at a great expence, and tries, by the prohibition of all trade, to force ready money back to its source. But a little liberty would make California the granary and market of the northern coasts of these seas, and the general resort of the ships which navigate them. Corn, oxen, salt, (at St. Quentin, Old California,) wine, the produce of which would increase the demand, give it in many respects a superiority over the Sandwich islands, though their situation, on the route between China and the northwest coast, is more advantageous. But industry and navigation, the offspring of liberty, would speedily transfer a profitable share in this trade to California, which possess the sea-otters in greater abundance than all the other coasts.

Yet California lies without industry, trade, and navigation, desert and unpeopled. It has remained neglected, without any importations from Mexico, during the six or seven years of the war between Spain and its colonies. The ship from St. Blas, which formerly brought supplies to these settlements yearly, arrived in Monterey only while we were there. The missions possess some bad barks in the harbour of San Francisco, built by foreign captives. Even the Presidio has not a single boat; and other havens are no better off. Strangers catch otter-skins even in the Spanish harbours; and only a smuggling trade, which the new governor of California, since his appointment (fourteen months ago) has tried to suppress, furnishes this province with the most indispensable articles.

Spain has given way in the affair of Nootka. England and the United States, without regarding its vain territorial possessions, are now negotiating about the colony at the mouth of the Columbia; and the Russian American Company have still a settlement a few leagues north of San Francisco.

But the maintenance of this colony is ascribed to another motive besides policy: namely, the pious intention of propagating the Christian religion, and the conversion of heathen nations. The governor of the province himself, informed us, that this was the real state of the case. Well, then, a good work has been here injudiciously begun and ill-executed.

The pious Franciscans, who hold the missions in New California, are not skilled in the arts and trades which they ought to exercise and teach, nor in any of the languages spoken by the nations to whom they are sent. They are monks, exactly like those in the convents of Europe. They direct a considerable agricultural establishment; (always two in each mission), perform divine service, and converse with those committed to their charge, by means of interpreters, who are themselves Indians. All property belongs to the community of the mission, and is administered by the fathers. The savage Indian derives no immediate advantage from his labours; no wages, if he happens to be let out as a day-labourer on the Presidio. The mission receives the money which he earns. He acquires no notion of property, and is not bound by it. We do not deny the mildness, the paternal anxiety of the missionaries, of which we have several times been witnesses. The relation still remains what is here represented; and, in our opinion, it would differ only in name, if the master of slaves kept them to work, and let them out at pleasure, he also would give them food.

The savage comes unthinkingly into the mission, receives the food which is willingly offered him, and listens to the instructions: he is still free. But as soon as he is baptized, he belongs to the church; and hence he looks with pain and longing to his native mountains. The church has an inalienable right to her children, and exercises this right with rigour.

The savage is unreflecting and inconstant, like a child. Work, to which he is unaccustomed, is too difficult for him; he repents of the step which binds him, and demands his pristine liberty. The love of home, is, in him, a ruling passion. The fathers allow their Indians, for the most part, twice a year, a leave of absence for some weeks to visit their friends, and their native place. On occasion of these journeys, which are undertaken in companies, apostates fall off, and new converts come in. The first, some of whom become the bitterest enemies to the Spaniards, the missionaries endeavour, on their excursions, to regain by gentle means; and if they do not succeed, they have recourse to the armed force. Hence many of the hostile events between the Spaniards and Indians.

The Indians die in the missions, in an alarming and increasing proportion. San Francisco contains about a thousand Indians: the number of deaths, in the last year, exceeded three hundred; it amounts already this year, (till October), to two hundred and seventy, of which forty occurred during the last month. But the number of proselytes must exceed that of the apostates and the excess of deaths. Five missions were named to us which have been founded in this province, since the time of Vancouver. On the other hand, several of the missions of the Dominicans in Old California, have ceased to exist; and the converted people may be considered as nearly extinct.

There is no medical assistance here, except bleeding, which is said to have been taught them by a ship's surgeon; and this remedy being since applied on every occasion, is more fatal than advantageous. Particularly one disorder, which, though the opinions are divided, has probably been spread by the Europeans, carries off its victim without opposition. It likewise prevails among the savage tribes: these latter do not, however, disappear from the earth with the same dreadful rapidity. The number of whites, on the other hand, increases.

The contempt which the missionaries have for the people, to whom they are sent, seems to us, considering their pious occupation, a very unfortunate circumstance. None of them appear to have troubled themselves about their history, customs, religions, or languages: "They are irrational savages, and nothing more can be said of them. Who would trouble himself with their stupidity? Who would spend his time upon it?"

In fact, these tribes are far below those on the north coast, and the interior of America. In their general appearance, they resemble each other, except the Tcholovonians, whom we soon learnt to distinguish by their marked physiognomy, which the fathers could not do. They have all a very savage look, and are of a very dark color. Their flat, broad countenance, with large staring eyes, is shaded by black, thick, long, and smooth hair. The gradations of color, the languages, which are radically different from each other; the mode of life, arts, arms, in some of them various lines tattooed about the chin and neck, the way in which they paint themselves for war and for the dance, distinguish the different tribes. They live among the Spaniards, and among themselves in different, friendly, or hostile relations. Among many of them their arms consist of bows and arrows; some of these are of extraordinary elegance, the bows light and strong, and covered with the sinews of animals on the convex side; among others it is merely of wood, and rudely made: some possess the art (women's work) of constructing neat and waterproof vessels of coloured blades of grass; but the Indian, for the most part, forgets his industry in the missions. They all go naked. They do not possess horses nor canoes of any kind; they only know how to fasten together bundles of rushes, which carry them over the water by their comparative lightness. Those who live near rivers subsist principally on salmon, which they catch in baskets; those in the mountains on wild fruits and grain. They neither sow nor reap, but burn their meadows from time to time to increase their fertility.

The South Sea islands, far distant from each other, and dispersed over nearly one-third of the torrid zone, speak one language. In America, here in

New California, tribes of one race, living near to each other, speak quite different languages. Every fragment of the history of man is of importance. We must leave it to our successors, as our predecessors have done to us, to collect more satisfactory information respecting the natives of California and their languages. We had proposed this as our object in a journey which we intended to make to some of the nearest missions. Business, however, of another kind kept us at San Francisco, and the period fixed for our departure came without our being able to afford time for this journey; for the rest we refer to the accounts of La Peyrouse and Vancouver, which we found very correct. Since their time there has been but little change in California. A fort, erected in a good situation, guards the harbour of San Francisco. The Presidio is newly built with stone, and covered with tiles. The building of the chapel has not been begun. In the missions they build in the same manner, and the barracks of the Indians at San Francisco are of similar construction. An artillerist has erected mills in the missions, worked by horses; but they are now for the most part out of order, and cannot be repaired. At San Francisco is a stone which a horse turns without mechanism over another stone, the only mill in order. The Indian women rub the corn between two stones for immediate use. A windmill of the Russian American Company's settlement creates astonishment, but does not find imitators. Some years ago, when artisans were brought here at a great expense to teach the necessary arts, the Indians profited more by their instructions than the *gente rational* (rational people) as the Spaniards call themselves.

We observed with regret, that the best understanding does not exist between the missions and the Presidio. The fathers consider themselves as the first in this country, and the Presidios merely sent for its protection. A soldier, who constantly carries and often uses arms, unwillingly bears the government of the church. The Presidio, living only on their pay, depend for the supply of their wants upon the missions, from which they purchase for ready money; they suffered distress in this latter period, neglected by the mother country, and accused the mission of not endeavoring to relieve them. Before we conclude, we must mention the generous hospitality with which both the military and the missionaries strove to supply our wants, and they willingly granted an unconstrained freedom, which we here enjoyed on Spanish ground. We dedicate these lines of remembrance and gratitude to our friends in California.

Port San Francisco and Its Inhabitants by Louis Choris

Early on September 20, 1816, we came within sight of the coast of New California. The land we first saw was what is known as Point Reyes, to the north of San Francisco. As the wind was favourable we soon passed the Farallones, which are dangerous rocks, and at four in the afternoon we entered San Francisco harbour. The fort, which is within the entrance and on the south shore, is thoroughly equipped for defense. The presidio of San Francisco is about one marine mile from the fort and on the same side; it is square in form and has two gates which are constantly guarded by a considerable company of men. The buildings have windows on the side towards the interior court only. The presidio is occupied by ninety Spanish soldiers, a commandant, a lieutenant, a commissary, and a sergeant. Most of these are married. The men and women are tall and well built. Very few of the soldiers have married Indians. They are all good horsemen and two of them can easily cope with fifty natives.

Two leagues to the southeast of the presidio and on the southern shore of the harbour is the Mission of San Francisco, which makes a fair-sized village. The mission church is large and is connected with the house of the missionaries, which is plain and reasonably clean and well kept. The mission always has a guard of three or four soldiers from the presidio. The village is inhabited by fifteen hundred Indians; there they are given protection, clothing, and an abundance of food. In return, they cultivate the land for the community. Corn, wheat, beans, peas, and potatoes—in a word, all kinds of produce—are to be found in the general warehouse. By authority of the superior, a general cooking of food takes place, at a given hour each day, in the large square in the middle of the village; each family comes there for its ration which is apportioned with regard to the number of its members. They are also given a certain quantity of raw provisions. Two or three families occupy the same house. In their free time, the Indians work in gardens that are given them; they raise therein onions, garlic, cantaloupes, watermelons, pumpkins, and fruit trees. The products belong to them and they can dispose of them as they see fit.

In winter, bands of Indians come from the mountains to be admitted to the mission, but the greater part of them leave in the spring. They do not like the life at the mission. They find it irksome to work continually and to have everything supplied to them in abundance. In their mountains, they live a free and independent, albeit a miserable, existence. Rats, insects, and snakes,—all these serve them for food; roots also, although there are few that are edible, so that at every step they are almost certain to find something to appease their hunger. They are too unskillful and lazy to hunt. They have no fixed dwellings; a rock or a bush affords sufficient protection for them from every vicissitude of the weather. After several months spent in the missions, they usually begin to grow fretful and thin, and they constantly gaze with sadness at the mountains which they can see in the distance. Once or twice a year the missionaries permit those Indians upon whose return they believe they can rely to visit their own country, but it often happens that few of these return; some, on the other hand, bring with them new recruits to the mission.

The Indian children are more disposed to adopt the mission life. They learn to make a coarse cloth from sheep's wool for the community. I saw twenty looms that were constantly in operation. Other young Indians are instructed in various trades by the missionaries. There is a house at the mission in which some two hundred and fifty women—the widows and daughters of dead Indians—reside. They do spinning. This house also shelters the wives of Indians who are out in the country by order of the fathers. They are placed there at the request of the Indians, who are exceedingly jealous, and are taken out again when their husbands return. The fathers comply with such requests in order to protect the women from mischief, and they watch over this establishment with the greatest vigilance.

The mission has two mills operated by mules. The flour produced by them is only sufficient for the consumption of the Spanish soldiers who are obliged to buy it from the fathers.

The presidio frequently has need of labourers for such work as carrying wood, building, and other jobs; the superior, thereupon, sends Indians who are paid for their trouble; but the money goes to the mission which is obliged to defray all the expenses of the settlement.

On Sundays and holidays they celebrate divine service. All the Indians of both sexes, without regard to age, are obliged to go to church; and worship. Children brought up by the superior, fifty of whom are stationed around him, assist him during the service which they also accompany with the sound of musical instruments. These are chiefly drums, trumpets, tabors, and other instruments of the same class. It is by means of their noise that they endeavour to stir the imagination of the Indians and to make men of these savages. It is, indeed, the only means of producing an effect upon them. When the drums begin to beat they fall to the ground as if they were half dead. None dares to move; all remain stretched upon the ground without making the slightest movement until the end of the service, and, even then, it is necessary to tell them several times that the mass is finished. Armed soldiers are stationed at each corner of the church. After the mass, the superior delivers a sermon in Latin to his flock.

On Sunday, when the service is ended, the Indians gather in the cemetery, which is in front of the mission house, and dance. Half of the men adorn themselves with feathers and with girdles ornamented with feathers and bits of shell that pass for money among them, or they paint their bodies with regular lines of black, red, and white. Some have half their bodies (from the head downward) daubed with black, the other half red, and the whole crossed with white lines. Others sift the down from birds on their hair. The men commonly dance six or eight together, all making the

CALIFORNIAN AIR

Tremblingly and Mysteriously

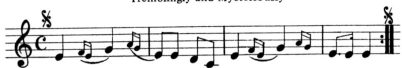

same movements and all armed with spears. Their music consists of clapping the hands together which has a charm for their ears; this is finally followed by a horrible yell that greatly resembles the sound of a cough accompanied by a whistling noise. The women dance among themselves, but without making violent movements.

The Indians are greatly addicted to games of chance; they stake their ornaments, their tools, their money, and, frequently, even the clothing that the missionaries have given them. Their games consist of throwing little pieces of wood which have to fall in an even or in an odd number, or others that are rounded on one side and as they fall on the flat or on the round side the player loses or wins.

Upon the demise of his father or mother, or of some kinsman, the Indian daubs his face with black in token of mourning.

From *Two Years Before the Mast* by Richard Henry Dana

Dana visited San Francisco Bay in 1835—probably the quietest time in the City's history. The Secularization Act of 1833 drastically depleted the population of Mission Dolores, and the Presidio languished under the neglect of the home government. The Anglo-American invasion was in the future, though William Richardson had already erected his house and trading post on present-day Grant Avenue.

None of this mattered to Dana, who had come to the Bay in search of hides. And when we read Dana's account, we learn much more about the business of fetching hides than of the city of Yerba Buena. But the modern reader can't help but marvel at the accuracy of his prophecy that "If California ever becomes a prosperous country, this bay will be the center of its prosperity." His remarks on the character of Russians, Indians, and *Californios* are bound to offend modern readers; but we are bound to remember that confidence in the superiority of one's own civilization was a hallmark of every civilization, Western and nonwestern alike, in the last century.

California and Its Inhabitants

In their domestic relations these people [the Mexicans of California] are not better than in their public. The men are thriftless, proud, extravagant, and very much given to gaming; and the women have but little education, and a good deal of beauty, and their morality, of course, is none of the best; yet the instances of infidelity are much less frequent than one would at first suppose. In fact, one vice is set over against another; and thus something like a balance is obtained. If the women have but little virtue, the jealousy of their husbands is extreme, and their revenge deadly and almost certain. A few inches of cold steel have been the punishment of many an unwary man, who has been guilty, perhaps, of nothing more than indiscretion. The difficulties of the attempt are numerous, and the consequences of discovery fatal, in the better classes. With the unmarried women, too, great watchfulness is used. The main object of the parents is to marry their daughters well, and to this a fair name is necessary. The sharp eyes of a duena, and the

39

ready weapons of a father or brother, are a protection which the characters of most of them—men and women—render by no means useless; for the very men who would lay down their lives to avenge the dishonour of their own family would risk the same lives to complete the dishonour of another.

Of the poor Indians very little care is taken. The priests, indeed, at the missions, are said to keep them very strictly, and some rules are usually made by the alcaldes to punish their misconduct; yet it all amounts to but little. Indeed, to show the entire want of any sense of morality or domestic duty among them, I have frequently known an Indian to bring his wife, to whom he was lawfully married in the church, down to the beach, and carry her back again, dividing with her the money which she had got from the sailors. If any of the girls were discovered by the alcalde to be open evil livers, they were whipped, and kept at work sweeping the square of the presidio, and carrying mud and bricks for the buildings; yet a few reals would generally buy them off. Intemperance, too, is a common vice among the Indians. The Mexicans, on the contrary, are abstemious, and I do not remember ever having seen a Mexican intoxicated.

Such are the people who inhabit a country embracing four or five hundred miles of sea-coast, with several good harbours, with fine forests in the north; the waters filled with fish, and the plains covered with thousands of herds of cattle; blessed with a climate, than which there can be no better in the world; free from all manner of diseases, whether epidemic or endemic; and with a soil in which corn yields from seventy to eighty-fold. In the hands of an enterprising people, what a country this might be! we are ready to say. Yet how long would a people remain so, in such a country? The Americans (as those from the United States are called) and Englishmen, who are fast filling up the principal towns, and getting the trade into their hands, are indeed more industrious and effective than the Mexicans; yet their children are brought up Mexicans in most respects, and if the "California fever" (laziness) spares the first generation, it is likely to attack the second.

San Francisco

Our place of destination had been Monterey, but as we were to the northward of it when the wind hauled ahead, we made a fair wind for San Francisco. This large bay, which lies in latitude 37° 58 ', was discovered by Sir Francis Drake, and by him represented to be (as indeed it is) a magnificent bay, containing several good harbours, great depth of water, and surrounded by a fertile and finely wooded country. About thirty miles from the mouth of the bay, and on the south-east side, is a high point, upon which the presidio is built. Behind this point is the little harbour, or bight, called Yerba Buena, in which trading-vessels anchor, and, near it, the Mission of Dolores. There was no other habitation on this side of the bay, except a shanty of rough boards put up by a man named Richardson, who was doing a little trading between the vessels and the Indians. Here, at anchor, and the only vessel, was a brig under Russian colours, from Sitka, in Russian America, which had come down to winter, and to take in a supply of tallow and grain, great quantities of which latter article are raised in the missions at the head of the bay. The second day after our arrival we went on board the brig, it being Sunday, as a matter of curiosity; and there was enough there to gratify it. Though no larger than the *Pilgrim,* she had five or six officers, and a crew of between twenty and• thirty; and such a stupid and greasy-looking set I never saw before. Although it was quite comfortable weather and we had nothing on but straw hats, shirts, and duck trousers, and were barefooted, they had, every man of them, double-soled boots coming up to the knees, and well greased; thick woolen trousers, frocks, waistcoats, pea-jackets, woolen caps, and everything in true Nova Zembla rig; and in the warmest days they made no change. The clothing of one of these men would weigh nearly as much as that of half our crew. They had brutish faces, looked like the antipodes of sailors, and apparently dealt in nothing but grease. They lived upon grease; ate it, drank it, slept in the midst of it, and their clothes were covered with it. To a Russian, grease is the greatest luxury. They looked with greedy eyes upon the tallow-bags as they were taken into the vessel, and, no doubt, would have eaten one up whole, had not the officers kept watch over it. The grease appeared to fill their pores, and to come out in their hair and on their faces. It seems as if it were this saturation which makes them stand cold and rain so well. If they were to go into a warm climate, they would melt and die of the scurvy.

The vessel was no better than the crew. Everything was in the oldest and most inconvenient fashion possible: running trusses and lifts on the yards, and large hawser cables, coiled all over the decks, and served and parcelled in all directions. The topmasts, topgallant-masts, and studding-sail booms were nearly black for want of scraping, and the decks would have turned the stomach of a man-of-war's-man. The galley was down in the forecastle; and there the crew lived, in the midst of the steam and grease of the cooking, in a place as hot as an oven, and apparently never cleaned out. Five minutes in the forecastle was enough for us, and we were glad to get into the open air. We made some trade with them, buying Indian curiosities, of which they had a great number; such as beadwork, feathers of birds, fur moccasins, etc. I purchased a large robe, made of the skins of some animal, dried and sewed nicely together, and covered all over on the outside, with thick downy feathers, taken from the breasts of various birds, and arranged with their different colours so as to make a brilliant show.

A few days after our arrival the rainy season set in, and for three weeks it rained almost every hour, without cessation. This was bad for our trade, for the collecting of hides is managed differently in this port from what it is in any other on the coast. The Mission Dolores, near the anchorage, has no trade at all; but those of San Jose, Santa Clara, and others situated on the large creeks or rivers which run into the bay, and distant between fifteen and forty miles from the anchorage, do a greater business in hides than any in California. Large boats, or launches, manned by Indians, and capable of carrying from five to six hundred hides apiece, are attached to the mission, and sent down to the vessels with hides, to bring away goods in return. Some of the crews of the vessels are obliged to go and come in the boats, to look out for the hides and goods. These are favourite expeditions with the sailors in fine weather; but now, to be gone three or four days in open boats, in constant rain, without any shelter, and with cold food, was hard service.

Having collected nearly all the hides that were to be procured, we began our preparations for taking in a supply of wood and water, for both of which San Francisco is the best place on the coast. A small island, about two leagues from the anchorage, called by us "Wood Island," and by the Mexicans "Isla de los Angeles," was covered with trees to the water's edge; and to this two of our crew, who were Kennebec men, and could handle an axe like a plaything, were sent every morning to cut wood, with two boys to pile it up for them. In about a week they had cut enough to last us a year, and the third mate, with myself and three others, were sent over in a large, schooner-rigged, open launch, which we had hired of the mission, to take in the wood, and bring it to the ship. We left the ship about noon, but owing to a strong head wind, and a tide which here runs four or five knots, did not get into the harbour, formed by two points of the island, where the boats lie, until sundown. No sooner had we come-to than a strong southeaster, which had been threatening us all day, set in, with heavy rain and a chilly air. We were in rather a bad situation: an open boat, heavy rain, and long night; for in winter, in this latitude, it was dark nearly fifteen hours. Taking a small skiff, which we had brought with us, we went ashore, but discovered no shelter, for everything was open to the rain; and, collecting a little wood, which we found by lifting up the leaves and brush, and a few mussels, we put aboard again, and made the best preparations in our power for passing the night. We unbent the mainsail, and formed an awning with it, over the after part of the boat, made a bed of wet logs of wood, and, with our jackets on, lay down, about six o'clock, to sleep. Finding the rain running down upon us, and our jackets getting wet through, and the rough, knotty logs rather indifferent couches, we turned out; and, taking an iron pan which we brought with us, we wiped it out dry, put some stones around it, cut the wet bark from some sticks, and striking a light, made a small fire in the pan. Keeping some sticks near to dry, and covering the whole over with a roof of boards, we kept up a small fire, by which we cooked our mussels, and ate them, rather for an occupation than from hunger. Still it was not ten o'clock, and the night was long before us, when one of the party produced an old pack of Spanish cards from his monkey-jacket pocket, which we hailed as a great windfall; and, keeping a dim, flickering light by our fagots, we played game after game, till one or two o'clock, when, becoming really tired, we went to our logs again, one sitting up at a time, in turn, to keep watch over the fire. Towards morning the rain ceased, and the air became sensibly colder, so that we found sleep impossible, and sat up, watching for daybreak. No sooner was it light than we went ashore, and began our preparations for loading our vessel. We were not mistaken in the coldness of the weather, for a white frost was on the ground—a thing we had never seen before in California—and one or two little puddles of fresh water were skimmed over with a thin coat of ice. In this state of the weather, and before sunrise, in the grey of the morning, we had to wade off, nearly up to our hips in water, to load the skiff with the wood by armfuls. The third mate remained on board the launch, two more men stayed in the skiff to load and manage it, and all the waterwork, as usual, fell upon the two youngest of us; and there we were, with frost on the ground, wading forward and back, from the beach to the boat, with armfuls of wood, barefooted, and our trousers rolled up. When the skiff went off with her load, we could only keep our feet from freezing by racing up and down the beach on the hard sand as fast as we could go. We were all day at this work, and towards sundown, having loaded the vessel as deep as she would bear, we hove up our anchor and made sail, beating out of the bay. No sooner had we got into the large bay than we found a strong tide setting us out to seaward, a thick fog which prevented our seeing the ship, and a breeze too light to set us against the tide, for we were as deep as a sand-barge. By the utmost exertions we saved ourselves from being carried out, and were glad to reach the leeward-most point of sea of the island, where we came-to, and prepared to pass another night more uncomfortable than the first, for we were loaded up to the gunwale, and had only a choice among logs and sticks for a resting-place. The next morning we made sail at slack water with a fair wind, and got on board by eleven o'clock, when all hands were turned-to to unload and stow away the wood, which took till night.

Having now taken in all our wood, the next morning a water-party was ordered off with all the casks. From this we escaped, having a pretty good siege with the wooding. The water-party were gone three days, during which time they narrowly escaped being carried out to sea, and passed one day on an island, where one of them shot a deer, great numbers of which overrun the islands and hills of San Francisco Bay.

While not off on these wood and water parties, or up the rivers to the missions, we had easy times on board the ship. We were moored, stem and stern, within a cable's length of the shore, safe from southeasters, and with little boating to do; and, as it rained nearly all the time, awnings were put over the hatchways, and all hands sent down between-decks, where we were at work, day after day, picking oakum, until we got enough to calk the ship all over, and to last the whole voyage. Then we made a whole suit of gaskets for the voyage home, a pair of wheel-ropes from strips of green hide, great quantities of spun yarn, and everything else that could be made between decks. It being now midwinter and in high latitude, the nights were very long, so that we were obliged to knock off at five in the evening, when we got supper; which gave us nearly three hours before eight bells, at which time the watch was set.

As we had now been about a year on the coast, it was time to think of the voyage home, and, knowing that the last two or three months of our stay would be very busy ones, and that we should never have so good an opportunity to work for ourselves as the present, we all employed our evenings in making clothes for the passage home, and more especially for Cape Horn. As soon as supper was over and the kids cleared away, and each man had taken his smoke, we seated ourselves on our chests round the lamp, which swung from a beam, and went to work each in his own way, some making hats, others jackets, etc., etc., and no one was idle. The boys who could not sew well enough to make their own clothes laid up grass into sinnet for the men, who sewed for them in return. Several of us clubbed together, and bought a large piece of twilled cotton, which we made into trousers and jackets, and, giving them several coats of linseed oil, laid them by for Cape Horn. I also sewed and covered a tarpaulin hat, thick, and strong enough to sit upon, and made myself a complete suit of flannel underclothing for bad weather. Those who had no southwester caps made them; and several of the crew got up for themselves tarpaulin jackets and trousers, lined on the inside with flannel. Industry was the order of the day, and every one did something for himself; for we knew that as the season advanced, and we went farther south, we should have no evenings to work in.

Friday, December 25th. This day was Christmas; and, as it rained all day long, and there were no hides to take in, and nothing especial to do, the captain gave us a holiday (the first we had had, except Sundays, since leaving Boston), and plumduff for dinner. The Russian brig, following the old style, had celebrated their Christmas eleven days before, when they had a grand blow-out, and (as our men said) drank, in the forecastle, a barrel of gin, ate up a bag of tallow, and made a soup of the skin.

Sunday, December 27th. We had now finished all our business at this port, and, it being Sunday, we unmoored ship and got under way, firing a salute to the Russian brig, and another to the presidio, which were both answered. The comandante of the presidio, Don Guadalupe Vallejo, a young man, and the most popular, among the Americans and English, of any man in California, was on board when we got under way. He spoke English very well, and was suspected of being favourably inclined to foreigners.

We sailed down this magnificent bay with a light wind, the tide, which was running out, carrying us at the rate of four or five knots. It was a fine day; the first of entire sunshine we had had for more than a month. We passed directly under the high cliff on which the presidio is built, and stood into the middle of the bay, from whence we could see small bays making up into the interior, large and beautifully wooded islands, and the mouths of several small rivers. If California ever becomes a prosperous country, this bay will be the centre of its prosperity. The abundance of wood and water; the extreme fertility of its shores; the excellence of its climate, which is as near to being perfect as any in the world; and its facilities for navigation, affording the best anchoring-grounds in the whole western coast of America—all fit it for a place of great importance.

The tide leaving us, we came to anchor near the mouth of the bay, under a high and beautifully sloping hill, upon which herds of hundreds and hundreds of red deer, and the stag, with his high branching antlers, were bounding about, looking at us for a moment, and then starting off, affrighted at the noises which we made for the purpose of seeing the variety of their beautiful attitudes and motions.

San Francisco in 1846-47.

VI

From *Reminiscences and Incidents of "The Early Days" of San Francisco* by John Henry Brown

Before Brown came to San Francisco, he had led an adventurous life travelling and living among the Cherokees. Once established in the City, though, he transformed himself into a moderately successful businessman. He lived to see the tiny, Mexican-controlled village of Yerba Buena evolve into a city of several hundred thousand, all within a span of some forty years. In 1886, he published his *Reminiscences,* a lively personal account of the events of the formative years of San Francisco.

How much of Brown's narrative is truth, and how much is good old Western yarn? It is difficult to say, but it matters little. Brown's account is lively and charming enough to brush aside the charge of truth-stretching. Whether gospel truth or good tales, Brown's anecdotes give us a fair insight into the life of early San Francisco.

The only pay the City officials received for their services, was that raised by fines, most of which was taken from sailors, who would remain on shore after sunset. The fine for this offense was usually five or ten dollars, as the case might be, and the money thus received was equally divided between the authorities. Captains and First officers were permitted to remain on shore as long as they pleased.

As stated elsewhere I was in the employ of Finch and Thompson, having charge of the bar, and also keeping the accounts. Mr. Finch was a man of but little education; in fact, he could neither read nor write, and he had a peculiar way of his own in keeping accounts. He had an excellent memory for names and was in the habit of noting any peculiarity about a person as regards his dress and general appearance. Captain Hinckley wore brass buttons on his coat and was represented on the books by a drawing of a button. A certain sawyer in the place was represented by a drawing of the top saws of a saw pit, and many others were thus represented according to their various characteristics or callings. Many of the drawings showed considerable ingenuity and originality. I remained with Finch about three weeks, during that time I became acquainted with Robert T. Ridley the proprietor of a liquor and billiard saloon. He made me an offer of fifty dollars per month to take charge of his place. I accepted the offer and commenced my work there in the early part of February, 1846.

The bark "Sterling" of Boston, Captain Vincent, Master; and William Smith, Super Cargo; arrived in port in February, with a full cargo. Ridley had made some large purchases of wines and liquors from Mr. Smith. The billiard-room was at that time the headquarters for all strangers in the city, both foreigners and Californians. All persons wishing to purchase lots would apply to Ridley: as the first map of surveyed land was kept in the bar-room, the names of those who had lots granted were written on the map. The map was so much soiled and torn from the rough usage it received, that Captain Hinckley volunteered to make a new one. He tried several times, but, being very nervous he could not succeed in making the lines straight, so he got me to do the work, according to his instructions. The original map was put away for safe keeping. The maps were left in the bar-room, until after the raising of the American Flag, when they were demanded of me by Washington A. Bartlett, of the United States Ship Portsmouth, by order of Captain Montgomery.

The first sermon delivered in the English language in Yerba Buena was preached by Samuel Brannan, who is well known, and will probably be remembered by many of the present day, and they will, no doubt, be surprised on hearing of his serving in this capacity. He preached on the last Sunday in July, 1846, as good a sermon as any one would wish to hear. The first wedding which took place after this city was under the protection of the American Flag, was celebrated in a building owned by the proprietors of the Portsmouth House. The ceremony was performed in a large room on the ground floor, which was generally used by the Mexicans as a calaboose or prison. The marriage took place among the Mormons, who had arrived so short a time before. The contracting parties were: Lizzie, the second daughter of Mr. Winner, and Mr. Basil Hall. The marriage ceremony was performed by Mr. Samuel Brannan, according to the Mormon faith. I was one of the guests, and I never enjoyed myself, at any gathering, as I did there. There was a general invitation extended to all, a large quantity of refreshments had been prepared, and as there was plenty of music and singing, we had lots of fun. The festivities were kept up until twelve o'clock, when everyone returned to their homes, perfectly satisfied, and ready to pronounce the first wedding a grand success. Mr. Hall, the bridegroom, had accumulated considerable wealth in this country, and he left here in 1850, for Washington city. On his return home, he purchased a colored woman, a slave. Mr. Winner told me that Mrs. Hall treated the colored woman brutally; and the woman, tired of her treatment, and determined to have revenge, one day put Mrs. Hall's feet into the fire, and held them there until she was burned to death.

As soon as the American Flag was hoisted, Captain Watson was sent on shore to guard the city with a file of marines from the ship Portsmouth.

Their headquarters being the adobe building, known as the old Custom-House. There was a captain here, by the name of Philips, from Boston, who had lost his vessel at Bodego, who did a very brave act; he took his boat with four men, went to the Presidio, where the old Mexican cannons were lying on the ground and "spiked" them, thinking that he was doing the Government a favor. He might have taken up his abode at the Fort without any difficulty, as there was not a Spaniard nearer than the Mission Dolores, to oppose him in any way. Washington A. Bartlett was elected by the votes of the sailors from the Portsmouth, who were sent ashore in boats to vote for him, as it was thought that Ridley would favor the Mexicans. After Captain Watson came ashore to guard the city he made it a rule every morning to fill his flask with good whiskey. It was usually at a very late hour when he called for it, and I would be in bed. His signal would be two raps on the shutter. As soon as I would answer him, he would say: "The Spaniards are in the brush," this was the pass-word, I would then get up and fill his bottle, and he would leave and go on duty. A short time after the arrival of so many whalers in port, there was about five captains who remained on shore to have a good time with some of the officers of the Portsmouth. Captain Watson being one of the number, and several prominent Californians, among whom were Guerrero and Sanchez. They kept me up two nights in succession, and when they finally departed, I decided to take a good night's rest, as there was no business doing after ten o'clock, so I took to my room an extra allowance of whiskey. I was sleeping sounder than usual, when there were a number of raps on the window shutter. I did not hear them, however, and as Watson, who had been imbibing freely, found the raps did no good, he fired off one of his pistols, and sang out at the top of his voice, "The Spaniards are in the brush!" The report of the pistol was heard at the Barracks, and they began to beat the long roll. I jumped out of bed, (more asleep than awake) filled Watson's flask, and was told that no one would hurt me, and to go to bed again. There were signals given from the Portsmouth that men would be sent ashore for duty. The Mormons had only arrived a few days prior to this event, and at the beat of the long roll they were all up and on hand with arms and ammunition, ready to furnish what service they could. They remained under arms for about three hours, in the yard of the Portsmouth House, and were then discharged. That night there were several shots fired by those on duty, thinking they were shooting at Californians; but, they found next day, to their great surprise, that instead of dead bodies, some scrub oaks had received the shots. The wind in bending the oaks hither and thither had made them suppose that "The Spaniards" were really in the "brush." Captain Watson called on me the next morning in the billiard-room, and told me that if I ever told, or even mentioned what happened the night previous, as long as I lived, I would be a dead man, as it would greatly injure his reputation if it were made public.

A few days later, while the Captain was in the billiard-room, Tom

Smith, (a man who made it a regular business to catch runaway sailors) informed the Captain that one of the men had deserted. The Captain was surprised and inquired what kind of a looking man he was. Tom told him he was a "seven footer," and after thinking a moment, the Captain made up his mind who it was. He then asked Smith what he got for bringing in runaway sailors. He said five dollars was the regular price. The Captain told him he thought five dollars was too much; but, he would be willing to give him two dollars and a half if he would let the runaway sailor go wherever he pleased to, as he was no earthly account aboard a ship. The same sailor, Mr. Peckham, got a situation with Captain Dring, as clerk in a store, where he studied law, and afterwards became one of the best lawyers in Santa Cruz, where he practiced and also served as County Judge.

An Incident in the American Occupation

A report arrived in town that the Californians were again mustering to take the city. It was only known by very few persons. Fonteroy being the principle one, he enlisted the following named persons to go with him to the Presidio. Captain King, Master of a vessel belonging to the Sandwich Island, and owned by Alexander G. Able, a Super-Cargo, by the name of Chever; Mr. Gordon, late of Boston, a newspaper agent; and Mr. Stetson. These gentlemen had provisions put up for their journey, and a bottle of whiskey for each. They engaged a man named Collins, the second steward of the hotel, to carry the refreshments for them. They had been enjoying themselves pretty well that evening, as they expected to start between eleven and twelve o'clock, and ordered breakfast to be ready for them at ten o'clock next morning. About three o'clock in the morning there was some heavy knocking at the front door of the hotel, and who should be there but those great warriors; and such looking men as they were would be hard to find anywhere. It commenced to rain soon after they left, and one of the heaviest showers set in, that I have ever seen in California, fortunately it lasted but a short time, however. Steward Collins deposited the firearms and provisions about a mile from town, and went after them the next morning. The next day there were two marines sent out to ascertain what was going on. They reported, on their return, that there was not a living soul in sight. The next thing that happened of any note, was the bursting of the coffee-pot in Brown's Hotel. Captain King, who arrived from the Islands, brought with him a newly patented coffee-pot, the like of which I had never seen before, nor since. It held about a gallon and a half. On the top was a large iron wheel, which fitted tight to the tin; over that was a cover; on the outside was a screw, which could be turned with the fingers. It could be screwed down so tight that no steam could escape. Captain King had with him a Kanaka steward, who had learned how to use the coffee-pot with safety, and had done so several times. It was their habit to make coffee in this pot every day; but, it so happened at this time that the steward had other work to do, and after fixing the coffee-pot, as he supposed, all right, he left it in charge of the second cook, with instructions if too much steam escaped to turn the screw tighter; and the cook turned it down so tight, that no steam could escape. The consequence was that the coffee-pot exploded, blowing the cook twenty yards from the kitchen; also, scattering the cooking utensils in different parts of the room. At that time Captain Hull's head-quarters were on the north side of the hotel. When he heard the explosion he ran immediately to the Barracks, (which were in the old Custom-House), and ordered the long roll to the beat, as the Spaniards had come to take the city. George McDougal and I were in the bar-room at the time, and on looking out of the window, we saw the cook lying on the ground badly scalded; we went immediately and picked him up, and we thought at first he was dead, as he could neither speak nor move. Captain King with two other gentlemen came to our assistance, and told me to run to the military quarters for a doctor. In the meantime Captain Hull demanded the call of the citizens, who very promptly responded, and he ordered them to form in line, and be ready to fire at the word of command. He also sent out some marines, as scouts, to find out the strength of the Californians. He made signals for the men on ship to be ready, if required on shore. When I arrived at the quarters, I met Captain Hull as I was going up the steps, and he began to scold me for not being on hand, one of the very first, as he thought I had as much at stake as anyone; I then told him he could stop beating his long roll, all I wanted was the doctor, as the coffee-pot had exploded in the hotel, and the cook was badly scalded; perhaps fatally burned. He turned to his company whom he had called together, and thanked them for their ready response to his call; and in case they should be needed in the future, he hoped they would show as great a readiness to respond as they had that day. They were then discharged from further duty. This, I think, was the last call to fight an imaginary battle in San Francisco.

Gambling, Drinking, Preaching

In the year 1847 the Bark Whiting arrived, which had on board as passengers the following persons: Charles Ross, and a young man, whose parents were very wealthy, and who had sent him out here to reform; but, I think it was a hard place in which to reform a young man. The captain left money with Robert A. Parker for his board, also a small sum to be given him as pocket money every week. Later on he left for Sutter's Fort, and I heard that he died at Cordeway's Ranch, now known as the city of Marysville. I have entirely forgotten the name of the young man; but, the captain told me that his father was one of the wealthiest merchants in the city of New York. On board the same ship, enroute for Oregon was a Methodist preacher by the name of Roberts, accompanied by his wife and daughter. While the vessel lay in the harbor, he often came ashore. He informed me that if it was convenient, and would be agreeable to the citizens to have him do so, he would like to hold services on Sunday. I told him he could have the use of the dining-room, and that I knew he would have a good congregation. On Sunday morning, June 1847, I posted a notice that there would be preaching that day at the hotel. The room was filled, and the Reverend Mr. Roberts preached a good sermon, and it was the first Methodist sermon ever preached in the city of San Francisco. The congregation was not very fashionable; but deeply attentive, and well pleased with the sermon. I can say that many who were at that meeting had not been to any place of worship for ten or fifteen years previous to that occasion. One old sailor, who was greatly pleased with the sermon put a five dollar gold piece in his own hat and went around the room and collected over fifty dollars, which he gave to the minister; and with the tears in his eyes, he tapped the minister on the shoulder in a sailor like way and exclaimed: "That was a d—m good sermon"; he further showed his appreciation by inviting the minister and his family to take dinner with him the next day at the hotel. The dining-room was in the center of the house; on the other side was a billiard-room and a saloon; on the other were two rooms, used for card-playing. I do not suppose another instance could be cited, where under the same roof there was preaching, drinking, card-playing and billiards all going on at the same time and hour. Those who did not wish to attend the religious services in the room had too much respect for the minister to make the least noise or disturbance. Let this much, at least be said to the credit of the early pioneers.

VII

From "Filings from an Old Saw" by Joseph Downey

In the 1850s San Francisco's leading literary magazine, *The Golden Era*, published a series of articles by Joseph Downey, who modestly cloaked his identity under the pseudonym "Filings from an Old Saw." Downey saw a good deal in the characters of the men who shaped early San Francisco. And in the first two sketches he draws quick protraits of some of the outstanding citizens and their amusements. It is truly remarkable how Downey can evoke such vivid recollections of men in so short a space, usually no more than a paragraph per person.

In the second selection, Downey gives us a humorist's glance at the first great event in San Francisco history: the American takeover. Downey hears more than the cannon and the brave speech; he hears the jackasses braying, the dogs barking, and the roar of the drunken celebrants in the local tavern as the city becomes American.

Our final extract from "Filings" describes the arrival of Sam Brannan's shipful of Mormon immigrants. The general excitement engendered by a curiosity about Mormon ways (especially polygamy) is followed by general disappointment when their women prove to be women, no more and no less.

Portraits

Thinking that a picture drawn from life (if not on stone) yet on paper, of Yerba Buena in 1845 may be recognized by at least a few of your readers, and be interesting to many, I have overhauled the locker of my memory, and among other rubbish discovered a few choice hand-fuls of filings, which have been most carefully laid away from time to time, embracing a period of eight years, and have come to the conclusion to scatter them about for the edification of the community.

First and foremost, then, the Harbor of San Francisco was just the same as it is now, only a little more so;—the rude hand of man and the march of civilization had not encroached upon the dominions of the King of the Sea, even in the slightest particular. Clark's point was then in reality a point, and not as now a dense mass of houses and rocks torn from their foundations. Landing at this place, it was almost a Sabbath day's journey to the first house, which combined all the qualities of a rum shop, bakery, grocery, and dwelling for a jolly lot of Dutchmen who rusticated there.

Pursuing your way through narrow paths and devious ways, if you had good fortune you might safely arrive on the square, where you would naturally stop and breathe. Now cast a good look around, and in one view you can take in the whole of this glorious city. Face to the east, and before you stands the venerable Adobe Custom House, sacred to the memory of many a dollar robbed from the government of Mexico, and many pleasant hours passed in the enjoyment of the light fandangoes and mazy waltzed by the dark eyed, semi-aborigines of California, who were wont to assemble from far and near at the beck and nod of those in authority, in crowds which could scarcely be counted, and "trip it on the light fantastic toe" for two or three days in succession, barely giving themselves time to partake of refreshments enough to sustain their fainting spirits; or, more properly speaking, to keep body and soul together.

On the hill just to the left stands a small wooden frame building, a bad imitation of New England cottage, and plumb in front of the door, seated on a porch, drawing away at a cigarrito from morn till night and from night till morn, sits the proprietor of the said house—the big gun of the village— the major domo—Alcalde, and Juez de Paz, Señor Don José Jesús de Noé, as fair, full and radiant a specimen of a beef-fed Californian as ever was put on exhibition. Heaven bless his portly figure and round, rosy cheeks; he may yet be seen perambulating around town, apparently lost in wonder at the modern improvements every day making, yet determined to preserve his identity in spite of wind and weather.

To the right about face—and on the left hand corner you will perceive a (heaven help the mark) house—a rum shop and ten-pin alley; let us enter there. Look at the face which first greets you; who is he?—Why, heaven bless your stupidity, that is Old Tinker, a fixture in Yerba Buena, a friend of the poor, the friend of the whole world, especially the friend of the sailors, who come on shore with pockets well lined and stomachs empty. How kind he always was to them—drenching them with rot-gut gin and knock-me-down whisky until they had lost all control of themselves, and then kindly permitting them to stretch themselves at full length upon the alley, and snore away *ad libitum* until they had dissipated the fumes of the liquor, and arise with swelled heads and parched throats to resume the onslaught upon king alcohol: and then when the money was all gone, and liberty hour expired, how affectionately he would remind them of these facts, and how liberally he would stand the last glass, promise to take best of care of sundry jackets, pants, and such gear as had been pawned to him; and to crown all, procure a wheel-barrow or hand-cart for the furthest gone in oblivion, and wheeling them down, dump them unceremoniously into the boat; and thanking God for the good riddance, return to his deserted shop and fill his own keg, and drowse away until the return of some future cargo of jolly dogs to enliven the scene.

Poor old Tinker, he was not the worst among the bad; was free and hearty; was an inveterate enemy to Rum, and in proof of his sincerity, he continued his attacks upon him until at last he was laid in his grave. Who does not remember his partner, the wily Thompson, still, sly, quiet, avaricious, industrious, scheming and unscrupulous, he wormed his way along, until at last, having acquired a competency, and smarter men coming along, forced him out of the country; his departure occasioned but few tears.

On the corner opposite, stands a small store, in which reposes, among a heterogeneous mass of dry goods, groceries, hardware, and raw hides, the representative of the majesty of the United States of America, in the person of Capt. W.A. Leidesdorff, one of those shrewd spirits which are often found forcing their way against all obstacles to a station which they hardly dream of. Watch him now, 'tis the Sabboth, dressed in his flashy Consular uniform, revelling in all the glory of navy blue, gold lace and gilt buttons, cane in hand, he hobbles about, the potentate, ruler, master and sovereign of a dozen half dressed Indians, who serve him with oriental obedience—his word is law, his nod is imperative, and the Czar of Russia is not more of a monarch over his thousands than is the Capt. over his Indian serfs. He too has passed away, and that too, at the very moment when the golden sun began to rise in all her majesty upon the Eureka State.

Here comes another of the dignitaries—see the air of grace with which he stalks down the street, and what patronizing nods, he dispenses on every hand,—his linen neat and spotless, his clothes fitting to his well made form, without a crease or wrinkle, while above all peers out his jolly, good-humored countenance. That is Robert T., or as he was familiarly called Bob Ridley, an Englishman by birth, but for many years a resident here, and a naturalized Mexican citizen; he has held high offices of trust under the Government, has married a California wife, and is to all intents and purposes, a California graft. He is now second Captain of the Port, and proprietor of the only respectable shanty for the sale of liquors, and the recreation of billiards in this great town. Bob is a jolly dog, knows everybody, and everybody knows him; but like Tinker, he too is a sworn enemy to rum, and in his many encounters has more than once been put "hors de combat," yet his strong constitution always enables him to come out (next morning) fresh and blooming as a rose.

There strolls another of the land marks in the person of Capt. Vioget, or as he is known familiarly, old Blucher, specs upon his nose, he peers around the corner, and greets the knot of ancient ones with a jocund laugh, which resounds all over the Plaza.

But who is this plodding through the Plaza with a bunch of greens, that!

why Soldier Jack—Juan Coopa, as the Spaniards term him—he is the gardener of the village, the only raiser of eatable vegetables in the region of town, and perforce a great man—Jack is a proud man too—but in his own peculiar way—he is proud in dress—proud of his eccentricity, and proud of his style—his white head everlastingly surmounted by a ringed, striped and streaked nightcap, that immortal pea jacket trailing almost to the ground, and those dungaree pants, complete his picture. Jack has a young wife too, and he is proud of her—nothing in the calico line, gaudy, gay, or flaring ever finds its way to this market but one pattern is sure to be exhibited by la Senora Cooper, and she is second to none of the dark eyed senoras in the fandango either for taste, fancy, or dress. She is some pumpkins sure.

Here come the balance of this jolly crowd; watch them sailing round the corner of the Custom House; are they the three Graces? Three better spirits never were permitted to roam this earth's wide surface—Bennet is the sole proprietor of the up town bowling alley, and is, in his own way, a diamond of the first water—his house is always open and his face ever on the smile to receive customers, no matter what their size, age, sex, or complexion, and when he laughs, ye Gods! 'tis the explosion of what would appear to be the quintessence of all that is cachinatory; Bennet has a family and they are all family too, one in which is contained most of the *bone* and *muscle* of Yerba Buena. They are rousers, male and female, and can work their way anywhere.—Dorente is on the German order, one of the right stripe, and he too, is a man of family; his wife is a belle, the belle, and the only bell in town at all musical; any hour of the day or night the passer by may find her up to her elbows in the wash tub, or driving a hot iron over the spotless linen, with a smile in her eye, and a carol flowing from her lungs, as if she lived alone on work and music. Gus is a carpenter and miller, he has a cottage and windmill on the hill, and consequently he commands a double respect, for his plane and saw will cover their heads, and his mill fill up their bodies. He must be a useful man.

The Dutch butcher, famous for sausages and fat beef. Baker, renowned for fresh bread and sweet pies; and even old Aleck the shoemaker, one by one stroll up and join the crowd, Sherreback brings up the rear; and having completed the groups we will leave them with you for a Sunday morning's chat, and promise, if we please you, to call again with our FILINGS.

All Was Life and Gaiety

These groups of worthies now gathered in the Plaza, at the date we speak of, constituted the major portion of the Grandees of the famous town of Yerba Buena. They one and all lived and loved together, and their eternal routine of drinking, smoking and dancing was never interrupted save by an occasional rodeo kicked up by the wild boys of the ranches, the periodical visitations of the hide drogers, or the rare appearance of a man-of-war, or whale ship in the harbor. They had enough of this world's goods to keep them content, and the spirit of rash speculation had not as yet developed itself. Did a revolution break out, it was but a change or rulers, they cared not. Worse they could not have, and there was a chance for better. Politics were nothing to them—Whigs or Democrats were unknown; true hospitality stalked through the length and breadth of the country, and to be a stranger was a sure passport to the kindliest feelings of their hearts.

Upon the arrival of one of the ships the California Telegraph (a fast horse) soon spread the news far and near, and for days and weeks the port was crowded with the sturdy rancheros, and their dark-eyed senoritas, rushing to purchase such goods as most pleased the fancy and suited their wants. The articles brought for sale were retained on board the ships, which were fitted up expressly for trade, and had each a large storeroom on the between decks, where the stock was displayed with a taste which would do honor to any establishment in the republic of the east. Obliging, attentive and handsone clerks were always on hand to wait upon the ladies, who thronged the ship from morning until sunset,—brought off by boats always in readiness at the Embarcadero, and many a one of the millionaires who now hold high their heads, laid the foundations of their fortunes on board the hide drogers, as supercargo's clerks.

No credit was ever asked or expected, but all bills were settled as soon as articles were delivered, by a draft on the bank of California, which was always paid in bank notes (i.e.) hides, horns and tallow minted from the backs and bodies of the thousands of cattle which swarmed in every valley of the country. When the rush ' of trade was over, launches were dispatched to each and every rancho, and invariably returned loaded with the above commodities, which were then transported to San Diego, the grand head-quarters, and there underwent the process of drying, salting and curing, previous to their final shipment to the States.

During the stay of one of these vessels in port, all was life and gaiety. Parties, fandangoes, bull-fights, and horse races were at once the order of the day, and upon their departure, every thing relapsed into its former monotony and simple contentment. One of the grand eras, however, was the appearance of a man-of-war, no matter of what nation.

Here was a chance for a grand display, and it was never allowed to pass without being improved. Washer-women swarmed to the Embarcadero to solicit custom. The baker and the butcher started into new life, and worked with renewed vigor to cater for the tastes of the strangers, especially the officers' messes. The cabarets of Tinker, Bennet, and the Dutcher baker, each received a new coat of whitewash; bottles which had not been cleaned for months were now rubbed and scrubbed, and furbished up; unknown quantities of liquor were ruthlessly dragged from their hiding places, and were forced to garnish the counters at which Jack was expected to lay down his dimes. Ten-pin alleys and *billiard table,* were put through an entire course of *scrub.* Balls were burnished, and cues new leathered, and every face wore a smiling aspect at the prospect before them. The Purser became (as if by magic) the great *I Am,* and his Steward, as well as the Stewards of the cabin and wardroom, were as near as could be deified, in consequence of the power which was wielded by them. During the stay of said war vessel here, the town assumed a new aspect, and to a superficial observer it would seem that naught but supreme happiness ever reigned here. Every house and every heart was opened to the stranger, and if he was not delighted with California customs, he was indeed hard to please.

Stars and Stripes

The morning of the 9th of July broke bright and beautiful, and long before the sun rose the crew of the Portsmouth were aroused from their hammocks, and contrary to the usual custom, the decks were left to their own fate for the nonce, for far more important affairs were on the *tapis* than the mere cleaning of decks and scouring of brass works. Breakfast was served at 6 A.M., and the word passed for all hands to clean in white frocks, blue pants, black hats and shoes and prepare for muster. Breakfast was soon dispatched, for every body was too much interested in the crowding events of the day to have much appetite, and long before the sound of the drum called us to muster the boys might be seen each in his respective station around the guns.

Precisely at eight the drum beat to quarters, and the Captain made a speech of (as one of the fore-topmen called it) 11 or 8 words, which conveyed to us the idea that he, in obedience to orders from the Commodore, should hoist the stars and stripes in the public square that day, and take possession in the name of the United States of America. The First Lieut. then called over a list of the carbineers, who were for the nonce to become soldiers and form a part of the escort. The Marines under the command of Lieut. Watson, were in full dress and every officer of the ship save two, who remained on board to fire a national salute, were to accompany the party. As soon as retreat was beaten the boats were ordered alongside, and the marines and carbineers filed into them.

We were landed on what is now Clark's Point, and when all were on shore, formed in sections, and to the soul-inspiring air of Yankee Doodle from our band, consisting of one drum and fife, with an occasional put in from a stray dog or disconsolate jackass on the line of march, trudged proudly up through Montgomery street to Clay, up Clay to the plaza, and formed a solid square, around a flag staff which stood some 50 yards north of where the present one now is, though nearly in the same line. Here we rested on our arms, while the Aides of the Commander-in-Chief disseminated themselves through town, and by entreaties, menaces and promises at last gathered some 30 or 40 persons of all nations, colors and languages and having penned them in the square formed by the soldier sailors, the Captain putting on all his peculiar dignity, walked up to the flag staff and gave a majestic nod to his second in command; the First Lieutenant gave a similar nod to one of our Quarter-Masters, who came forward, flag in hand and bent it on the halyards.

This was an eventful moment—something was about to be done that could not be easily undone, and as I gazed upon that crowd of manly faces, I fancied I could read a settled determination to do or die in defence of the act of this day, should it become necessary.

Capt. M. had a proclamation all ready prepared, and our First Lieutenant now read it to the assembled crowd, and when he had finished gave the signal, and in a moment, amid a roar of cannon from the ship, and hurrahs of the ship's company, the *vivas* of the Californians, the cheers of the Dutchmen, the barking of dogs, braying of jackasses and a general confusion of sounds from every living thing within hearing, that flag floated proudly up, which has never yet been lowered to mortal foe.

When the ceremony was over and the Captain had proclaimed himself Governor of the northern portion of Upper California, he constituted the aforesaid Lieutenant Watson of the Marines, Military Commandant of the town of Yerba Buena, and giving him a garrison of 24 rank and file marines, installed him into the Adobe Custom House, which from thenceforth assumed the name of the barracks, and made him at once from a poor Lieutenant of Marines, the great and noble potentate of the village.

The "Jacks," whose imbibing propensities are so well known to the whole world, were not permitted to stroll about, but were marched at once down to the landing, where, notwithstanding various and sundry wistful looks and longings were cast toward the several rummeries, they were embarked, and before noon were again on board ship. "Filings" was one of those who were detailed for shore duty, and consequently had an opportunity to see the end of the fun.

As soon as the "Jacks" had marched away, a guard was placed at the foot of the flag staff, and the assembled crowd of the free and enlightened citizens of Mexico, at last forced into their brains that they had by some magical proceeding suddenly been metamorphosed into citizens of the U. States, and unanimously wanted to go where liquor could be had, and drink a health and long life to that flag. The Indians consequently rushed frantically to one pulperee, Capt. Leidesdorff and the aristocracy to Bob Ridley's bar-room, and the second class and the Dutch to Tinker's. These houses being on three of the four corners of the square, one in the door of the barracks could see the manoeuvres in each of them.

For the first hour things went quiet enough, but soon the strong water began to work, and such a confusion of sounds could never have been heard since the Babel Tower arrangement, as came from these three corners. First would be heard a drunken *viva* from an Indian who would come out of Pulperee No. 1, gaze up at the flag and over he would go at full length upon the grass, for reader there was grass on the square then. Then the aristocrats would raise a hip, hip, hip and a cheering, "three times three," then from Tinker's a strange jumble of words, in which hurrah, viva, hip, pah and Got verdam, were only too plainly distinguishable. This Pandemonium lasted for some hours, in fact until sundown, when the Commandant sent a guard to warn the revellers that as the town was now under martial law, they must cease their orgies and retire to their respective homes. But few, however were able to do so, and the greater part of them either slept in Tinker's alley or on the grass in the plaza, and only woke with the morning's first beams, to wonder what was the cause of yesterday's spree.

The Mormon Arrival

The arrival of Mormons in Yerba Buena, a sect of whom we had heard so much, was an event which caused great surprise and no little share of excitement in our little colony. Curiosity was raised to the highest pitch, and surmises ran rife among all the inhabitants. The stories of their adventures in Illinois and Missouri had preceded them, and a vague idea seemed to predominate in the minds of all that they were a sort of wild, desperate people, and that trouble would soon arise from their arrival.

Capt. M., however, was a man equal to any emergency, and with him to will was to do, consequently he at once decided upon a plan to curb them if hostile, or to foster them if they came in peace. Our boat was again despatched to the Brooklyn, and soon returned, having on board their leader, a man who has since won himself an enviable name and a princely fortune, viz: SAMUEL BRANNAN, and two or three of his coadjutors, who were designated as Elders, and being ushered into the recesses of the private cabin of the Portsmouth, the views and plans of the newcomers were at once explained, preliminaries arranged, the harmony so necessary to good government concerted, and the parties departed for their own ship again.

The next day being the Sabbath, no work could be done, but as before stated, our Captain being of a truly Christian turn, in default of a chaplain, always mustered the crew for church and read the service of the Episcopal persuasion, and afterwards a printed sermon, of which he had a copious supply on hand. This Sunday was to be a memorable one to us, for we were to have strangers on board. The newcomers, male and female, were to visit us, and anxiety to see and examine the female portion of this strange sect, was apparent on the faces of all. At the appointed hour the quarter-deck was cleared, the awnings spread, and the chairs from ward room and cabin placed for the ladies, the capstan-bars ranged as seats for the men, and the boats called to bring visitors.

When on their return with their live cargoes they hauled alongside the gangway, the whole ship's company was collected on the larboard side of the spar deck, and every eye was fixed on the ladder, anxious to get a first peep at that portion of the human family which is generally denominated the better half of man. Over they came, and as they followed one after another, curiosity appeared to fade away, and ere the last had seated herself in the chair appropriated for her, a long drawn sigh of disappointment escaped from that large crowd, and a dilapidated specimen of a Quarter-Gunner growled out, in no very sweet tones, "D-mnation, why they are just like other women." And so they were; sect, creed or religion had not changed the human form divine, and they sat as meek and smiling as though they had no religion at all. Service over, they one and all partook of a lunch with the Captain and Lieutenants, inspected the ship all over, and then took their leave, having created a most favorable impression among the hardy Tars of the good ship Portsmouth.

There arrived also in the Brooklyn, several other passengers, but none who ever created much sensation in the country save Frank Ward, a jolly, good hearted, enterprising young man, who, imbued with a strong love of adventure, had laid in a small but very select and valuable lot of goods, and came to this almost unknown land to try his fortune here. Frank was one of those choice spirits who are welcome everywhere, and he soon made himself a pet with the officers and men.

On Monday morning, all the boats of the ship were despatched to aid in disembarking the Mormons and their plunder, and before night they were all snugly on shore, and their white tents were pitched in the lot bounded by Kearny, Montgomery, Clay and Washington streets, directly opposite the Barracks, and presented to the eye quite a military appearance. Indeed, to a stranger, ignorant of the majority of the sex in occupation, it would have seemed that a large force was concentrated here, and that Uncle Sam had determined that the Army of Occupation of the Northern District should be strong enough to defy all attempts of the doughty Mexicans to dislodge them.

The cargo of the Brooklyn consisted of the most heterogeneous mass of materials ever crowded together; in fact, it seemed as if, like the ship of Noah, it contained a representative for every mortal thing the mind of man had ever conceived. Agricultural, mechanical and manufacturing tools were in profuse abundance; dry goods, groceries and hardware, were dug out from the lower depths of the hold, and speedily transferred on shore, our men working with a will which showed the good feeling they bore for the parties to whom they belonged. A Printing Press and all its appurtenances, next came along, and last though not least, three beautiful pieces of brass cannon, six pounders, mounted in the style of light artillery, with the necessary complement of powder and shot, round, fixed and grape, gave token to the reflecting mind of what would or might have been done, had the flag of Mexico, instead of our own, waved over the port of Yerba Buena upon their arrival.

VIII

Selections from the *California Star*

The people's literature of San Francisco was and is the newspaper. The early San Franciscans, isolated as they were from the mainstream of civilization, read voraciously, supporting more newspaper in the 1850s than London.

The early newspapers were frankly commercial enterprises that doubled as vehicles for editorializing by their owners. Today, news manipulation is a far more subtle craft, able to pump adrenaline into millions of bloodstreams by judicious selection and amplification of news items and a careful nuancing of adjectives. In the days of the *California Star,* moralizing and joking took precedence over reportage ("Starting in the World" and "A Secret," in the following pages are taken from the *front page* of the *Star!*). Any reporting of current events was necessarily limited to local news, since it took several months to reach San Francisco from the East Coast, Europe, or the Orient.

Yerba Buena, January 16, 1847

Starting in the World

Many an unwise parent labors hard and lives sparingly all his life for the purpose of leaving enough to give his children a start in the world, as it is called. Setting a young man afloat with money left him by his relatives is like tying bladders under the arms of one who cannot swim, ten chances to one he will lose his bladders and go to the bottom. Teach him to swim and he will never need the bladders. Give your child a sound education and you have done enough for him. See also, that his morals are pure, his mind cultivated and his whole nature made subservient to laws which govern man, and you have given what will be of more value than the wealth of the Indies. You have given him a start which no misfortunes can deprive him of. The earlier you teach him to depend on his own resources, the better.

The Iron Master

I delve in the mountain's dark recess,
And build my fires in the wilderness;
The red rock crumbles beneath my blast,
While the tall trees tremble and stand aghast;
At the midnight hour my furnace glows,
And the liquid ore in a red stream flows,
Till the mountain's heart is melted down,
And seared by fire is its sylvan crown.

Old Cyclops worked in his cavern dire,
To tip the arrows of Jove with fire;
But I in my mountain crevice toil,
And make the rocks in my cauldron boil,
That man may hurl on his fiercest foes,
The iron rain and the sabre blows;
And send on the long and quivering wire
The silent thought with a wing of fire.

I burn the woods, and I melt the hills,
While the liquid ore from the earth distils,
That over the railroad track may run
The iron horse to outstrip the sun:
That ponderous wheels may dash the brine,
And play with monsters of the Line;
While islands of coral seem to be
But milestones placed in the deep blue sea.

When night comes on and the storm is out,
And the rain falls merrily about,
My mountain fires with a ruddier glow,
Are seen to burn by the drones below;
And as my merry men pass around,
Their shadows seem on the bright back ground,
Each like a Vulcan huge and dire,
Forging a thunderbolt of fire.

Richer than Danae's golden rain,
Is the wealth I send to the fertile plain,
The Press that gives to the nations light;
The wheel that turns with a thousands might;
The plough that furrows the stubborn field;
The sickle that reaps the harvest's yield,
Are hidden now in that shapeless *bloom*
Which I have borne from the cavern's gloom.

The miser may squander his golden hoard,
And the warrior fall on his bloody sword;
The iron horse may be stiff and chill,
And the wheels of a thousand mills be still;
The steamer may sink on her ocean way,
And the fire refuse on its wire to play;
With me, the earth would forget to mourn,
And leap at a blast of my mountain horn.

Yerba Buena, February 6, 1847

School

We would again call the attention of the citizens of Yerba Buena to the importance of establishing a public school in the town. We trust that they will take this matter in hand and display their usual liberality.

At a public meeting about two weeks since a committee of five was appointed to ascertain the best means of raising a sufficient amount of money to build a school house, and to pay a teacher. We believe that nothing has yet been done by them. We belong to the committee, but we have had so much other business to attend to that we have not had time to attend to this.—We therefore plead guilty of a neglect of duty in this respect, and promise to do our part during the coming week.

Yerba Buena, February 13, 1847

A Secret

"How do you do, Mrs. Tome, have you herd that story about Mrs. Ludy?" "Why, no really, Mrs. Gad, what is it—do tell." "Oh, I promised not to tell it for all the world!—No, I must never tell on't. I'm affraid it will get out." "Why, I'll never tell on't as long as I live, just as true as the world; what it it, come, tell." "Now you won't say any thing about it, will you?" "No, I'll never open my head about it—never. Hope to die this minute." "Well, if you'll believe me, Mrs. Fundy told me last night, that Mrs. Trot told her that her sister's husband was told by a person who dreamed it, that Mrs. Trouble's oldest daughter told Mrs. Nichens that her grandmother herd by a letter she got from her third sister's second husband's oldest brother's step-daughter, that it was reported by the captain of a clam boat just arrived from the Feejee Islands, that the mermaids about that section wore shark skin bustles stuffed with pickled eel's toes."

Distressing News

By Capt. J.A. Sutter's Launch which arrived here a few days since from Fort Sacramento—We received a letter from a friend at that place, containing a most distressing account of the situation of the emigrants in the mountains, who were prevented from crossing them by the snow,—and of a party of eleven who attempted to come into the valley on foot. The writer who is well qualified to judge, is of the opinion that the whole party might have reached the California valley before the first fall of snow, if the men had exerted themselves as they should have done. Nothing but a contrary and contentious disposition on the part of some of the men belonging to the party prevented them from getting in as soon as any of the first companies.

The following particulars we extract from the letter:

The company is composed of twenty three waggons, and is a part of Col. Russell's company, that left the rendezvous on Indian Creek near the Missouri line on the 13th day of May last. They arrived at Fort Bridger in good time, some two weeks earlier than the last company on the road. From that point they took the new road by the south end of the Great Salt Lake, which was then being marked out by some seventy five waggons with Messrs Hastings and Headspath as pilots. They followed on in the train until they were near the "Weber River canion," and within some 4 or 5 days travel of the leading waggons, when they stopped and sent on three men, (Messrs Reed, Stanton and Pike) to the first company, (with which I was then travelling in company,) to request Mr. Hastings to go back and show them the pack trail from the Red Fork of Weber River to the Lake. Mr. H. went back and showed them the trail, and then returned to our company, all of which time we remained in camp, waiting for Mr. Hastings to show us the rout. They then commenced making the new road over the Lake on the pack trail, so as to avoid the Weber river canion, and Mr. Reed and others who left the company, and came in for assistance, informed me that they were sixteen days making the road, as the men would not work one quarter of their time. Had they gone on the road that we had made for them, they would have easily overtaken us before we reached the old road on Mary's river. They were then but some 4 or 5 days travel behind the first waggons; which were travelling slow, on account of being obliged to make an entire new rout for several hundred miles through heavy sage and over mountains, and delayed four days by the guides hunting out passes in the mountains; and these waggons arrived at the settlement about the first of October. Had they gone around the old road, the north end of the great Salt Lake, they would have been in the first of September. After crossing the long drive of 75 miles without water or grass, and suffering much from loss of oxen, they sent on two men (Mssrs. Stanton and McCutcher.) They left the company recruiting on the second long drive of 35 miles, and came in to Capt. J.A. Sutter's Fort, and asked for assistance. Capt. Sutter in his usual prompt and generous manner, furnished them with 7 of his best mules and two of his favorite Indian vaqueros, and all of the flour and beef that they wanted. Mr. C.S. Stanton, a young gentleman from Syracuse, New York, although he had no interest in the company, took charge of the vaqueros and provisions, and returned to the company. Afterwards Mr. Reed came in almost exhausted from starvation; he was supplied with a still larger number of horses and mules and all the provisions he could take. He returned as far as the Bear river valley, and found the snow so deep, that he could not get to the company. He cached the provisions at that place and returned. Since that time (the middle of November,) we heard nothing of the company, until last week, when a messenger was sent down from Capt. Wm. Johnson's settlement, with the astounding information that five women and two men had arrived at that point entirely naked, their feet frost bitten—and informed them that the company arrived within three miles of the small log cabin near Trucky's Lake on the east side of the mountains, and found the snow so deep that they could not travel, and fearing starvation, sixteen of the strongest, (11 males and 5 females,) agreed to start for the settlement on foot. Scantily clothed and provided with provisions they commenced that horrid journey over the mountains that Napoleon's fete on the Alps was childs play compared with it. After wandering about a number of days bewildered in the snow, their provisions gave out, and long hunger made it necessary to resort to that horrid recourse casting lots to see who should give up life, that their bodies might be used for food for the remainder. But at this time the weaker began to die which rendered it unnecessary to take life, and as they died the company went into camp and *made meat of the dead bodies of their companions.* After travelling thirty days, 7 out of the 16 arrived within 15 miles of Capt. Johnson's, the first house of the California settlements; and most singular to relate, all the females that started, 5 women came in safe, and but two of the men, and one of them was brought in on the back of an Indian. Nine of the men died and seven of them were eaten by their companions—The first person that died was Mr. C.S. Stanton, the young man who so generously returned to the company with Capt. Sutter's two Indian vaqueros and provisions; his body was left on the snow. The last two that died was Capt. Sutter's two Indian vaqueros and their bodies were used as food by the seven that came in. The company left behind, numbers sixty odd souls; ten men, the ballance women and children. They are in camp about 100 miles from Johnson's, the first house after leaving the mountains, or 150 from fort Sacramento. Those who have come in say that Capt. Sutter's seven mules were stolen by the Indians a few days after they reached the company, and that when they left, the company had provisions sufficient to last them until the middle of February. The party that came in, were at one time 36 hours in a snow storm without fire; they had but three quilts in the company. I could state several most horrid circumstances connected with this affair: such as one of the women being obliged to eat part of the body of her father and brother, another saw her husband's heart cooked &c.; which would be more suitable for a hangmans journal than the columns of a family newspaper. I have not had the satisfaction of seeing any one of the party that has arrived; but when I do, I will get more of the particulars and send them to you. As soon as we received the information we drew up the appeal of which I enclose you a copy, called a meeting in the armory of the Fort, explained the object of the meeting and solicited the names of all that would go. *We were only able to raise seven here,*—they started this morning for Johnson's to join the party raised there. Capt. J.A. Sutter in his usual generous manner ordered his overseer to give this brave band of men, all the provisions they could carry. They took as much beef, bread, and sugar, as they thought they could carry and started in good spirits on their long and perilous trip. Capt Kern the commander of the Sacramento District, will go up as far as Johnson's to-morrow to assist in starting the party, and may go as far as the Bear River Valley.

Yerba Buena, February 13, 1847

Forms of Intemperance.

There is the intemperance of mirth, and then its victim is a silly buffoon.

The intemperance of seriousness, and then he is a gloomy ascetic.

The intemperance of ambition, and then he is the laureled hero of a hundred, a mad-cap poet, or mountebank statesman.

The intemperance of love, and then he is a good for nothing driveler.

The intemperance of anger, and then he is a frothing madman.

The intemperance of dress and manners, and then he is a glittering fop.

The intemperance of the purse, and then he is a sordid miser.

The intemperance of the plate, and then he is a filthy glutton.

Yerba Buena, February 20, 1847

A PROCLAMATION
to the Inhabitants
of the Northern District of California

It having come to the knowledge of the Commander in Chief of this district, that certain persons have been and still are imprisoning and holding to service Indians against their will, and without any legal contract, and without a due regard to their rights as freeman when not under legal contract for service.—It is hereby ordered, that all persons so holding or detaining Indians shall release them, and permit them to return to their own homes, unless they can make a contract with them which shall be acknowledged before the nearest Justice, which contract, shall be binding upon both parties.

The Indian population must not be regarded in the light of slaves, but it is deemed necessary that the Indians within the Settlement shall have employment, with the right of choosing their own master and employer; and after having made such choice, they must abide by it, unless they can obtain permission in writing to leave, or the Justice on their complaint shall consider they have just cause to anuul the contract, and permit them to obtain another employer.

All Indians must be required to obtain service, and not be permitted to wander about the country in idle and disolute manner; if found doing so, they will be liable to arrest and punishment by labor on the PUBLIC WORKS at the direction of the Magistrate.

All Officers, civil or military, under my command, are required to execute the terms of the order, and take notice of every violation thereof.

Given at head quarters in Yerba Buena.

Sept. 15th 1846

(Signed) . . . . . . JOHN B. MONTGOMERY.

Commanding District of San Francisco.

Published for the government
of all concerned.
WASH'N. A. BARTLETT.
Magistrate of San Francisco.

"Perils of the Wilderness"—the hazards of coming out West, as imagined by photographer George Barker.

PART TWO

From the Gold Rush to the Completion of the Transcontinental Railroad

I

Introduction

In 1848, San Francisco was a small village with less than 1,000 souls. Five years later the population would reach 25,000; and by 1870 the city would pass the 100,000 mark. As everyone knows, the story can be told in a single word: GOLD. But gold alone—and later, silver from Nevada—cannot explain why San Francisco continued to thrive while other towns, like Bodie, withered into ghost towns. After the rush was over, San Francisco remained the locus of trade while countless other overnight gold towns diminished. As Dana foresaw, San Francisco was destined to become a major port. The discovery and mining of gold only hurried the inevitable.

It was during these years, from 1848-1869, that San Francisco matured into a full-fledged city, blessed and stricken with all the glories and degradations that beset any city. But whereas most cities are allowed many decades, even centuries, to work through their growing pains, San Francisco had to rush through its childhood in twenty short years. In 1869, the railroad connected San Francisco inexorably to the East Coast. The City rejoiced that its isolation had ended, and that real Progress would now lift its people to new heights, driven by the power of the steam locomotive.

In the short period of 1849-1869, San Francisco developed a style of living uniquely its own: the Darwinian democracy. The people who flooded through the Golden Gate and out to the gold fields had one urge, one common goal: to get as rich as possible as fast as possible, then to return home in triumph and splendor and live out life as gentlemen and good ladies of means. It was a democracy in that no title, no pedigree, no race, no education made any difference, at least initially. Everyone had an equal chance to get rich. But this greedy democracy was no community of ideals; it was Darwinian in the strict sense of survival and success. Those who used their intelligence and will to the best advantage usually succeeded; the others were destined, at best, to become bricks in other men's walls.

The life of San Francisco in the early 1850s was suited to the life style that evolved in the placers. Both were a gamble of big risks for big gains. The small city of 25,000 sported close to 1,000 gambling halls and saloons, and averaged, for months on end, about two murders per day. The entire city was burned to the ground six times between 1849 and 1851. Twice the citizens rose up to form the purely anarchic association known as the Committee of Vigilance of San Francisco. Men outnumbered women by at least ten to one, possibly more. Europeans, Latin Americans, Indians, American whites and blacks, Chinese—all jostled each other in the streets, saloons, and business enterprises for a place in the sun.

Look at any old photograph of San Francisco in its early years. No one

73

building tries to overtop its neighbors. Up until the building of the Montgomery Block in 1856, almost all the structures are one-, two-, or three-story affairs, each crowding up against its neighbors, striving for a place but not domineering or overshadowing. The skyline is as democratic as the society.

But early San Francisco was a democracy of diversity, of strongly-felt individual interests and nationalistic pride. Rosales, De Russailh, Taylor, Delano ("Old Block"), and (somewhat later) Mulford all describe the Gold Rush City; but what a difference there is among them! National and cultural prejudices stand out in strong relief, over and above the considerable personal differences among these five men. Yet in spite of their radically different outlooks, there is an unmistakable continuity of community in all their works. This common feeling, which might be described (with the necessary exaggeration) as "grand hopes in the golden violence," was surely common to every man and woman who sailed through the Golden Gate in those wild years.

The forces were soon at work, though, that segregated San Francisco into two distinct classes: the United States-born white, and the rest of the world. Mining taxes, directed against foreigners, were passed to assure that the wealth of California would stay with the United States. Laws were passed in the 1850s forbidding black, Asian, or Indian people to testify against whites in court (these laws would be overturned in the next decade). And by the time the second era in the life of the City came to a close, all the class distinctions known to every civilization were well established in San Francisco. But, for a few brief years, San Francisco had known a life without a ruling class or castes—a privilege granted to few other cities in the course of history.

It is worth remembering that those first 25,000 avaricious dreamers formed the nucleus of what has grown into the San Francisco of the present. The grand schemes, the toleration of other folk's fantasies, the hope that this may really be the promised land they just knew *had* to exist—these are the values of the 49ers, and their best (or most foolish) legacy to people who live here now.

By the 1860s, the chaos of individualism had subsided into a quieter urban existence. The frontier was almost a thing of the past; and with the coming of the railroad in 1869, San Francisco's hour of independence and glory was over. In one sense, the story of the next century in San Francisco history would be the gradual submergence of her identity into the larger megalopolitan physiognomy of the American City.

II

The Annals of San Francisco by Frank Soulé, John Nesbit, and John H. Gihon

It is no exaggeration to say that *The Annals of San Francisco* is the cornerstone of San Francisco's literary past. Published in 1854, *The Annals* provided to all thoughtful people a compendium of events that would serve as the foundation of thought about the City's character. The book's 800 pages given an admirable history of the Spanish and Mexican periods and, best of all, a vivid first-hand account of San Francisco during the Gold Rush. Here the reader will find the source of all those events from the near-mythological beginnings of the City: the extravagance and fever of gambling, rats and prostitutes, criminals and fires. The more sober element of the city, too, had its place in the annals: churches and schools, biographies of influential citizens and business enterprise. But it was the extraordinary vitality, the *spirit* of the city of San Francisco that most fascinated the authors of the Annals, and continues to intrigue us today.

CHAPTER IX.
1849.

Increase of population.—No proper homes.—Character of the houses.—Condition of the streets.—Employments of the people.—Every thing in apparent confusion; still nobody idle, and much business accomplished.—How the inhabitants lived.—Money rapidly made and freely spent.—Gambling.

The population of the State, and of San Francisco in particular, had been largely increasing during the last six months. Between the 1st of January, 1849, and the 30th of June following, it was estimated that fifteen thousand had been added to the population of the country; of which number nearly ten thousand came by sea, and landed at San Francisco. Only about two hundred of these were females. The next half year gave an average of four thousand immigrants per month, by sea alone, about five hundred of whom, in all, were females; and the whole of which numbers landed at San Francisco. In the early part of 1849, the arrivals were principally from Chili, Mexico, and other countries on the Pacific coasts of America; but later in the year, an immense number of Americans came direct from the Atlantic States, around Cape Horn, or by way of Panama, while many foreigners also arrived from China and from various parts of Europe. Hitherto the departures were comparatively few. Altogether nearly forty thousand immigrants landed at San Francisco during 1849. Besides that great number, some three thousand or four thousand seamen deserted from the many hundred ships lying in the bay. Probably two-thirds of all these proceeded to the mines, or to various parts of the interior; but, on the other hand, numerous fortunate diggers, or those who had tried gold digging and been disappointed, visited town, to spend their gains, recruit their health, or follow out some new pursuit there. It will be remembered also that somewhere about thirty thousand American immigrants had reached California across the plains, many of whom ultimately settled in San Francisco. Therefore, it may be reasonably estimated, that, at the close of 1849, the population of the town numbered, at least, twenty, and probably nearer twenty-five thousand souls. A very small proportion of these were females—a still smaller one, children of either sex; while the vast majority of inhabitants were adult males, in the early prime of manhood. This circumstance naturally tended to give a peculiar character to the aspect of the place and habits of the people.

There was no such thing as a *home* to be found. Scarcely even a proper *house* could be seen. Both dwellings and places of business were either common canvas tents, or small rough board shanties, or frame buildings of one story. Only the great gambling saloons, the hotels, restaurants, and a few public buildings and stores had any pretensions to size, comfort or elegance. The site on which the town is built was then still covered with numberless sand-hills. The streets were therefore uneven and irregular. By the continued passage of men, and of horses and drays with building materials and goods, while the rainy season (which commenced earlier than usual, and was remarkably severe) was shedding torrents from the clouds, the different thoroughfares were soon so cut up as to become almost, if not quite impassible. Indeed both horse, or mule and dray were sometimes literally swallowed up in the mud, while their owner narrowly escaped a similar fate. The town authorities caused numberless cart loads of brushwood and limbs of trees to be cut from the surrounding hills, and thrown into the streets; but these only answered a limited and temporary purpose. The difficulty could not thus be remedied. Nobody troubled himself to remove any rubbish from the way; but inmates of tents and houses satisfied themselves with placing a few planks, tobacco-boxes, bags of coffee, barrels of spoiled provisions, or any other available object, across and along the worst parts of the roads, to enable them safely to reach their own dwellings. It was not for every body, however, to attempt to navigate these perilous places, or hope to keep on the narrow, slippery, unsteady, and often interrupted path which spanned the unfathomed abysses of mud and water which lay on all sides. Lanterns were indispensable to pedestrians at night, and even in daylight not a few would lose their footing, and find it difficult to extricate themselves from their unpleasant predicaments.

In those miserable apologies for houses, surrounded by heaps and patches of filth, mud and stagnant water, the strange mixed population carried on business, after a fashion. It is not to be supposed that people could or did manage matters in the strict orderly manner of older communities. Very few were following that particular business to which they had been bred, or for which they were best fitted by nature. Every immigrant on landing at San Francisco became a new man in his own estimation, and was prepared to undertake any thing or any piece of business whatsoever. And truly he did it; but it was with a deal of noise, bustle and unnecessary confusion. The great recognized orders of society were tumbled topsy-turvy. Doctors and dentists became draymen, or barbers, or shoe-blacks; lawyers, brokers and clerks, turned waiters, or auctioneers, or perhaps butchers; merchants tried laboring and lumping, while laborers and lumpers changed to merchants. The idlest might be tempted, and the weakest were able, to do something—to drive a nail in frame buildings, lead a burdened mule, keep a stall, ring a bell, or run a message. Adventurers, merchants, lawyers, clerks, tradesmen, mechanics, and every class in turn kept lodging-houses, eating and drinking houses, billiard rooms and gambling saloons, or single tables at these; they dabbled in "beach and water lots," fifty-vara blocks, and new town allotments over the whole country; speculated in flour, beef, pork and potatoes; in lumber and other building materials; in dry goods and soft, hard goods and wet; bought and sold, wholesale and retail, and were ready to change their occupation and embark in some new nondescript undertaking after two minutes' consideration. All things seemed in the utmost disorder. The streets and passages, such as they were, and the inside of tents and houses, were heaped with all sorts of goods and lumber. There seemed no method in any thing. People bustled and jostled against each other, bawled, railed and fought, cursed and swore, sweated and labored lustily, and somehow the work was done. A spectator would have imagined the confusion inextricable, but soon had reason to change his opinion. Every body was busy, and knew very well what he himself had to do. Heaps of goods disappeared, as if by magic, and new heaps appeared in their place. Where there was a vacant piece of ground one day, the next saw it covered with half a dozen tents or shanties. Horses, mules and oxen forced a way through, across, and over every obstruction in the streets; and men waded and toiled after them. Hundreds of rude houses and tents were daily in the course of erection; they nestled between the sand-hills, covered their tops, and climbed the heights to the north and west of the town.

As we have said, there were no *homes* at this period in San Francisco, and time was too precious for any one to stay within doors to cook victuals.

Consequently an immense majority of the people took their meals at restaurants, boarding-houses and hotels—the number of which was naturally therefore very great; while many lodged as well as boarded at such places. Many of these were indeed miserable hovels, which showed only bad fare and worse attendance, dirt, discomfort, and high prices. A few others again were of a superior class; but, of course, still higher charges had to be made for the better accommodation. At best all were inconveniently crowded, heated and disagreeable. The whole population was constantly moving, and always visible, which added greatly to its apparent numbers. If only people did not sleep in public, they at least worked, eat, and amused themselves in crowds. But even at night, they lay from half a dozen to two score in a room, on the floor, in rows of cots, or contracted and filthy bunks fastened to the weather-boards from floor to ceiling, in which were immense swarms of fleas and other troublesome vermin. At some lodging-houses and hotels, every superficial inch— on floor, tables, benches, shelves, and beds, was covered with a portion of weary humanity.

While wages and profits were so high, and there was no comfort at their sleeping quarters, men spent money freely at different places of riotous excess, and were indeed forced to pass their hours of leisure or recreation at drinking bars, billiard rooms and gambling saloons. Such places were accordingly crowded with a motley crew, who drank, swore, and gamed to their hearts' content. *Every body did so;* and that circumstance was a sufficient excuse, if one were needed, to the neophyte in debauchery. To vary amusements, occasionally a fancy-dress ball or masquerade would be announced at high prices. There the most extraordinary scenes were exhibited, as might have been expected where the actors and dancers were chiefly hot-headed young men, flush of money and half frantic with excitement, and lewd girls freed from the necessity of all moral restraint. A concert or a lecture would at other times help to entertain the weary spirits of the town. But of all their haunts, the gambling saloons were the most notorious and best patronized.

Gambling was a peculiar feature of San Francisco at this time. It was *the* amusement—*the* grand occupation of many classes—apparently the life and soul of the place. There were hundreds of gambling saloons in the town. The bar-room of every hotel and public house presented its tables to attract the idle, the eager and covetous. Monté, faro, roulette, rondo, rouge et noir and vingt-un, were the games chiefly played. In the larger saloons, beautiful and well-dressed women dealt out the cards or turned the roulette wheel, while lascivious pictures hung on the walls. A band of music and numberless blazing lamps gave animation and a feeling of joyous rapture to the scene. No wonder the unwary visitor was tempted and fell, before he had time to awake from the pleasing delusion. To make a fortune in the turning of a card was delightful—the very mingled hope and fear of eventual success was a charming excitement. For the moment, men felt as great conquerors may be supposed sometimes to feel; they manoeuvred on the green cloth,—the field of their operations;—thinking their own skill was playing the game, when chance alone gave the result. At the end of a long evening's campaign of mingled victories and defeats—petty skirmishes—they would either draw off their forces to renew the game next day, or hazard their all, thousands of dollars perhaps, on the issue of one great battle, and a moment afterwards leave the table richer or poorer by a moderate fortune. Again and again, were such campaigns fought, till the excitement and intense desire of playing became chronic. When great sums could no longer be had, small ones served the same purpose; and were, in the end, lost like the others. Gambling became a regular business; and those who followed it professionally were really among the richest, most talented and influential citizens of the town.

The sums staked were occasionally enormous. One evening sixteen thousand dollars' worth of gold dust was laid upon a faro table as a bet. This was lost by the keeper of the table, who counted out the money to the winner without a murmur, and continued his business with a cheerful countenance, and apparently with as good spirits as though he had incurred no more than an ordinary loss. As high as twenty thousand dollars, it is said, have been risked upon the turn of a card. Five thousand, three thousand, and one thousand dollars were repeatedly ventured. The ordinary stakes, however, were by no means so high as these sums—from fifty cents to five dollars being the usual amount; and thus the common day laborer could lay his moderate stake as stylishly as a lord. It was only when the rich gamester was getting desperate, or a half tipsy miner had just come from the diggings with a handsome "pile," that the larger sums were put on the cloth. Generally speaking, the keepers of the tables, or "bankers," had no objection to these heavy stakes; they knew the game better than the player, and were well aware of all the chances in their own favor. But it was scarcely necessary for the professional gambler to encourage particularly large stakes. The combined amount of all the usual small ones was very large; while every two minutes there was a new game formed, and new stakes put down. The extensive saloons, in each of which ten or a dozen such tables might be placed, were continually crowded, and around the tables themselves the players often stood in lines three or four deep, every one vieing with his neighbors for the privilege of reaching the board, and staking his money as fast as the wheel and ball could be rolled or the card turned. The professional gamblers, who paid great rents for the right of placing their tables in these saloons, made large fortunes by the business. Their tables were piled with heaps of gold and silver coin, with bags of gold dust, and lumps of the pure metal, to tempt the gazer. The sight of such treasures, the occasional success of players, the music, the bustle, heat, drink, greed and deviltry, all combined to encourage play to an extent limited only by the great wealth of the community. Judges and clergymen, physicians and advocates, merchants and clerks, contractors, shopkeepers, tradesmen, mechanics and laborers, miners and farmers, all adventurers in their kind—every one elbowed his way to the gambling-table, and unblushingly threw down his golden or silver stake. The whole of the eastern side of Portsmouth Square, three-fourths of the northern, and a portion of the southern sides were occupied by buildings specially devoted to gambling. At these portions of the plaza were perhaps the greater saloons, but all around the neighborhood there were numberless other places, where the same system was carried on, and where the proceedings were exposed to the careless look of every passer-by.

While such scenes, in hundreds of distinct places, were night and day being acted in public, the better or richer classes, who at first had openly appeared and gambled among the crowds at the general saloons, began to separate and confine themselves to semi-private play in the rear of the Parker House, and at similar places. There, if the external excitement of moving crowds and music was wanting, the interest in the sport arising from larger stakes was correspondingly increased, if that were possible. The amounts ventured in such secluded circles were immense; and almost surpass belief. Men had come to California for gold; and, by hook or by crook, gold they would have. It was a fair and honest game, they thought, to hazard one's own money against that of another. Therefore, they staked and lost—staked and won—till in the end they were rich indeed, or penniless. But poor or rich, the speculative spirit continued—(there was surely something infectious in the air!)—and either in direct gambling, or in nearly similar operations in mercantile, land-jobbing, or general business, the inhabitants of San Francisco, at this period of its history, seemed to be one great horde of gamesters. There were exceptions indeed, and some men scorned to enter a gambling saloon, or touch a card, but these were too few comparatively to be specially noticed in the general hubbub and speculative disposition of the place.

Steamer-Day

Once a fortnight, at the beginning and middle of every month, San Francisco, which is never without some feverish excitement, gets gradually worked up to a crisis. Different places have also their occasional periods of intense interest. What in other countries may be the annual fair to a village belle, a great saint's day of obligation to devout Roman Catholics, the solitary "cheap pleasure trip" to the artisan who has toiled and moiled unceasingly for a twelvemonth, the last day of grace to a tottering merchant who must meet his bill—but what need is there of comparisons? STEAMER-DAY in San Francisco stands alone; it is *sui generis*. Every body, man, woman, and child, native and foreigner, merchant and miner, general dealer, laborer, and non-descript adventurer, old resident, and recent immigrant—*every body* is deeply interested in this day. Mails in the Atlantic cities start oftener, and affect only particular sections of the comunity; but the great eastern mails that leave San Francisco depart at long intervals, while they directly concern all classes. The people who live here are not yet independent, either in business or in home

Departure of a Steamship.

and affectionate feelings, of the connections of their native countries. Hence, an immense amount of correspondence is written and forwarded every two weeks.

Some days before the 1st or the 16th of the month, the merchant, who must send returns for the goods he has received, and perhaps sold, begins to consider how best he can "raise the wind." He is not a Prospero, who, by waving his wand, consulting his book, and muttering a few conjurations, can command the elements; but he summons his "faithful Ariel," his managing clerk, and the two take a long *spell* of a different description. Daily, hourly, obstinate debtors are dunned; and are alternately beseeched, wheedled and bullied, to come down with the *dust*—the one precious product and export of California. One's own funds are failing, and money every where has suddenly and alarmingly become scarce. Debtors are doubtful, and no credit is given the unfortunate cash-hunter himself. Yet money must be had for steamer-day. This is essential to the merchant's honor and his continuance in business. Cash bargains are therefore hurried through at any sacrifice, and temporary loans effected, upon tangible security always, at usurious rates—from four to five, up to ten or twelve *per cent* per month. Every means is taken to collect a given sum. While the merciless creditor assails his shuffling debtor, he himself turns a dull ear to reproaches, entreaties and threats of his own creditors and dunners. Every man for himself in such matters. All the businessmen in San Francisco are bustling about; every body is abusing another for dilatoriness in making payments. What should have been paid before last steamer-day not yet forthcoming!—what was a *cash* transaction two days ago not yet settled for! Why, it was shameful, unbusiness-like, atrocious conduct! Where did such people expect to go to when they died? So the angry dunner says to one neighbor, and so another speaks to the poor enraged man a few minutes afterwards. The agony and the "hope deferred" of making up the required sum continue to grow in intensity until the last moment that bank, post, and express arrangements permit the remittance to be made. When the gun of the departing steamer is heard, the merchant feels once more at ease. His excited nervous system becomes relaxed; and for another week, or ten days, he cares not though he receives not a cent. He smiles again on his delinquent debtor; they drink lovingly together, and exchange segars, and chat and joke, in the most friendly manner, of their individual troubles and throes in providing for the dread steamer-day. There is little business done the day before the mail leaves, and none on the forenoon of the day of its departure. Not only is time consumed in attending to the indispensable remittances, but numerous business letters must be answered, the state of the markets described, account sales made out, suggestions given to foreign merchants for particular shipments, and new orders sent on one's personal account. The business letters alone of an extensive mercantile house must closely occupy the time of the heads of the firm for at least a whole day before the mail is closed.

The purely business letters may be the most urgent and pecuniarily important communications, but those between the mere resident and his friends *at home* are the most interesting. Many residing here have left wives and families in far distant countries. To such the opportunity is invaluable of telling of their various movements, of their speculations, hopes and fears, their health and comforts, and to express all their affectionate wishes and love towards those most dear to them. But besides the married and family man, all have more or fewer acquaintances and dear friends whom they wish should know of their "whereabouts." When emigrants leave home to settle permanently in a new land, they very soon cease to feel interest in their native place and old friends, and gradually give up the first habit of communicating by letter with them. But many of the San Franciscans have the surety of speedily rejoining the friends and country they had left, whilst most of them hope and expect that they will be enabled to do so in a few years at farthest. Hence, all these find it their interest, as they feel it their pleasure, to keep up a familiar correspondence with the mother country. The answers that will appear by and by to their several communications will be eagerly looked for, and perused over and over again. To continue to receive such interesting epistles, they must be faithfully acknowledged. Replies and other letters are accordingly multiplied for each mail. With many people, the entire day before the sailing of the steamer is consumed in writing these. No wonder that the occasion is looked forward to with much interest.

But it is not merely epistolary communications and the necessity of remitting that give lifelike interest and excitement to steamer-day. Always two, and often three, large vessels leave upon that occasion, conveying together from a thousand to sometimes nearly two thousand persons. That alone is an immense body of people, who are naturally very much excited by thoughts of the long passage, and the peculiar circumstances attending their departure. Besides these it may be supposed that at least thrice the same number of persons are directly interested as the nearest friends of the actual passengers, while the whole city entertains some kind of curiosity as to who are leaving and a general feeling of interest on the subject. Numbers have come from the mines and interior towns to take their departure from San Francisco; and these crowd the hotels and boarding-houses for a few days until the steamer sails. From every large lodging-house there is somebody departing, while in almost every house there are companions and confidants of those leaving. These must commune and prepare; they must drink, smoke and palaver; buy and interchange gifts, and make solemn promises of future communications. All is eagerness and excitement, on both sides, until steamer-day has come and gone.

III

From *Reminiscences and Incidents of "The Early Days" of San Francisco* by John Henry Brown

Most of the writing from the gold rush era comes from outsiders, foreign adventurers (including Americans) for whom San Francisco, at least at first, was just a jumping off place to the mines. John Henry Brown's memoirs are here for the sake of continuity with the pre-rush times and to give the reader an idea of how a "native" of Yerba Buena dealt with the influx into his city. Though he is recalling the events after a span of over thirty-five years, he recalls, with remarkably few errors, names, places, and incidents with an honesty and accuracy that have endeared his name to generations of historians.

When gold dust was first brought to Yerba Buena I had no idea of what its real value was, and most people had an idea that gold dust would depreciate in value, judging from the quantity which was brought to the city; consequently I would pay out the gold dust as fast as possible, fearing I might lose by keeping it; selling it often at the rate of ten to twelve dollars per ounce. Cash seemed to be money, but gold dust was looked at more in the light of merchandise. I have often purchased it for six dollars per ounce. In the Fall of 1848 the miners began to come to Yerba Buena for the purpose of spending the winter, and they continued to come until the latter part of December. In those days there were no towns or houses at the mines, and the only place that afforded any shelter was at Sutter's Fort, which afforded room for only a small number, however, I think I can say with safety, that there were that winter between eighty and ninety boarding and lodging at the City Hotel. At the commencement of the winter the miners would pass the time away by playing billiards; but they soon tired of that, and wished me to take the billiard-table out and turn it into a gambling saloon. They said they would pay me two hundred dollars per day; or pay five dollars an hour after six o'clock up to twelve at night; later than that, they would pay ten dollars per hour. The size of this room was thirty feet by twenty-four. I got eight tables made for this room, and before the tables were finished they were all taken. One man was so afraid he would not be able to obtain one that he gave me one hundred dollars in advance to secure one. When it was in full blast, we found that there were not tables enough to accommodate all who wished to join in the games. I could have rented, in the same room a dozen tables; but the room was not large enough. I had three more tables made and placed them in an adjoining room. All three rooms were used for gambling purposes; such games as Monte, Faro, Roulette and others being played. Most of these tables were spoken for in advance; sometimes they were engaged by the week, and I could then have rented as many more if I had had room for them. There were two other rooms used for gambling purposes, in the back of the hotel. I remember one instance where a gambler gave five hundred dollars premium for a room with a lease on it for three months. I feel almost ashamed to put in print some of the things which happened in those early days, as they seem almost incredible, and still it is the truth.

I am almost afraid you will hardly believe that in those days money could be made so easily, and in so short a time. In the bar-room alone, they were taking from two thousand five hundred to over three thousand dollars every day. There were also ten gambling tables, which would each pay from seventy to one hundred dollars per day. At the commencement of my taking gold dust, I thought it would be to my advantage to send it away; I did not expect it was going to bring me over twelve dollars per ounce; but, to my great surprise, I did not ship any that brought less than sixteen dollars per ounce; and often more than that amount. You can see by this, that the first cost of goods was really nothing, as my cash returns were over and above first cost. A basket of champagne wine was sold in the bar for one hundred and twenty dollars. The only thing which would buy these wines was gold coin. In that way I could purchase it for from twenty-four dollars per basket. Most merchants, in purchasing a cargo of goods, found it a very difficult task to raise the cash for the payment of duties, and I was offered a good chance to purchase such goods as I wanted, at my own figures, if I would pay for them in coin, by a gentleman, who was one of the wealthiest merchants in this city. He could not raise the cash to pay the duties on goods, which he had purchased. He sold me dust at ten dollars per ounce, and for the balance he deposited gold dust, at ten dollars per ounce; and when the time came for him to redeem the dust, he could not do so; consequently, it was sold at public auction for ten dollars and twenty-five cents per ounce. Mr. Shalabie, from the Sandwich Islands, was the purchaser. This same merchant must have had, at the same time in his possession, not less than five hundred pounds of gold dust.

I had a great advantage over most persons in obtaining coin. During the latter part of the summer, a great many persons came to the city, all of whom had coin, and we accommodated as many as we possibly could at the hotel. The only money they had was coin, and I think I may say, that one-half of the cash which was brought here by the passengers was spent in the hotel. I was well acquainted with the captains with whom I had dealings, and had full confidence in their honesty; and felt quite sure that I ran no risk in trusting them with the gold dust; the percentage, aside from the freight, was ten per cent on the cash returns, and ten per cent on the goods purchased.

We must not neglect to mention the first fire that took place during the early days of this city. A house, by the name of "The Shades," used as a boarding and lodging saloon, caught fire one morning about two o'clock. An alarm was given, and it being the first fire that had happened in the city, it seemed as though every person was on hand, rendering all the assistance possible. A new building, some four feet distance from "The Shades," caught fire several times; but, through the perseverance of Robert A. Parker, Dave Whaling and Tom Smith, (the owner of the property), the new building was saved; but "The Shades" was entirely destroyed. The men who were so perservering in saving the new building had their hair singed and the coats on their backs were burned. The men went so far as to cover themselves with wet blankets, cutting holes in the blankets to enable them to see, while they threw water on the burning building. When the building was out of danger three loud and hearty cheers were given for "the brave firemen." It was only a few days after the fire, when the rebuilding of "The Shades" was commenced and when completed, it was a much finer building than the one previous to the fire. In the winter of '48, most of the persons who had gone to the mines, returned to the city, and by the latter part of November there were over one hundred and sixty persons in the hotel. Bennett's house was also crowded; so much so, that the bowling alleys were used as sleeping apartments. We had to put two beds or more in a room; and, as we rented the rooms for twenty dollars per week, it made no difference to us, how many slept in them. Those who gambled, would use the beds during the day, and others would occupy them at night, so they were well taken up, night and day. I will here mention a few persons, whom you may well say, threw their money away. One man who went by the name of Dancing Billy, would station himself on the front verandah, and dance by the hour, and would only stop long enough, to treat all, who would spend their time looking at him. I know of one instance, where he gave a man fifty dollars, to play for him one hour. Another one who was known by the name of Flaxhead. This man brought down from the mines, that winter, over twenty pounds of gold dust. He was a hard drinker; but never was known to gamble, so he found it very difficult to get rid of his dust. After the winter was over, in the month of February, 1849, he made up his mind to return to the mines. He wanted to know the amount of his bill at the Hotel. He also wished me to charge him with one box of claret wine, one box of whiskey, and to cook him provisions enough to take him to the mines; also, to pay his passage to Sacramento. After taking everything out that he was in debt for there was over six pounds of dust left. I was ordered to put that away until next morning, or he would get rid of it before he left here. He had an idea that if he left the city, with any money, he would get bad luck. The next morning he purchased a pair of boots. He gave me one to put under the counter. He then asked me for his bag of dust. He emptied the dust in the boot. He put a stick through the ears of the boot, and throwing it over his shoulder, went from the City Hotel to the Parker House (the Parker House bar was then open). He would treat all who would drink with him, and would give in pay gold dust, all your conscience would take. I had a good many talks with him in regard to his throwing away his money in such a manner; but his reply would be, that there was plenty more at the mines. In the year of 1851 I went to Monterey, on business for Middleton and Joyce, to get a deed fixed up on the Union Hotel. While E. V. Joyce and myself were walking up the street, a man called after me, and on coming up, we shook hands, and he called me by name. I told him he had the advantage of me in name. He said he was the man I used to call a fool, for putting the gold dust in the boot. He then took me to the hotel and called for the best in the house, cost what it would. He informed me that he was married, and had two children. He also said he had bought a nice home, and had thirty pounds of gold dust buried in his orchard. I will mention another circumstance which took place in the winter of 1848. Major James Savage and John Murphy were stopping at the hotel, and on one rainy day, got to talking about the things that had happened at the gold mines. John Murphy was doing an extensive business with the Indians and often would take in per day from twenty to twenty-five pounds of gold dust. Major Savage found out the extensive trade, that was carried on, and tried to take from Murphy part of the trade; but found out he could do nothing with the Indians, and almost gave up every hope, and made up his mind to leave the camp and try his luck in some other place. John Murphy had a tin cup which he held in his left hand, while he would hold on his right hand a pair of blankets. The Indians would put gold dust in the cup until Murphy would say enough. He would move his hands up and down, like a balance beam on a pair of scales. A thought struck Major Savage that he could sell the blankets for half the amount of gold dust that Murphy got, and then it would pay him a very large profit. He got a tin cup made, with a small strap, so he could fasten the cup on his foot. When he laid on his back, the cup would be in such a position that his Indian customers could put in it their gold dust. His idea was only to take one-half the amount in gold dust that Murphy took. When the first Indian came to his tent, the major thought it a good time to try his new experiment, so he lay on his back with the cup strapped to his foot, and he lifted his legs with such rapidity as to make the Indian believe that it would not take as much weight to balance the feet as it would his hands. He then put a pair of blankets on one foot lifting the other one high so the Indian could put in his gold dust, and when he thought he had about half the amount which Murphy generally took, he would tell the Indian to stop. The Indian thought it only took half as much to balance the legs as it did the arms, and in a very few days the Major got most of the Indian trade, and Murphy left that part of the country for better pasture. I will make mention of one more circumstance which happened in 1848. A person arrived here from the Sandwich Islands, by the name of Montgomery, who carried on the business of auctioneering, and he found it very profitable, as some goods that were brought here would not sell for any price, and he would often purchase them by private sale, and would lay them over until they were in demand. He would go for a month or more without liquor, but whenever he got started he knew no bounds, and would keep on a spree for one or two weeks. One time he rode up to the bar-room window (which was very large), and said he was going to ride through. I informed him that if he did so it would be a very dear ride. He then asked how much it would cost him. I made the figures rather high, thinking it would keep him from coming through. The price was $500. The words were hardly out of my mouth, when he threw a bag of dust through the window to me, and said, "Weigh out your $500, and take enough out for a basket of wine," and before I could pick up the bag he and his horse was through the window into the bar-room. It would be impossible to relate all things that happened in '48 and '49, as persons were very extravagant in their conversation regarding gold dust, and would often lead new-comers to believe that gold dust could be picked up anywhere, even in the public streets. I know of one instance where a party, after night, placed on the ground, in a spot where he would know well where to find it, some two or three ounces of gold dust. It happened to be in front of the Parker House, and he took several strangers to show them that gold could be found in the streets. Some forty or fifty persons followed him to the spot, when he took a pan of dust from the street, and on washing it out he got nearly two ounces of gold dust; this created quite an excitement among all new-comers, who went and purchased tin pans, with which to commence gold washing. One of the party was lucky; he got about twenty cents in his first pan. There were some forty or fifty who worked hard all day; but could not obtain the color of gold. It was afterwards discovered that the parties who had the tin pans for sale, and the parties who washed out the gold dust were in partnership, and they made money by selling all the tin pans they had, for two dollars each. The same can be purchased now for ten cents each. This, they called a Yankee trick.

It sounds almost incredible now, the many stories that are told of the manner in which persons would waste the gold dust in those early times; but it was the truth, nevertheless. In front of Mr. Howard's store, on Montgomery street, from the sweepings of the floor a man got over fifty dollars in one day. Another instance occurred in the City Hotel bar-room. The man who did the sweeping would save the sweepings in a barrel, until full; and on washing it out he obtained over two hundred dollars in gold dust.

In the early part of '49 I found it very difficult to get stewards or cooks, for, as fast as they could obtain money enough, they would be off for the mines. It was so difficult to keep help, that I wanted to give up the boarding department entirely. An Englishman arrived from the Sandwich Islands, who had with him twelve Chinamen, whom he could engage to work in the hotel. He made a proposition for himself and Chinamen, at the rate of twelve hundred dollars per month, for as he could speak their language, he would be able to obtain them for that amount; but, even with them, I could only make a bargain a month at a time. I think this must have been the first importation of Chinese to California. At that time I felt very much pleased that I was able to obtain Chinamen. They remained with me about three months, and they did very well and gave general satisfaction.

At "The Verandah" there was a man employed at fifty dollars per night, who played at one time five different musical instruments. He was a complete band by himself. In '49, Dave Broderick and Fred. Kohler arrived. They carried on an assayer's office, which was the first one started here. The office and works were on Clay street, opposite Portsmouth Square, in one of the wings of the City Hotel building; they also coined fifty dollar slugs and ten and five dollar pieces for the Miners' Bank, which was run by John Thompson, (who found most of the capital) Sam. Haight and Stephen Wright. They lent the money on the best of security, at the rate of ten per cent per month, and many times over that. This extravagant charge for interest usually broke all who had connection with the bank. I have known many a gambler to pay for the loan of money, as high as ten per cent interest per hour. I have loaned it myself to many at that rate. When they borrowed the money, they would have to pay the interest until the capital, with interest was left in the bar-room, and then the interest would stop. I have often read in the newspapers, about the hounds in San Francisco, but the true history, I have never seen in print. At first, the merchants of San Francisco tried every way to protect the captains and to keep the sailors from leaving the ships. The merchants raised a company of ten persons, and signed a paper, in which they promised to pay them twenty-five dollars for every runaway sailor they brought back. These men were called the Regulators. This paper was signed by Edward Harrison, W.D.M. Howard, James Layton, Captain Folsom, Robert A. Parker, and many others. The only purpose for which this company was formed was for the protection of captains of vessels, as the sailors would run away every chance they got, and the Regulators were found to be of great service, both by the shipping and city. They were not called regulators very long, however, as they took a new name, and were known as "The Hounds." Some very desperate characters joined the company, most of whom have been hung in this country for murder and other depredations, which they had committed. I will mention some of the leading characters: Captain Roberts, Jacob Powers, Tom Edward, (who to my certain knowledge, has murdered three men in this city), a man named Curly and four others from Sydney, named Red Davis, Curley Billy, Sam Terry and Barney Ray. Soon after these men joined the company, I would see them pass the hotel very often with a quantity of clothing. In conversation with one of them, he said they had taken the clothing as confiscated goods, as the Mexicans would not pay them for their share for keeping the town in good order. There were many Mexicans and other foreigners who lived in tents on Sacramento street, between Kearny and Montgomery. They complained very much of the brutal usage they received from these hounds. They would first demand money, and if they had none, they would take whatever goods they could lay their hands on. They made many complaints to the Hon. T.M. Leavensworth, who was then Alcalda of the city. He did all he could by talking to them, to stop such proceedings, and would have punished them, if he could have had the support of the city; but he found they were too many and too strong to undertake it alone.

IV

From *California Adventure*
by Vicente Pérez Rosales

Vicente Pérez Rosales was one of the great adventurers of the last century. Born in a declining aristocratic family in Santiago, Chile, he studied in Paris, then returned to Chile to try, in succession, farming, trade, writing, smuggling, mining, theater, and distilling liquor. Undaunted by his failures, Rosales, along with his three brothers, a brother-in-law, and two servants, left for San Francisco when the news of the gold rush reached Chile.

At the outset, he was brimming with confidence in himself and the new world of Alta California. "In California," he wrote, "there were no evils which courage could not repair—at first. Later on it was another matter." In his impressions of the early San Francisco we can read a mixture of pride in the Chileno character, amazement at the dizzying rise of the city of Saint Francis, and disgust with the Americans who had begun to discriminate against all foreigners in the frantic search for riches. In the end, Rosales laments, he "went out for wool, only to be shorn."

After his misadventures in San Francisco, though, the stars were kind to him. Following a successful mission to Germany for the Chilean government, he was elected to the senate, and finished out his life in the prosperity he had sought for half a century.

How different was the San Francisco of my second visit! The city of canvas and a few more or less pretentious structures had disappeared. Tents and shelters had been metamorphosed into buildings in regular rows, though of hurried and rough construction. Foundations had been laid for splendid hotels; and the streets, formerly cut off by mire at the high water level, had been extended out over the water by the means of piers resting on redwood logs driven into the bottom. Lots that had diligently been given away were now measured by feet, and their value was more than sky high.

The progress of this town, especially surprising to men like ourselves accustomed only to the tortoise pace of the Chilean villages, convinced me of our mistake in having refused the property offered us on condition we put up on it our fine tents. Could I do otherwise than regret underestimating what was to be worth so much in so short a period? It may be said here, with no intention of injuring feelings, that in California the only men to heap up fortunes were those who had not the daring to go out and seek them in the face of hunger, exertion and danger. Instead, some accepted free lots, others bought up property for next to nothing, and some simply stood in ambush behind goods that chance rather than design had led them to bring; and it was these men who found themselves over night the possessors of positive riches.

The bay was crowded with ships, all of them deserted. Passengers and crews were raising the unstable population to over 30,000. And so intense was the activity of transient and permanent residents alike, that the city was growing and being transformed as if by magic. Long wharves had already been built out over huge redwood piles, but were being lengthened; and others, only half finished as yet, ran out from every street that came down to the water's edge, disputing with the mud of low tide room for thoroughfare and new building. Owing to the shortage of other material right at hand for pier construction, boxes and sacks of earth were heaped up at the muddy waterline in one place, while in another spot piers, warehouses and streets were improvised by grounding a row of ships in a line from the ends of the city streets. Shops were then built over beams and boards resting upon the ships.

One of the inventors of this method of changing ships into land dwellings was the young Chilean Wenceslao Urbistondo. He made use of a full moon to prolong with his deserted and useless ship the street situated at the base of a hill that forms the lefthand boundary of the port, and created a bridge with his masts in order to cross the mud lying between his stern and the street. Since there were no cheaper or quicker sidewalks to be had, footpaths were made in the streets even with bundles of jerked beef, sunk into the clay along the houses to provide passage without the necessity for plunging up to the knees in mud.

Business in the city rose and fell with the tides. On some occasions the water invaded everything and in its fullness made light of the solidest values. At other times it left things high and dry. It was impossible for the most forehanded to escape the ruinous tricks played by unexpected rise and fall. As one man became rich without knowing how, another would be crushed in spite of the shrewdest foresight. I remember building materials were so scarce that preconstructed houses were ordered from Chile. When they arrived, there were already so many houses in San Francisco that the persons who had sent for them had to pay some one to take them and unload them from the ships. I am a witness and victim of what I relate.

Yet no one was dismayed. For in order to restore the value of wares least in demand, it was enough to extemporize the opportune fires that broke out from one day to the next and exposed everything to the danger of complete destruction.

In this theater of the noisiest international carnival that human memory records, no actor played the role that had fallen to his lot in his own country. The master became a servant; the lawyer, a mover of freight; the doctor, a porter; the sailor, a ditchdigger; and the philosopher abandoned the limitless void to become a toiler in the solid matter of reality. I have seen without surprise, but with pardonable pride as a Chilean, the soft and effeminate fop from Santiago, the gold chain that had adorned his vest at balls in the capital now dangling from the buttonhole of a sweat-drenched woolen shirt, unload the belongings of a muscular sailor in waterproofs while standing with sea water up to his waist; I have seen him smile, accept pay for his job, and hurry to offer his services to some other plain fellow.

Everywhere pretentious advertisements were posted. Over a mean barrack one read the name *Hotel Fremont;* over the waving canvas of a tent belonging for all one knew to a mere gravedigger, *X, Physician and Surgeon;* over that of a well known insurance broker of Valparaíso, *Y, Counselor-at-Law;* everywhere *Z and Co., Commission Brokers;* and over the shack of a former barber in Santiago, *French Hotel!* In the latter's footsteps followed other immigrants from Chile, few of whose principal families escaped similar displays of their names in California.

The hordes of men, always men, for women had as yet not come into fashion, had made it necessary to establish at least a pretense of civil government in this Tower of Babel. Indeed, an approach was created in the office of the alcade, an officer whose duties were exactly those of our old sheriffs. All that distinguished the former from the latter was the fact that the latter's orders and decrees, just or unjust, were carried out, whereas only convenience gave any weight to those of the Californian or San Franciscan alcalde.

Brought to the scene once by the bustle, shouting and swearing of a crowd of people I saw that they were pushing one of their number into the presence of the Alcalde. Casually joining them, I went with the rest into the courtroom, a large, bare hall with a door at one end and a low window at the other, where the judge sat. The latter, after a brief exchange of words with plaintiffs and defendant, considered himself informed—again *time was money*—and standing up, loudly said, "Hear, hear! I condemn the culprit to fifty lashes, to be administered at once!"

At the mention of fifty lashes, another voice, alcoholic and broken by hiccoughs, also pronounced a "Hear, hear!" All of us turned to the direction from which the bellow had issued, and saw with amazement that it came from an Oregonian who, precariously poised on a speaker's platform made by the shoulders of three heavy-faced companions, after another command of "Hear, hear!" cried out: "Citizens! Inasmuch as the Alcalde is in favor of the immediate application of fifty strokes to this citizen of the United States, I propose that ten of us escort the Alcalde for a distance of one mile with kicks in the ____ !"

"Hurray!" exclaimed all present with one voice. The culprit himself and all the rest rushed toward the Alcalde, who, swifter than a hare, leaped out the window and evaporated among the adjoining alleys. With such judges and such litigants, it was not surprising that suits of the first and second instance were adjusted with pistols and knives.

Relations between Chileans and Americans were in no way cordial. And the decree of General Persifer Smith, sent up from Panama and voicing the decision that "every foreigner henceforth be deprived of the right to exploit mines in California," capped the list of injuries to the peaceful and defenseless Chileans. Business and authorities in alarm proposed that foreigners acquire citizenship in the Union, a status dispensed at the cheap rate of ten dollars. But such a safe-conduct was only partially useful in the place where it was issued, and elsewhere more an object of mockery than a protection. Shortly afterward the provisional goverment at San José declared mining open to foreigners on the sole payment by each of twenty dollars a month in advance. The receipt for this sum was to afford adequate authorization to work. But how many conflicts arose from this resolution between collectors and contributors!

The animus of the average American toward the natives of other countries, and particularly toward the Chileans, had increased as a result. A simple and conclusive argument was adduced: The Chileans were descendants of the Spaniards; the Spaniards had Moorish blood; *ergo*, the Chileans were Hottentots at the very least, or, to give them the utmost one possibly could, something very like the timid and humble Californians. The Americans had found it hard to swallow the Chileans' intrepidity. Compliant in their own country, Chileans cease to be so abroad, even in the face of a pistol aimed at their hearts, provided only they can lay hand on the knife hilt at their belts. The Chileans in turn detested the Americans, whom they constantly averred to be cowards; and this mutual detestation explains the bloody disasters and attrocities that we saw at every step in the land of gold and hope.

Soon a society of bandits was formed in San Francisco, known as the Hounds and composed of vagrants, gamblers and drunkards united by the fellowship of thieves and boasting the motto *Get what you want*. They were everywhere preceded by the loathing and fear inspired by their offensive presence; and wherever they pitched their camps followed terrorism, violence and outrage.

But they did not always *get what they wanted* on the little point of land to the right where, apart from the rest of the city, a kind of miniature Chile had been created. The evil Hounds therefore determined to administer a forceful drubbing; and since *time was money* in California, the conscienceless malefactors fell upon the defenseless Chileans of that district with clubs and pistols.

The disturbance and outcry raised by so brutal and unwarranted an assault can be imagined. When they had recovered from the shock, the Chileans began to shower stones on their attackers. One respectable Chilean gentleman, unable to escape by the door of his tent owing to the entrance of several Hounds about to seize him, laid low with a pistol shot the first to approach, ripped open the canvas with his knife, and was fortunately able to join the body of his friends uninjured.

The ex-Mormon Brannan, owner of the unforgettable *Dysymy-nana,* was informed by some Chileans of the tragedy on the point. Boiling with indignation, he strode up to the roof of his house and shouted for the town to gather below. Briefly and energetically he asserted that it was high time to make an example of the perpetrators of these unheard-of outrages against the citizens of a friendly nation that daily exported to San Francisco not only the finest flour, but the best hands in the world at making bricks! He added a proposal that in order to give more complete satisfaction for the injury, all willing Chileans under the leadership of American citizens go at once to arrest the disturbers of the peace.

A general shout of approval from the point and the almost instantaneous presence of the posse put an end to a bit of savagery that might have brought the most disastrous consequences. Eighteen bandits forcibly removed from their lairs were imprisoned aboard the sloop *Warren* of the American squadron, and peace was reestablished.

Three days later, when I was making every effort to find means to return to my associates, I read to my terror in the San Francisco daily a report to the following alarming effect: "American blood shed by vile Chileans in the goldfields! Citizens be on your guard!" Next day the news had assumed dreadful proportions, and by nightfall it was rumored that not only had the Chileans been forcibly expelled from the San Joaquin, but the same band of criminals that had driven them away, still thirsting for vengeance and plunder, was headed for my compatriots on the tributaries of the American River.

Judge what must have been my situation when, as I nervously pondered what was left for me to do in this anxious plight, an acquaintance brought me a wild tale of indescribable atrocities just perpetrated against the Chileans at the Mill! I confess my weakness; neither the distance that lay between the Mill and San Francisco, a distance I knew so well, nor the obvious impossibility of sending news through the air, were sufficient to make me doubt what I heard. It was a question of my brothers. How could I do other than lose my power of reason? My brothers, my unfortunate brothers alone there, and I unable to share their misfortunes! Frantic, carrying only my weapons, and with no hope beyond that of avenging my family, I paid $200 for a boat to take me to Sacramento. And deaf to the counsels of prudence, daring to make no reflections, I cast myself into the hands of fate. Where was I going? What did I mean to do? I cannot say. I remember that anything seemed possible, anything easy, except to return to Chile without my brothers.

We rowed day and night without rest. We reached Sacramento. I jumped into the water without waiting to come up alongside the landing. And with anxiety in my heart I ran till I reached Gillespie's house. There, judge what must have been my surprise! God had not abandoned me! My brothers had arrived the day before in Sacramento, poor and stripped of all they possessed, but unharmed. They had been discussing with Gillespie how to join me as soon as possible in San Francisco. To arrive, to see them, to count them, and to faint with emotion, was all the work of an instant. One would have to have been in my situation to understand it!

As we lay together that evening under a modest shelter of *sarapes* and reported our mutual adventures, joy was not long in coming to reassure us that all that had happened was only a black and ridiculous nightmare. Indeed, we were well and sound, and by actual count not one of us was missing. What more could we ask? The Americans had not needed recourse to extreme violence to expel the unwanted Chileans from the Mill. To be sure, they had robbed them and taken from them all that they had, but this in California was of no great moment.

The rest of our associates had dispersed. That very night we sat in committee to decide what was now to be done. No one was in favor of a return to Chile; rather it was unanimously determined to reenter the struggle against adverse fortune, changing our plan of attack until finally victorious.

Chinese miners panning for gold near Placerville.

From *Last Adventure*
by Albert Benard de Russailh

De Russailh's life reads like a de Maupassant short story. When the news of the gold rush reached Paris, many Parisians, including his brother, left France for fortune. But young de Russailh was in love with an English-woman of quality whom he could not bear to leave. Finally, realizing that their romance was hopeless because of the disparity between her titles and his indigence, he left for California to win his own fortune so that he could be worthy of his lady's love.

Once here, he enjoyed the high times in San Francisco more than the thought of grinding labor in the fields. He kept a diary in which his selective eye heavily favors the French contributions to San Francisco. But he writes with the seemingly innate French flair for accuracy, and can describe a wharf as clearly as he can a "fancy dress ball." He also had the privilege of observing first-hand the workings of the Vigilance Committee of 1851. We can find in de Russailh's short description more of the visceral anger and resentment that generated the Vigilance Committee, than in all the ponderous volumes of official records kept by the Committee itself.

His English fiancee would never hear any of this from the lips of her young French adventurer. He died in a cholera epidemic in California in 1852.

Here I am at the end of my voyage, after six months less four days at sea. At least I am in this El Dorado that the whole world has been talking about. I am now walking on ground filled with an immense quantity of gold, and perhaps I may find the wealth I have come from so far away to seek.

I went ashore the evening of my arrival, Tuesday, the fourth of April. By nine o'clock I was walking on the Long Wharf. I at once began to look for a hotel where I might spend the night. My friend Louis and two other cabin-passengers came ashore with me. We followed the Wharf, crossed Montgomery Street, went up Commercial and, going through Portsmouth Square, reached Dupont Street, where there is a French hotel; L'Hôtel de l'Alliance. We had been assured that we could find fairly comfortable beds there. As I walked through the city, my impressions were very favorable. It

Albert Benard de Russailh, *The Last Adventure*. Translated by Clarkson-Crane. San Francisco: The Westgate Press, 1931.

could have been scarcely otherwise: after a sea voyage of six months, and so long a time spent looking at the same faces and things, the poorest Indian village would seem like a magnificent city. The brilliance of the lights on Commercial Street and the life we saw everywhere, astonished me. I had expected something quite different. Like so many other emigrants, I had thought to find on my arrival here only the beginnings of a town, a cluster of tents and rude shacks, where I should scarcely obtain shelter from bad weather. But I was greatly surprised to see, instead, large and fine streets, well laid-out, and wooden and brick houses, all in regular order. Instead of on muddy clay ground, I walked on board sidewalks, roughly made, of course, but very practicable. While I was taking all this in, I reached Dupont Street with my friends; we went into L'Hôtel de l'Alliance and asked for a night's lodging only, since we were uncertain if we should stay longer. They gave us a room and put four mattresses on the floor with a blanket apiece: these were the beds we had looked forward to.

We had been so engrossed with the novelty of the scenery during our last dinner on board that we had eaten very lightly. Now, late in the evening, our stomachs all felt the need of nourishment, and our first thought was to order a supper that would make up for all the privations we had undergone during our voyage. Lobster with mayonnaise, a roast chicken, a few slices of cold meat, and several bottles of fairly good Bordeaux, soon set us up. At one o'clock in the morning we were still at table, nearly forgetting that we had just come ashore in a foreign port, six thousand leagues from France. Poverty might await us, and riches might prove only an illusion, but we did not care. Our natural good humor revived by the end of the meal, and we became quite hilarious when we were shown to our bedroom. At daybreak we were still laughing at would-be clever remarks that the wine had put into our heads.

We knew that we should have to wait several days for our belongings, as there is a great deal of red-tape connected with the Customs House, and it is not very easy to pass through it. Accordingly, we had plenty of time to walk around the city, and get our bearings, and see just what we could do to make the best of the business and achieve the purpose we had in coming out here. We went out early in the morning bursting with curiosity and eagerness, like any traveler in an entirely new country. On leaving the hotel, we were amazed to find ourselves on regular, closely-built streets. From Dupont Street, where we had spent the night, we walked down Washington to Portsmouth Square, a large *plaza,* around which are handsome brick houses, already fairly old. Among these are the gambling halls: El Dorado, The Verandah, The Bella Union, the Parker House, The Empire, and The California Exchange. There are great sums of gold in evidence, which, of course, the gamblers never win, but only increase every day, by adding to them the fruit of their laborious and painful work. I shall return to this subject later on, when I take up the matter of gambling. We went on down Washington Street and were soon on Montgomery, which is the Rue St. Honore of San Francisco. It extends nearly the whole length of the city. The chief banks, and all the important commercial houses are on this street. At every step one hears the clinking of gold, and everywhere a tremendous activity makes one realize the importance of the business that is transacted in San Francisco. There are many attractive stores on this street, and the numerous flags and banners, flying from nearly every house, create a strange, holiday atmosphere.

We left Montgomery, and turned to the left on Commercial Street to go to the waterfront and the Wharf. This very busy street is an interesting sight. Shops right out on the pavement, and counters before every door filled with all kinds of food-stuff, from across the bay, make it a regular market place. Wagons in unending lines drive along this street from morning till evening, taking provisions for the mines to steamers that run to Sacramento, Stockton, Marysville, Trinidad, and Humboldt, and bringing back the cargoes of ships that have just come from Europe. Nearly the entire length of the street is occupied by stores, all heaped high with goods. Everywhere flags are floating, and make the city look as if an eternal fair were going on.

The Long Wharf is a wooden pier, built on piles, and splashed with water every day at high tide. The larger part of San Francisco, especially the district from Montgomery Street to the bay, is also built entirely on piles. Some years ago the points nearest the shore began to be filled in; a bit of land was reclaimed every day after that; and the area of the city was gradually enlarged by these additions.

There is a magnificent view from the end of the Wharf. Thousands of ships of every nationality crowd the harbor, which stretches farther than the eye can see. Several fleets could easily manoeuvre in it. Steamers are constantly moving back and forth, taking out and bringing back miners who are going to the Yuba, the Feather River, or the Calaveras and the Stanislaus, to work the veins of gold buried in the earth. The islands, Yerba Buena, Angel, and Alcatraz, are very arid, but help break the monotony of the open harbor. On the opposite shore of the bay, across from the city, rise the hills of the Mt. Diablo range.

There is a bustling activity everywhere in town; business is very flourishing, and the various commercial transactions must bring fine profits to those who have capital enough to take part in them, because there are excellent opportunities for markets.

The principal streets of San Francisco are: Montgomery Street, Commercial Street, where many Frenchmen live, and which is consequently called Frenchtown; Washington Street, Kearny Street, Sansome Street, Sacramento and California Streets; Pacific and Jackson Streets have also a certain importance. The busiest wharves are: the Long Wharf, Pacific Wharf, and Cunningham Wharf. Since the various fires that have destroyed San Francisco, and especially since last year's fire of May 4, Pacific Wharf and Cunningham Wharf, both a little distance from the center of town, have assumed great importance.

The chief public building of San Francisco is the Customs House, a large three-story affair, half brick and half wood, built like a chalet, with outside stairways. This is on the corner of Montgomery and California Streets, and rises above all the other houses in the city. Emigrants learn from the American flag floating from its roof that it is a public building, and one that they will soon get to know very well. Unluckily for them, they have to go there often during the first month after their arrival, and at every visit they leave behind some of the money they have brought from France. They have to pay exorbitant duties on things that have no value whatever. The charges are entirely arbitrary, since no law yet exists in California regulating the duties on imported objects. Everything is left to the discretion of the Collector, who doesn't hesitate to charge as much as he can. This makes the job of customs-collector extremely desirable. A story goes around of a collector, who, after three months at his honorable work, retired with $800,000. The Customs House in San Francisco is a regular Coudy Forest where at every turn you are held up and robbed.

As I have said, the city is surrounded by most beautiful and picturesque mountains. The bay is also magnificent, and we are never tired of admiring it.

Public Dances

It is easy for pleasure-loving people to find amusement in San Francisco. There are the French and American theatres and the circus; women and good restaurants abound; and the streets swarm with horses and carriages. For a time there were no public dances. Shortly before my arrival this defect was remedied by the proprietors of the California Exchange, who had the happy idea of giving dances in this large hall where much business is transacted by day and which is used as a stock-exchange. Now absolutely nothing is lacking, and a perpetual carnival reigns.

These entertainments are usually fancy-dress balls, and take place twice a week, on Wednesdays and Saturdays. They are very popular. Although Americans are generally awkward and unbending, they enjoy dancing, and above all they love to watch other people dance. All the women in town appear, French, American, and Mexican; the men gather in crowds; and one often sees beautiful costumes richly adorned with lace, which the women make themselves or order from dressmakers for each occasion. A masked ball naturally permits a certain freedom, but here the feverish atmosphere of the city produces an abandon I have never seen elsewhere. Three distinct quadrilles are always in progress simultaneously, French, American, and Mexican, and the races mingle only in waltzes, polkas, and gallops. The American quadrille is danced with Anglo-Saxon stiffness and impassivity; the Mexican with a southern languor and indolent grace; but the French quadrille is a centre of genuine gaiety and animation. I often notice how American men steal away from their own group and enviously watch the vivacious French women, who do not hesitate to let themselves go, when they see they are being admired. I am occasionally reminded of our balls at the Salle Valentine on the Rue St. Honoré. There is one important dif-ference: Parisian rowdies often come to blows; but in San Francisco hardly an evening passes without drunken brawls during which shots are fired.

The music is fairly good and is certainly noisy. Eight or ten passable musicians play all the popular dance tunes for quadrilles, waltzes, and polkas. The price of admission is $3.00, and, as I have said, the hall is always crowded.

The Vigilance Committee

In my description of San Francisco, with its business and amusements, I have frequently mentioned an important class of its citizens. The time has now come to devote a little more space to the undesirable race of bandits who take such a spectacular part in California life.

Immediately after the discovery of gold, the dregs of every nation, from Australia to Europe, rushed to San Francisco and began to exercise their profession on a grand scale. I am sure no other city in the world contains so many rogues and cut-throats. The streets and public places are infested with them; notorious thieves and murderers brush by you on the wooden sidewalks; it often seems as if the earth's entire supply of brigands had been dumped here. For all these men the gambling-halls provide the chief means of livelihood. Their favorite method is to hang around a table and to start a fight; and when the brawl is raging, they manage to snatch money from the bank and slip away. Powerful secret organizations, such as the *Do or Die,* or *The Society of Death,* bind them together, and they have a leader in Sacramento whom they obey unquestioningly. You must never walk through the outlying streets of the city at night, for robbers are always prowling about armed to the teeth, and they do not hesitate to use their weapons at the slightest provocation. They are good shots and deadly with the knife. At any darker corner, they may fall upon you; and nobody will answer your cries for help. We are so used to hearing shots during the night in this terrible country that we never even get up, but only turn over in bed and breathe a prayer for the victim.

Charles Duane, who is supposed to come from a good New Orleans family, is one of the most notorious bandits in San Francisco. People say that he was uncontrollable as a boy, and that before he was fifteen he already had two murders to his credit. His relatives tried every method of coercion and punishment, but his savage character remained unchanged, and finally they sent him away, glad to be rid of such a devil. Now he is like a tiger, always thirsting for blood.

Last April (1851) the actors in the French Theatre got up a ball, and Charles Duane, who is presentable and has good manners, made one of the party. Halfway through the evening, in the midst of the laughing and stamping of the dance, a quarrel broke out between Charles Duane and an actor, Monsieur Fayolle, who had by accident stepped on Duane's foot. In fear, everyone stopped dancing. Fayolle was very apologetic, but Charles Duane's rage flared up when he saw that the Frenchman wanted to avoid a fight. Some men intervened, separated the two, and pacified Charles Duane, who seemed ready to leap at Fayolle. At last everyone thought the quarrel was ended for good, but they had not taken into account the thirst for blood that maddens Charles Duane. A quadrille began. He moved aside and stood behind Monsieur Fayolle, who was dancing. When the dance was over, Duane coldly drew his revolver and shot Fayolle in the back. The actor fell severely wounded and lay in a pool of blood. At the sound of the shot the women ran away or fainted. As for Duane, he stood calm and impassive beside his victim, apparently contemplating his work with satisfaction, and quietly took a cigar from his pocket. He was about to light it when the other men at the ball seized him. They handed him over to the police, but the authorities are so afraid of him that he did not stay even twenty-four hours in jail, and was released almost immediately on $10,000 bail. A month or two later the trial took place and he was acquitted. The case was appealed to a superior court and he was once again acquitted by the jury. The trials made a great stir; the French and American newspapers took up the matter, and did not hesitate to demand his condemnation. I do not know how justice could declare him innocent, but the fact remains that he was finally acquitted by the Supreme Court, as he had been after the first trial. Justice had spoken; henceforth the newspapers had to be silent. Today Charles Duane rides impudently through the streets of San Francisco in his own carriage drawn by two magnificent black horses. He drives them himself, and he has a Negro groom in livery behind him. He seems to defy the people. Although he has committed innumerable murders, and has often been tried, he has always found a way to escape hanging. Let us hope a day will soon come when he will not be so lucky, and when he will receive the punishment he has so well earned.

Another famous character was John Jenkins, a former inhabitant of Sidney. After having perpetrated a number of crimes that went unpunished, he slipped into a store on the Long Wharf on the night of June 10, 1851, and stole some merchandise. Caught red-handed when he was returning for another load, he was rushed to the corner of Sansome and Bush Streets. There a jury was immediately impaneled; his trial was held on the spot, and he was condemned to be hanged. The rumor that an execution was about to take place soon spread through the city. A great crowd gathered in Portsmouth Square, where the hanging was to take place. Nearly all the good citizens of San Francisco were there, all eager to make sure that such a dangerous bandit would be safely strung up. He had long been a pest. Everybody was disgusted with official apathy and weakness; enough robberies and murders had gone unpunished; now honest people were determined that an example should be made. At two o'clock John Jenkins was led onto the Plaza, and his death-sentence was read aloud. He listened with cynical scorn. When the judge asked if he had anything to say in his defense, he smiled.

"I have nothing to say," he replied calmly, "but I'd like a cigar and a glass of brandy."

This final request was granted, although the people grumbled that he was being too well treated. He drank his brandy, lit the cigar, and waited. The noose was slipped around his neck. With a yell the crowd seized the rope and heaved him into the air. This time the law had not cheated them. John Jenkin's body dangled in Portsmouth Square until evening, while the good citizens of San Francisco gesticulated and shouted with joy underneath.

Two months later San Francisco had another opportunity to enjoy a good hanging, though without the approval of official justice. For long the police authorities had been asleep; public welfare was neglected; robbers, murderers, and incendiaries were allowed to stroll about unmolested. Although the newspapers and the public angrily complained, nothing could arouse the judges from their profound apathy. As usual, San Francisco was infested with a horde of blood-thirsty criminals, but the authorities seemed wholly indifferent, and paid no attention to the brawls and murders that occurred nearly every day in the streets.

All this disorder finally stirred the leading business men to action. They held a meeting and drew up and signed a forcefully worded proclamation, publicly denouncing the judges' neglect of duty. But the protest seemed useless: crimes went on, and the authorities showed no signs of life. Then the leading citizens organized the Vigilance Committee, and assumed the task of patrolling the streets, resolved to take justice into their own hands. They did not have long to wait.

A murder was committed on Broadway, and two notorious criminals, Samuel Whittaker and Robert McKenzie, were rightly suspected. They had the reputation of desperate characters who would stop at nothing. After some delay, the men were arrested by the police and turned over to the legal authorities; but in spite of overwhelming and undeniable proof, the court acquitted them.

On Sunday, August 24, 1851, at two-thirty in the afternoon, a carriage left the jail of Pacific Street, turned onto Dupont Street, and dashed across town, the horses at a gallop. In it sat Whittaker and McKenzie, securely bound, and guarded by members of the Vigilance Committee with drawn revolvers. The carriage stopped on Sansome Street near Bush. The two men were taken out and led up to the second floor. There the death sentence was read, and the noose slipped around their necks. More than fifteen thousand people gathered to witness this double hanging. When all was over, the crowd drifted away, praising the energetic conduct of the Vigilance Committee, whose members had dared to assume the responsibility of ridding the city of two rogues.

The legal authorities were enraged by this summary execution and threatened to prosecute the men who were implicated. But the entire Vigilance Committee came before the court in a body and assumed complete responsibility for the affair. They were all certain that they had served humanity by punishing two murderers. Their attitude, their number, their position in San Francisco, their clear, firm answers, undermined the judge's confidence. Moreover, the proof of the criminals' guilt was unquestionable. Finally, the judge realized that he could do nothing, and admitted that the court had been in the wrong.

The Vigilance Committee still exists in San Francisco, and also in the valley towns, whose inhabitants have recognized the value of taking justice into their own hands. It is an excellent institution. It may prevent many disasters in California; and perhaps a day will come when you can take a walk without being armed to the teeth, or travel through the country without danger of death. It is even possible that some time in the future San Francisco and the other California towns will become well governed cities, where murders will be the exception rather than the rule. At present, this seems an idle dream. But let us hope that it will be fulfilled.

From what I have said, you can imagine the corruption of California justice. Every judge can be bribed: for a small sum a man can have his enemy imprisoned, and escape punishment himself. And as for foreigners, God help them if they have any legal difficulties with Americans. No matter how strong their case may be, they have no chance. The spirit of nationalism is all-powerful here. The great American people is free, but one must admit that this liberty is put to strange uses.

The Police

As for the police, I have only one thing to say. The police force is largely made up of ex-bandits, and naturally the members are interested above all in saving their old friends from punishment. Policemen here are quite as much to be feared as the robbers; if they know you have money, they will be the first to knock you on the head. You pay them well to watch over your house, and they set it on fire. In short, I think that all the people concerned with justice or the police are in league with the criminals. The city is in a hopeless chaos, and many years must pass before order can be established. In a country where so many races are mingled, a severe and inflexible justice is desirable, which would govern with an iron hand.

A dive on the Barbary Coast during Gold Rush days.

VI

From *El Dorado, Or Adventures in the Path of Empire* by Bayard Taylor

In 1849, the *New York Tribune* sent its young ace reporter, Bayard Taylor, to the gold country. The rumors that drifted back East were too dazzling to be believed, and many people suspected the whole business to be a land promoter's plot to lure emigrants. Taylor, one of the outstanding reporting talents of the last century, was ready to send back an accurate, sensible account that would correct the bizarre tall tales concocted in California.

What he found in the city of San Francisco strained his credulity to the breaking point. The incredibly energetic populace, the churning mixture of races, the inversion of ordinary social values, the exorbitant prices charged for everything—Taylor had come to check out wild exaggerations, only to find that the reality was far more hallucinatory, more exhilarating, than the most breathless rumor vented in the east coast newspapers.

Fortunately, his reportorial talents were up to the task of describing, in detail and with breadth of perspective, the inchoate city of San Francisco. He gives us two pictures of the City—once on his way to the gold fields, and again on his way back. No one has better conveyed the *feeling* of the surging growth of San Francisco than Bayard Taylor in his two portraits of the City in *El Dorado*.

First Impressions of San Francisco

At last the voyage is drawing to a close. Fifty-one days have elapsed since leaving New York, in which time we have, in a manner, coasted both sides of the North-American Continent, from the parallel of 40° N. to its termination, within a few degrees of the Equator, over seas once ploughed by the keels of Columbus and Balboa, of Grijalva and Sebastian Viscaino. All is excitement on board; the Captain had just taken his noon observation. We are running along the shore, within six or eight miles' distance; the hills are bare and sandy, but loom up finely through the deep blue haze. A brig bound to San Francisco, but fallen off to the leeward of the harbor, is making a new tack on our left, to come up again. The coast trends somewhat more to the westward, and a notch or gap is at least visible in its lofty outline.

111

An hour later; we are in front of the entrance to San Francisco Bay. The mountains on the northern side are 3,000 feet in height, and come boldly down to the sea. As the view opens through the splendid strait, three or four miles in width, the island rock of Alcatraz appears, gleaming white in the distance. An inward-bound ship follows close on our wake, urged on by wind and tide. There is a small fort perched among the trees on our right, where the strait is narrowest, and a glance at the formation of the hills shows that this pass might be made impregnable as Gibraltar. The town is still concealed behind the promontory around which the Bay turns to the southward, but between Alcatraz and the island of Yerba Buena, now coming into sight, I can see vessels at anchor. High through the vapor in front, and thirty miles distant, rises the peak of Monte Diablo, which overlooks everything between the Sierra Nevada and the Ocean. On our left opens the bight of Sausalito, where the U.S. propeller *Massachusetts* and several other vessels are at anchor.

At last we are through the Golden Gate—fit name for such a magnificent portal to the commerce of the Pacific! Yerba Buena Island is in front; southward and westward opens the renowned harbor, crowded with the shipping of the world, mast behind mast and vessel behind vessel, the flags of all nations fluttering in the breeze! Around the curving shore of the Bay and upon the sides of three hills which rise steeply from the water, the middle one receding so as to form a bold amphitheatre, the town is planted and seems scarcely yet to have taken root, for tents, canvas, plank, mud and adobe houses are mingled together without the least apparent attempt at order and durability. But I am not yet on shore. The gun of the *Panama* has just announced our arrival to the people on land. We glide on with the tide, past the U.S. ship *Ohio* and opposite the main landing, outside of the forest of masts. A dozen boats are creeping out to us over the water; the signal is given—the anchor drops—our voyage is over. . .

The *Ohio's* boat put us ashore at the northern point of the anchorage, at the foot of a steep bank, from which a high pier had been built into the bay. A large vessel lay at the end, discharging her cargo. We scrambled up through piles of luggage, and among the crowd collected to witness our arrival, picked out two Mexicans to carry our trunks to a hotel. The barren side of the hill before us was covered with tents and canvas houses, and nearly in front a large two-story building displayed the sign: "Fremont Family Hotel."

As yet, we were only in the suburbs of the town. Crossing the shoulder of the hill, the view extended around the curve of the bay, and hundreds of tents and houses appeared, scattered all over the heights, and along the shore for more than a mile. A furious wind was blowing down through a gap in the hills, filling the streets with clouds of dust. On every side stood buildings of all kinds, begun or half-finished, and the greater part of them mere canvas sheds, open in front, and covered with all kinds of signs, in all languages. Great quantities of goods were piled up in the open air, for want of a place to store them. The streets were full of people, hurrying to and fro, and of as diverse and bizarre a character as the houses: Yankees of every possible variety, native Californians in *sarapes* and sombreros, Chileans, Sonorians, Kanakas from Hawaii, Chinese with long tails, Malays armed with their everlasting creeses and others in whose embrowned and bearded visage it was impossible to recognize any especial nationality. We came at last into the plaza, now dignified by the name Portsmouth Square. It lies on the slant side of the hill, and from a high pole in front of a long one-story adobe building used as the Custom House, the American flag was flying. On the lower side stood the Parker House—an ordinary frame house of about sixty feet front—and towards its entrance we directed our course.

Our luggage was deposited on one of the rear porticos, and we discharged the porters, after paying them two dollars each—a sum so immense in comparison to the service rendered that there was no longer any doubt of our having actually landed in California. There were no lodgings to be had at the Parker House—not even a place to unroll our blankets; but one of the proprietors accompanied us across the plaza to the City Hotel, where we obtained a room with two beds at $25 per week, meals being in addition $20 per week. I asked the landlord whether he could send a porter for our trunks. "There is none belonging to the house," said he; "every man is his own porter here." I returned to the Parker House, shouldered a heavy trunk, took a valise in my hand and carried them to my quarters, in the teeth of the wind. Our room was in a sort of garret over the only story of the hotel; two cots, evidently of California manufacture, and covered only with a pair of blankets, two chairs, a rough table and a small looking-glass, constituted the furniture. There was not a space enough between the bed and bare rafters overhead, to sit upright, and I gave myself a severe blow in rising the next morning without the proper heed. Through a small roof-window of dim glass, I could see the opposite shore of the bay, then partly hidden by the evening fogs. The wind whistled around the eaves and rattled the tiles with a cold, gusty sound, that would have imparted a dreary character to the place, had I been in a mood to listen.

Many of the passengers began speculation at the moment of landing. The most ingenious and successful operation was made by a gentleman of New York, who took out fifteen hundred copies of The Tribune and other papers, which he disposed of in two hours, at one dollar a-piece! Hearing of this I bethought me about a dozen papers which I had used to fill up crevices in packing my valise. There was a newspaper merchant at the corner of the City Hotel, and to him I proposed the sale of them, asking him to name a price. "I shall want to make a good profit on the retail price," said he, "and can't give more than ten dollars for the lot." I was satisfied with the wholesale price, which was a gain of just four thousand per cent!

I set out for a walk before dark and climbed a hill back of the town, passing a number of tents pitched in the hollows. The scattered houses spread out below me and the crowded shipping in the harbor, backed by a lofty line of mountains, made an imposing picture. The restless, feverish tide of life in that little spot, and the thought that what I then saw and was yet to see will hereafter fill one of the most marvellous pages of all history, rendered it singularly impressive. The feeling was not decreased on talking that evening with some of the old residents, (that is, of six months' standing,) and hearing their several experiences. Every new-comer in San Francisco is overtaken with a sense of complete bewilderment. The mind, however it may be prepared for an astonishing condition of affairs, cannot immediately push aside its old instincts of value and ideas of business, letting all past experience go for naught and casting all its faculties for action, intercourse with its fellows or advancement in any path of ambition, into shapes which it never before imagined. As in the turn of the dissolving views, there is a period when it wears neither the old nor the new phase, but the vanishing images of the one and the growing perceptions of the other are blended in painful and misty confusion. One knows not whether he is awake or in some wonderful dream. Never have I had so much difficulty in establishing, satisfactorily to my own sense, the reality of what I saw and heard.

I was forced to believe many things, which in my communications to The Tribune I was almost afraid to write, with any hope of their obtaining credence. It may be interesting to give here a few instances of the enormous and unnatural value put upon property at the time of my arrival. The Parker House rented for $110,000 yearly, at least $60,000 of which was paid by gamblers, who held nearly all the second story. Adjoining it on the right was a canvas-tent fifteen by twenty-five feet, called "Eldorado," and occupied likewise by gamblers, which brought $40,000. On the opposite corner of the plaza, a building called the "Miner's Bank," used by Wright & Co., brokers, about half the size of a fire-engine house in New York, was held at a rent of $75,000. A mercantile house paid $40,000 rent for a one-story building of twenty feet front; the United States Hotel, $36,000; the Post-Office, $7,000, and so on to the end of the chapter. A friend of mine, who wished to find a place for a law-office, was shown a cellar in the earth, about twelve feet square and six deep, which he could have at $250 a month. One of the common soldiers at the battle of San Pasquale was reputed to be among the millionaires of the place, with an income of $50,000 *monthly.* A citizen of San Francisco died insolvent to the amount of $41,000 the previous Autumn. His administrators were delayed in settling his affairs, and his real estate advanced so rapidly in value meantime, that after his debts were paid his heirs had a yearly income of $40,000. These facts were indubitably attested; every one believed them, yet hearing them talked of daily, as matters of course, one at first could not help feeling as if he had been eating of "the insane root."

The prices paid for labor were in proportion to everything else. The car-man of Mellus, Howard & Co. had a salary of $6,000 a year, and many others made from $15 to $20 daily. Servants were paid from $100 to $200 a month, but the wages of the rougher kinds of labor had fallen to about $8. Yet, notwithstanding the number of gold-seekers who were returning enfeebled and disheartened from the mines, it was difficult to obtain as many workmen as the forced growth of the city demanded. A gentleman who arrived in April told me he then found but thirty or forty houses; the population was then so scant that not more than twenty-five persons would be seen in the streets at any one time. Now, there were probably five hundred houses, tents and sheds, with a population, fixed and floating, of six thousand. People who had been absent six weeks came back and could scarcely recognize the place. Streets were regularly laid out, and already there were three piers at which small vessels could discharge. It was calculated that the town increased daily by from fifteen to thirty houses; its skirts were rapidly approaching the summits of the three hills on which it is located.

A curious result of the extraordinary abundance of gold and the facility with which fortunes were acquired, struck me at the first glance. All business was transacted on so extensive a scale that the ordinary habits of solicitation and compliance on the one hand and stubborn cheapening on the other, seemed to be entirely forgotten. You enter a shop to buy something; the owner eyes you with perfect indifference, waiting for you to state your want; if you object to the price, you are at liberty to leave, for you need not expect to get it cheaper; he evidently cares little whether you buy it or not. One who has been some time in the country will lay down the money, without wasting words. The only exception I found to this rule was that of a sharp-faced Down-Eastern just opening his stock, who was much distressed when his clerk charged me seventy-five cents for a coil of rope, in-stead of one dollar. This disregard for all the petty arts of money-making was really a refreshing feature of society. Another equally agreeable trait was the punctuality with which debts were paid, and the general confidence which men were obliged to place, perforce, in each other's honesty. Perhaps this latter fact was owing, in part, to the impossibility of protecting wealth, and consequent dependence on an honorable regard for the rights of others.

About the hour of twilight the wind fell; the sound of a gong called us to tea, which was served in the largest room of the hotel. The fare was abundant and of much better quality than we expected—better, in fact, than I was able to find there two months later. The fresh milk, butter and excellent beef of the country were real luxuries after our sea-fare. Thus braced against the fog and raw temperature, we sailed out for a night-view of San Francisco, then even more peculiar than its daylight look. Business was over about the usual hour, and then the harvest-time of the gamblers commenced. Every "hell" in the place, and I did not pretend to number them, was crowded, and immense sums were staked at the monte and faro tables. A boy of fifteen, in one place, won about $500, which he coolly pocketed and carried off. One of the gang we brought in the Panama won $1,500 in the course of the evening, and the other lost $2,400. A fortunate miner made himself conspicuous by betting large piles of ounces on a single throw. His last stake of 100 oz. was lost, and I saw him the following morning dashing through the streets, trying to break his own neck or that of the magnificent *garañon* he bestode.

Walking through the town the next day, I was quite amazed to find a dozen persons busily employed in the street before the United States Hotel, digging up the earth with knives and crumbling it in their hands. They were actual gold-hunters, who obtained in this way about $5 a day. After blowing the fine dirt carefully in their hands, a few specks of gold were left, which they placed in a piece of white paper. A number of children were engaged in the same business, picking out the fine grains by applying to them the head of a pin, moistened in their mouths. I was told of a small boy having taken home $14 as the result of one day's labor. On climbing the hill to the Post Office I observed in places, where the wind had swept away the sand, several glittering dots of the real metal, but, like the Irishman who kicked the dollar out of his way, concluded to wait till I should reach the heap. The presence of gold in the streets was probably occasioned by the leakings from the miner's bags and the sweepings of stores; though it may also be, to a slight extent, native in the earth, particles having been found in the clay thrown up from a deep well.

The arrival of a steamer with a mail ran the usual excitement and activity of the town up to its highest possible notch. The little Post Office, half-way up the hill, was almost hidden from sight by the crowds that clustered around it. Mr. Moore, the new Postmaster, who was my fellow-traveler from New York, barred every door and window from the moment of his entrance, and with his sons and a few clerks, worked steadily for two days and two nights, till the distribution of twenty thousand letters was completed. Among the many persons I met, the day after landing, was Mr. T. Butler King, who had just returned from an expedition to the placers, in company with General Smith. Mr. Edwin Bryant, of Kentucky, and Mr. Durivage, of New Orleans, had arrived a few days previous, the former by way of the Great Salt Lake, and the latter by the northern provinces of Mexico and the Gila. I found the artist Osgood in a studio about eight feet square, with a head of Captain Sutter on his easel. He had given up gold-digging, after three months of successful labor among the mountains.

I could make no thorough acquaintance with San Francisco during this first visit. Lieutenant Beale, who held important Government dispatches for Colonel Fremont, made arrangements to leave for San José on the second morning, and offered me a seat on the back of one of his mules. Our fellow-passenger, Colonel Lyons, of Louisiana, joined us, completing the mystic number which travelers should be careful not to exceed. We made hasty tours through all the shops on Clay, Kearny, Washington and Montgomery streets, on the hunt of the proper equipments. Articles of clothing were cheaper than they had been or were afterwards; tolerable blankets could be had for $6 a pair; coarse flannel shirts, $3; Chilean spurs, with rowels two inches long, $5, and Mexican *sarapes,* of coarse texture but gay color, $10. We could find no saddle-bags in the town, and were necessitated to pack one of the mules. Among our camping materials were a large hatchet and plenty of rope for making lariats; in addition to which each of us carried a wicker flask slung over one shoulder. We laid aside our civilized attire, struck long sheath-knives into our belts, put pistols into our pockets and holsters, and buckled on the immense spurs which jingled as they struck the ground at every step. Our "animals" were already in waiting; an *alazan,* the California term for a sorrel horse, a beautiful brown mule, two of a cream color and a dwarfish little fellow whose long forelock and shaggy mane gave him altogether an elfish character of cunning and mischief.

San Francisco by Day and Night

A better idea of San Francisco, in the beginning of September, 1849, cannot be given than by the description of a single day. Supposing the visitor to have been long enough in the place to sleep on a hard plank and in spite of the attacks of innumerable fleas, he will be awakened at daylight by the noises of building, with which the hills are all alive. The air is temperate, and the invariable morning fog is just beginning to gather. By sunrise, which gleams hazily over the Coast Mountains across the Bay, the whole populace is up and at work. The wooden buildings unlock their doors, the canvas houses and tents throw back their front curtains, the lighters on the water are warped out from ship to ship; carts and porters are busy along the beach; and only the gaming-tables, thronged all night by the votaries of chance, are idle and deserted. The temperature is so fresh as to inspire an active habit of body, and even without the stimulus of trade and speculation there would be a few sluggards at this season.

As early as half-past six the bells begin to sound to breakfast, and for an hour thenceforth, their incessant clang and the braying of immense gongs drown all the hammers that are busy on a hundred roofs. The hotels, restaurants and refectories of all kinds are already as numerous as gaming-tables, and equally various in kind. The tables d'hote of the first class, (which charge $2 and upwards the meal,) are abundantly supplied. There are others, with more simple and solid fare, frequented by the large class who have their fortunes yet to make. At the United States and California restaurants, on the plaza, you may get an excellent beefsteak, scantily garnished with potatoes, and a cup of good coffee or chocolate, for $1. Fresh beef, bread, potatoes, and all provisions which will bear importation, are plenty; but milk, fruit and vegetables are classed as luxuries, and fresh butter is rarely heard of. On Montgomery street, and the vacant space fronting the water, venders of coffee, cakes and sweetmeats have erected their stands, in order to tempt the appetite of sailors just arrived in port, or miners coming down from the mountains.

By nine o'clock the town is in the full flow of business. The streets running down to the water, and Montgomery street which fronts the Bay, are crowded with people, all in hurried motion. The variety of characters and costumes is remarkable. Our own countrymen seem to lose their local peculiarities in such a crowd, and it is by chance epithets rather than by manner, that the New-Yorker is distinguished from the Kentuckian, the Carolinian from the Down-Easten, the Virginian from the Texan. The German and Frenchman are most easily recognized. Peruvians and Chileans go by in their brown ponchos, and the sober Chinese, cool and impassive in the midst of excitement, look out of the oblique corners of their long eyes at the bustle, but are never tempted to venture from their own line of business. The eastern side of the plaza, in front of the Parker House and a canvas hell called the Eldorado, are the general rendezvous of business and amusement—combining 'change, park, club-room and promenade all in one. There, everybody not constantly employed in one spot, may be seen at some time of the day. The character of the groups scattered along the plaza is oftentimes very interesting. In one place are three or four speculators bargaining for lots, buying and selling "fifty varas square" in towns, some of which are canvas and some only paper; in another, a company of miners, brown as leather, and rugged in features as in dress; in a third, perhaps, three or four naval officers speculating on the next cruise, or a knot of genteel gamblers, talking over the last night's operations.

The day advances. The mist which after sunrise hung low and heavy for an hour or two, has risen above the hills, and there will be two hours of pleasant sunshine before the wind sets in from the sea. The crowd in the streets is now wholly alive. Men dart hither and thither, as if possessed with a never-resting spirit. You speak to an acquaintance—a merchant, perhaps. He utters a few hurried words of greeting, while his eyes send keen glances on all sides of you; suddenly he catches sight of somebody in the crowd; he is off, and in the next five minutes has bought up half a cargo, sold a town lot at treble the sum he gave, and taken a share in some new and imposing speculation. It is impossible to witness this excess and dissipation of business, without feeling something of its influence. The very air is pregnant with the magnetism of bold, spirited, unwearied action, and he who but ventures into the outer circle of the whirlpool, is spinning, ere he has time for thought, in its dizzy vortex.

But see! the groups in the plaza suddenly scatter; the city surveyor jerks his pole out of the ground and leaps on a pile of boards; the venders of cakes and sweetmeats follow his example, and the place is cleared, just as a wild bull which has been racing down Kearny street makes his appearance. Two *vaqueros,* shouting and swinging their lariats, follow at a hot gallop; the dust flies as they dash across the plaza. One of them, in mid-career, hurls his lariat in the air. Mark how deftly the coil unwinds in its flying curve, and with what precision the noose falls over the bull's horns! The horse wheels as if on a pivot, and shoots off in an opposite line. He knows the length of the lariat to a hair, and the instant it is drawn taut, plants his feet firmly for the shock and throws his body forward. The bull is "brought up" with such force as to throw him off his legs. He lies stunned a moment, and then, rising heavily, makes another charge. But by this time the second *vaquero* has thrown a lariat around one of his hind legs, and thus checked on both sides, he is dragged off to slaughter.

The plaza is refilled as quickly as it was emptied, and the course of business is resumed. About twelve o'clock, a wind begins to blow from the north-west, sweeping with most violence through a gap between the hills, opening towards the Golden Gate. The bells and gongs begin to sound for dinner, and these two causes tend to lessen the crowd in the streets for business an hour or two. Two o'clock is the usual dinnertime for business men, but some of the old and successful merchants have adopted the fashionable hour of five. Where shall we dine today? The restaurants display their signs invitingly on all sides; we have choice of the United States, Tortoni's, the Alhambra, and many other equally classic resorts, but Delmonico's, like its distinguished original in New York, has the highest prices and the greatest variety of dishes. We go down to Kearny street to a two-story wooden house on the corner of Jackson. The lower story is a market; the walls are garnished with quarters of beef and mutton: a huge pile of Sandwich Island squashes fills one corner, and several cabbage-heads, valued at $2 each, show themselves in the window. We enter a little door at the end of the building, ascend a dark, narrow flight of steps, and find ourselves in a long, low room, with ceiling and walls of white muslin and a floor covered with oil-cloth.

There are about twenty tables disposed in two rows, all of them so well filled that we have some difficulty in finding places. Taking up the written bill of fare, we find such items as the following:

Soups.

Mock Turtle	$ .75
St. Julien	1.00

Fish.

Boiled Salmon Trout, Anchovy sauce $1.75

Boiled.

Leg Mutton, caper sauce 1.00
Corned Beef, Cabbage 1.00
Ham and Tongues................................... .75

Entrees.

Fillet of Beef, mushroom sauce 1.75
Veal Cutlets, breaded 1.00
Mutton Chop 1.00
Lobster Salad 2.00
Sirloin of Venison 1.50
Baked Macaroni .... .75
Beef Tongue, sauce piquante........................ 1.00

So that, with a moderate appetite, the dinner will cost us $5, if we are at all epicurean in our tastes. There are cries of "steward!" from all parts of the room—the word "waiter" is not considered sufficiently respectful, seeing that the waiter may have been a lawyer or merchant's clerk a few months before. The dishes look very small as they are placed on the table, but they are skilfully cooked and very palatable to men that have ridden in from the diggings. The appetite one acquires in California is something remarkable. For two months after my arrival, my sensations were like those of a famished wolf.

In the matter of dining, the tastes of all nations can be gratified here. There are French restaurants on the plaza and Dupont street; an extensive German establishment on Pacific street; the *Fonda Peruana;* the Italian Confectionery; and three Chinese houses, denoted by their long three-cornered flags of yellow silk. The latter are much frequented by Americans, on account of their excellent cookery, and the fact that meals are $1 each, without regard to quantity. Kong-Sung's house is near the water; Whang-Tong's in Sacramento Street, and Tong-Ling's in Jackson street. There the grave Celestials serve up their chow-chow and curry, besides many genuine English dishes; their tea and coffee cannot be surpassed.

The afternoon is less noisy and active than the forenoon. Merchants keep within-doors, and the gambling-rooms are crowded with persons who step in to escape the wind and dust. The sky takes a cold gray cast, and the hills over the bay are barely visible in the dense, dusty air. Now and then a watcher, who has been stationed on the hill above Fort Montgomery, comes down and reports an inward-bound vessel, which occasions a little excite-ment among the boatmen and the merchants who are awaiting consignments. Towards sunset, the plaza is nearly deserted; the wind is merciless in its force, and a heavy overcoat is not found unpleasantly warm. As it grows dark, there is a lull, though occasional gusts blow down the hill and carry the dust of the city out among the shipping.

The appearance of San Francisco at night, from the water, is unlike anything I ever beheld. The houses are mostly canvas, which is made transparent by the lamps within, and transforms them, in the darkness, to dwellings of solid light. Seated on the slopes of its three hills, the tents pitched among the chaparral to the very summits, it gleams like an amphitheatre of fire. Here and there shine out brilliant points, from the decoy-lamps of the gaming-houses; and through the indistinct murmur of the streets comes by fits the sound of music from their hot and crowded precincts. The picture has in it something unreal and fantastic; it impresses one like the cities of the magic lantern, which a motion of the hand can build or annihilate.

The only objects left for us to visit are the gaming-tables, whose day has just fairly dawned. We need not wander far in search of one. Denison's Exchange, the Parker House and Eldorado stand side by side; across the way are the Verandah and Aguila de Oro; higher up the plaza the St. Charles and Bella Union; while dozens of second-rate establishments are scattered through the less frequented streets.

The greatest crowd is about the Eldorado; we find it difficult to effect an entrance. There are about eight tables in the room, all of which are thronged; copperhued Kanakas, Mexicans rolled in their *sarapes* and Peruvians thrust through their ponchos, stand shoulder to shoulder with the brown and bearded American miners. The stakes are generally small, though when the bettor gets into "a streak of luck," as it is called, they are allowed to double until all is lost or the bank breaks. Along the end of the room is a spacious bar, supplied with all kinds of bad liquors, and in a sort of gallery, suspended under the ceiling, a female violinist tasks her talent and strength of muscle to minister to the excitement of play.

The Verandah, opposite, is smaller, but boasts an equal attraction in a musician who has a set of Pandean pipes fastened at his chin, a drum on his back, which he beats with sticks at his elbows, and cymbals in his hands. The piles of coin on the monte tables clink merrily to his playing, and the throng of spectators, jammed together in a sweltering mass, walk up to the bar between the tunes and drink out of sympathy with his dry and breathless throat. At the Aguila de Oro there is a full band of Ethiopians serenaders, and at the other hells, violins, guitars or wheezy accordions, as the case may be. The atmosphere of these places is rank with tobacco-smoke, and filled with a feverish, stifling heat, which communicates an unhealthy glow to the faces of the players.

We shall not be deterred from entering by the heat and smoke, or the motley characters into whose company we shall be thrown. There are rare chances here for seeing human nature in one of its most dark and exciting phases. Note the variety of expression in the faces gathered around this table! They are playing monte, the favorite game in California, since the chances are considered more equal and the opportunity of false play very slight. The dealer throws out his cards with a cool, nonchalant air; indeed, the gradual increase of the hollow square of dollars at his left hand is not calculated to disturb his equanimity. The two Mexicans in front, muffled in their dirty *sarapes,* put down their half-dollars and dollars and see them lost without changing a muscle. Gambling is a born habit with them, and they would lose thousands with the same indifference. Very different is the demeanor of the Americans who are playing; their good or ill luck is betrayed at once by involuntary exclamations and changes of countenance, unless the stake should be very large and absorbing, when their anxiety, though silent, may read with no less certainty. They have no power to resist the fascination of the game. Now counting their winnings by thousands, now dependent on the kindness of a friend for a few dollars to commence anew, they pass hour after hour in those hot, unwholesome dens. There is no appearance of arms, but let one of the players, impatient with his losses and maddened by the poisonous fluids he has drunk, threaten one of the profession, and there will be no scarcity of knives and revolvers.

There are other places, where gaming is carried on privately and to a more ruinous extent—rooms in the rear of the Parker House, in the City Hotel and other places, frequented only by the initiated. Here the stakes are almost unlimited, the players being men of wealth and apparent respectability. Frequently, in the absorbing interest of some desperate game the night goes by unheeded and morning breaks upon haggard faces and reckless hearts. Here are lost, in a few turns of a card or rolls of a ball, the product of fortunate ventures by sea or months of racking labor on land. How many men, maddened by continual losses, might exclaim in their blind vehemence of passion, on leaving these hells:

> "Out, out, thou strumpet, Fortune! All you gods,
> In general synod, take away her power;
> Break all the spokes and felloes from her wheel,
> And bowl the round knave down the hill of heaven,
> As low as to the fiends!"

San Francisco, Four Months Later

Of all the marvellous phases of the history of the Present, the growth of San Francisco is the one which will most tax belief of the Future. Its parallel was never known, and shall never be beheld again. I speak only of what I saw with my own eyes. When I landed there, a little more than four months before, I found a scattering town of tents and canvas houses, with a show of frame buildings on one or two streets, and a population of about six thousand. Now, on my last visit, I saw around me an actual metropolis, displaying street after street of well-built edifices, filled with an active and enterprising people and exhibiting every mark of permanent commercial prosperity. Then, the town was limited to the curves of the Bay fronting the anchorage and bottom of the hills. Now, it stretched to the topmost heights, followed the shore around point after point, and sending back a long arm through a gap in the hills, took hold of the Golden Gate and was building its warehouses on the open strait and almost fronting the blue horizon of the Pacific. Then, the gold-seeking sojourner lodged in muslin rooms and canvas garrets, with a philosophic lack of furniture, and ate his simple though substantial fare from pine boards. Now, lofty hotels, gaudy with verandas and balconies, were met with in all quarters, furnished with home luxury, and aristocratic restaurants presented daily their lone bills of fare, rich with the choicest technicalities of the Parisian cuisine. Then, vessels were coming in day after day, to lie deserted and useless at their anchorage. Now scarce a day passed, but some cluster of sails bound *outward* through the Golden Gate, took their way to all corners of the Pacific. Like the magic seed of the Indian juggler, which grew, blossomed and bore fruit before the eyes of his spectators, San Francisco seemed to have accomplished in a day the growth of half a century.

When I first landed in California, bewildered and amazed by what seemed an unnatural standard of prices, I formed the opinion that there would be before long a great crash in speculation. Things, it appeared then, had reached the crisis, and it was pronounced impossible that they could remain stationary. This might have been a very natural idea at the time, but the subsequent course of affairs proved it to be incorrect. Lands, rents, goods, and subsistence continued steadily to advance in cost, and as the credit system had been meanwhile prudently contracted, the character of the business done was the more real and substantial. Two or three years will pass, in all probability, before there is a positive abatement of the standard of prices. There will be fluctuations in the meantime, occasioning great gains and losses, but the fall in rents and real estate, when it comes, as it inevitably must in the course of two or three years, will not be so crushing as I at first imagined. I doubt whether it will seriously injure the commercial activity of the place. Prices will never fall to the same standard as in the Atlantic States. Fortunes will always be made by the sober, intelligent, industrious, and energetic; but no one who is either too careless, too spiritless or too ignorant to succeed at home, need trouble himself about emigrating. The same general rule holds good, as well here as elsewhere, and it is all the better for human nature that it is so.

Not only was the heaviest part of the business conducted on cash principles, but all rents, even to lodgings in hotels, were required to be paid in advance. A single bowling-alley, in the basement story of the Ward

House—a new hotel on Portsmouth-Square—prepaid $5,000 monthly. The firm of Findley, Johnson & Co. sold their real estate, purchased a year previous, for $20,000, at $300,000; $25,000 down, and the rest in monthly installments of $12,500. This was a fair specimen of the speculations daily made. Those on a lesser scale were frequently of a very amusing character, but the claims on one's astonishment were so constant, that the faculty soon wore out, and the most unheard-of operations were looked upon as matters of course. Among others that came under my observation, was one of a gentleman who purchased a barrel of alum for $6, the price in New York being $9. It happened to be the only alum in the place, and as there was a demand for it shortly afterwards, he sold the barrel for $150. Another purchased all the candle-wick to be found, at an average price of 40 cts. per lb., and sold it in a short time at $2.25 per lb. A friend of mine expended $10,000 in purchasing barley, which in a week brought $20,000. The greatest gains were still made by the gambling tables and the eating-houses. Every device that art could suggest was used to swell the custom of the former. The latter found abundant support in the necessities of a large floating population, in addition to the swarm of permanent residents.

For a month or two previous to this time, money had been very scarce in the market, and from ten to fifteen percent monthly, was paid, with the addition of good security. Notwithstanding the quantity of coin brought into the country by emigrants, and the millions of gold dust used as currency, the actual specie basis was very small compared with the immense amount of business transacted. Nevertheless, I heard of nothing like a failure; the principal firms were prompt in all their dealings, and the chivalry of Commerce—to use a new phrase—was as faithfully observed as it could have been in the old marts of Europe and America. The merchants had a 'Change and News-room, and were beginning to cooperate in their movements and consolidate their credit. A stock company which had built a long wharf at the foot of Sacramento St. declared a dividend of ten percent within six weeks after the wharf was finished. During the muddy season, it was the only convenient place for landing goods, and as the cost of constructing it was enormous, so were likewise the charges for wharfage and storage.

There had been a vast improvement in the means of living since my previous visit to San Francisco. Several large hotels had been opened, which were equal in almost every respect to houses of the second class in the Atlantic cities. The Ward House, the Graham House, imported bodily from Baltimore, and the St. Francis Hotel, completely threw into the shade all former establishments. The rooms were furnished with comfort and even luxury, and the tables lacked few of the essentials of good living, according to a 'home' taste. The sleeping apartments of the St. Francis were the best in California. The cost of board and lodging was $150 per month—which was considered unusually cheap. A room at the Ward House cost $250 monthly, without board. The principal restaurants charged $35 a week for board, and there were lodging houses where a berth or "bunk"—one out of fifty in the same room—might be had for $6 a week. The model of these establishments—which were far from being "model lodging-houses"—was that of a ship. A number of staterooms, containing six berths each, ran around the sides of a large room, or cabin, where the lodgers resorted to read, write, smoke and drink at their leisure. The staterooms were consequently filled with foul and unwholesome air, and the noises in the cabin prevented the passengers from sleeping, except between midnight and four o'clock.

The great want of San Francisco was society. Think of a city of thirty thousand inhabitants, peopled by men alone! The like of this was never seen before. Every man was his own housekeeper, doing, in many instances, his own sweeping, cooking, washing and mending. Many home-arts, learned rather by observation than experience, came conveniently into play. He who cannot make a bed, cook a beefsteak, or sew up his own rips and rents, is unfit to be a citizen of California. Nevertheless, since the town began to assume a permanent shape, very many of the comforts of life in the East were attainable. A family may now live there without suffering any material privations; and if every married man, who intends spending some time in California, would take his family with him, a social influence would soon be created to which we might look for the happiest results.

Towards the close of my stay, the city was as dismal a place as could well be imagined. The glimpse of bright, warm, serene weather passed away, leaving in its stead a raw, cheerless, southeast storm. The wind now and then blew a heavy gale, and the cold, steady fall of rain, was varied by claps of thunder and sudden blasts of hail. The mud in the streets became little short of fathomless, and it was with difficulty that the mules could drag their empty wagons through. A powerful London dray-horse, a very giant in harness, was the only animal able to pull a good load; and I was told that he earned his master $100 daily. I saw occasionally a company of Chinese workmen, carrying bricks and mortar, slung by ropes to long bamboo poles. The plank sidewalks, in the lower part of the city, ran along the brink of pools and quicksands, which the Street Inspector and his men vainly endeavored to fill by hauling cart-loads of chapparal and throwing sand on the top; in a day or two the gulf was as deep as ever.

The sidewalks, which were made at the cost of $5 per foot, bridged over the worst spots, but I was frequently obliged to go the whole length of a block in order to get on the other side. One could not walk any distance, without getting at least ankle-deep, and although the thermometer rarely sank below 50°, it was impossible to stand still for even a short time without a death-like chill taking hold of the feet. As a consequence of this, coughs and bronchial infections were innumerable. The universal custom of wearing the pantaloons inside the boots threatened to restore the knee-breeches of our grandfathers' times. Even women were obliged to shorten their skirts, and wear high-topped boots. The population seemed to be composed entirely of dismounted hussars. All this will be remedied when the city is two years older, and Portsmouth Square boasts a *pavé* as elegant as that on the dollar side of Broadway.

The severe weather occasioned a great deal of sickness, especially among those who led an exposed life. The city overflowed with people, and notwithstanding buildings were continually growing up like mushrooms, overnight, hundreds who arrive were obliged to lodge in tents, with which the summits of the hills were covered. Fever-and-ague and dysentery were the prevailing complaints, the great prevalence of which was owing undoubtedly to exposure and an irregular habit of life. An association was formed to relieve those in actual want, many of the wealthiest and most influential citizens taking an honorable part in the matter. Many instances of lamentable destitution were by this means brought to light. Nearly all the hospitals of the place were soon filled, and numbers went to the Sandwich Islands to recruit. The City Hospital, a large, well ventilated and regulated establishment, contained about fifty patients. The attending physician described to me several cases of nearly hopeless lunacy which had come under his care, some of them produced by disappointment and ill-luck, and others by sudden increase of fortune. Poor human nature!

In the midst of the rains, we were greeted one morning with a magnificent spectacle. The wind had blown furiously during the night, with violent falls of rain, but the sun rose in a spotless sky, revealing the Coast Mountains across the bay wrapped in snow half-way down their sides. For two days they wore their dazzling crown, which could be seen melting away hour by hour, from their ridges and cloven ravines. This was the only snow I saw while in San Francisco; only once did I notice any appearance of frost. The grass was green and vigorous, and some of the more hardy plants in blossom; vegetables, it is well known, florish with equal luxuriance during the winter season. At one of the restaurants, I was shown some remarkable specimens of the growth of California soil—potatoes, weighing from one to five pounds each; beets and turnips eight inches in diameter, and perfectly sweet and sound; and large, silver-skinned onions, whose delicate flavor the most inveterate enemy of this honest vegetable could not but have relished. A gentleman who visited the port of Bodega, informed me that he saw in the garden of Capt. Smith, the owner of the place, peavines which had produced their third crop from the same root in one summer.

As the rains drove the deer and other animals down from the mountains, game of all kinds became abundant. Fat elks and splendid black-tailed does hung at the doors of all the butcher-shops, and wild geese, duck and brant, were brought into the city by the wagon-load. "Grizzly bear steak," became a choice dish at the eating-houses; I had the satisfaction one night of eating a slice of one that had weighed eleven hundred pounds. The flesh was of a bright red color, very solid, sweet, and nutritious; its flavor was preferable to that of the best pork. The large native hare, a specimen of which occasionally found its way to the restaurants, is nowise inferior to that of Europe. As an illustration of the money which might be spent in procuring a meal no better than an ordinary hotel-dinner at home, I may mention that a dinner for fifteen persons, to which I was invited, at the "Excelsior," cost the giver of it $225.

The effect of a growing prosperity and some little taste of luxury was readily seen in the appearance of the business community of San Francisco. The slouched felt hats gave way to narrow-brimmed black beavers; flannel shirts were laid aside, and white linen, though indifferently washed, appeared instead; dress and frock coats, of the fashion of the previous year in the Atlantic side, came forth from trunks and sea-chests; in short, a San Francisco merchant was almost as smooth and spruce in his outward appearance as a merchant anywhere else. The hussar boot, however, was obliged to be worn, and a variation of the Mexican sombrero—a very convenient and becoming headpiece—came into fashion among the younger class.

The steamers which arrived at this time, brought large quantities of newspapers from all parts of the Atlantic States. The speculation which had been so successful at first, was completely overdone; there was a glut in the market, in consequence whereof newspapers came down to fifty and twenty-five cents apiece. The leading journals of New York, New Orleans and Boston were cried at every street-corner. The two papers established in the place issued editions "for the Atlantic Coast," at the sailing of every steamer for Panama. The offices were invaded by crowds of purchasers, and the slow hand-presses in use could not keep pace with the demand. The profits of these journals were almost incredible, when contrasted with their size and the amount of their circulation. Neither of them failed to count their gains at the rate of $75,000 a year, clear profit.

My preparations for leaving San Francisco were made with the regret that I could not remain longer and see more of the wonderful growth of the Empire of the West. Yet I was fortunate in witnessing the most peculiar and interesting stages of its progress, and I took my departure in the hope of returning at some future day to view the completion of these magnificent beginnings. The world's history has no page so marvellous as that which has just been turned in California.

There are some features of Society in California, which I have hitherto failed to touch upon in my narrative, but which deserve a passing notice before I take my final leave of that wonderful land. The direct effect of the state of things growing out of the discovery of the placers, was to develop new qualities and traits of character, not in single individuals, but in every individual of the entire community—traits frequently most unlooked-for in those who exhibited them in the most marked degree. Society, therefore, was for the time cast into new forms, or, rather, deprived of any fixed form. A man, on coming to California, could no more expect to retain his old nature unchanged than he could retain in his lungs the air he had inhaled on the Atlantic shore.

The most immediate and striking change which came upon the greater portion of the emigrants was an increase of activity, and opportunity, of reckless and daring spirit. It was curious to see how men hitherto noted for their prudence and caution took sudden leave of those qualities, to all appearance, yet only prospered the more thereby. Perhaps there was at bottom a vein of keen, shrewd calculation, which directed their seemingly heedless movements; certain it is, at least, that for a long time the rashest speculators were the most fortunate. It was this fact, no doubt, that seemed so alarming to persons newly-arrived, and gave rise to unnumbered predictions of the speedy and ruinous crash of the whole business fabric of San Francisco. But nothing is more contagious than this spirit of daring and independent action, and the most doleful prophets were, ere long, swallowed up in the same whirlpool against which they had warned others.

The emigrants who arrive in California, very soon divide into two distinct classes. About two-thirds, or possibly three-fourths of them are active, hopeful and industrious. They feel this singular intoxication of society, and go to work at something, no matter what, by which they hope to thrive. The remaining portion see everything "through a glass, darkly." Their first bright anticipations are unrealized; the horrid winds of San Francisco during the dry season, chill and unnerve them; or, if they go to the placers, the severe labor and the ill success of inexperienced hands, completes their disgust. They commit a multitude of sins in the shape of curses upon every one who has written or spoken favorably of California. Some of them return home without having seen the country at all, and others, even if they obtain profitable situations, labor without a will. It is no place for a slow, an over-cautious, or a desponding man. The emigrant should be willing to work, not only at one business, but many, if need be; the grumbler or the idler had far better stay at home.

It cannot be denied that the very activity of California society created a spirit of excitement which frequently led to dangerous excesses. The habits of the emigrants, never, even at home, very slow and deliberate, branched into all kinds of wild offshoots, the necessary effect of the sudden glow and expansion which they experienced. Those who retained their health seemed to revel in an exuberance of animal spirits, which carried them with scarce a jar over barriers and obstacles that would have brought others to a full stand. There was something exceedingly hearty, cordial and encouraging in the character of social intercourse. The ordinary forms of courtesy were flung aside with a bluntness of good-fellowship infinitely preferable, under the circumstances. I was constantly reminded of the stories of Northern History—of the stout Vikings and Jarls who exulted in their very passions and made their heroes of those who were most jovial at the feast and most easily kindled with the rage of battle. Indeed, it required but little effort of the imagination to revive those iron ages, when the rugged gold-diggers, with their long hair and unshorn beards, were grouped around some mountain camp-fire, revelling in the ruddy light and giving full play to a mirth so powerful and profound that it would not have shamed the Berserkers.

The most common excesses into which the Californians run, are drinking and gambling, I say drinking, rather than drunkeness, for I saw very little of the latter. But a single case came under my observation while I was in the gold region. The man's friends took away his money and deposited it in the hands of the Alcalde, then tied him to a tree where they left him till he became sober. The practice of drinking, nevertheless, was widely prevalent, and its effects rendered more destructive by the large amount of bad liquor which was sent into the country. Gambling, in spite of a universal public sentiment against it, grew and flourished; the disappointment ruin of many emigrants were owing to its existence. The gamblers themselves were in many instances men who had led orderly and respectable lives at home. I have heard some of them frankly avow that nothing would induce them to acquaint their friends and families with the nature of their occupation; they would soon have enough, they said, and then they would wash their hands of the unclean stain, and go home to lead more honorable lives. But alas! it is not so easy to wash out the memory of self-degradation. If these men have in truth any sentiment of honor remaining, every coin of the wealth they have hoarded will awaken a shameful consciousness of the base and unmanly business by which it was obtained.

In spite, however, of all these dissipating and disorganizing influences, the main stock of society was sound, vigorous, and progressive. The rank shoots, while they might have slightly weakened the trunk, only showed the abundant life of the root. In short, without wishing to be understood as apologizing in any degree for the evils which existed, it was evident that had the Californians been more cool, grave and deliberate in their temperament—had they lacked the fiery energy and impulsive spirit which pushed them irresistibly forward—the dangers which surrounded them at the outset would have been far more imminent. Besides, this energy did not run at random; it was in the end directed by an enlightened experience, and that instinct of Right, which is the strength and security of a self-governed People. Hundreds of instances might be adduced to show that the worst passions of our nature were speedily developed in the air of California, but the one grand lesson of the settlement and organization of the country is of a character that ennobles the race.

The unanimity with which all united in this work—the frankness with which the old prejudices of sect and party were disclaimed—the freshly-awakened pride of country, which made every citizen jealously and disinterestedly anxious that she should acquit herself honorably in the eyes of the Nation at large—formed a spectacle which must claim our entire admiration. In view of the splendid future which is opening for California, it insures her a stable foundation on which to build the superstructure of her wealth and power.

After what has been said, it will appear natural that California should be the most democratic country in the world. The practical equality of all the members of a community, whatever might be the wealth, intelligence or profession of each, was never before thoroughly demonstrated. Dress was no gauge of respectability, and no honest occupation, however menial in its character, affected a man's standing. Lawyers, physicians and ex-professors dug cellars, drove ox-teams, sawed wood and carried luggage; while men who had been Army privates, sailors, cooks or day laborers were at the head of profitable establishments and not infrequently assisted in some of the minor details of Government. A man who would consider his fellow beneath him, on account of his appearance or occupation, would have had some difficulty in living peaceably in California. The security of the country is owing, in so small degree, to this plain, practical development of what the French reverence as an abstraction, under the name of *Fraternité*. To sum up all, in three words, LABOR IS RESPECTABLE: may it never be otherwise, while a grain of gold is left to glitter in California soil!

I have dwelt with the more earnestness of these features of Society because they do not seem to be fully appreciated in this side of the Continent. I cannot take leave; in the regular course of my narrative, of a land where I found so much in Nature to admire and enjoy, without attempting to give some general, though imperfect view of Man, as he appeared under those new and wonderful influences.

VII

From *Pen-Knife Sketches, or Chips of the Old Block,* by Alonzo Delano

Though only five feet, six inches tall, Alonzo Delano had a nose well over three feet long. He had to ask friends to scratch its tip; it picked up the scent of gold in California for its owner who resided in Illinois; its fame preceded the name of Old Block by several years and several miles.

"Old Block"—Alonzo Delano's pseudonym—came to California in search of better health and, of course, a little gold, if he could find it. As for health, he almost died crossing the Rockies, where he was forced to eat "rats and other nutritious vegetables." And when he reached the promised land of gold, he learned quickly that mining life was lean and bitter, and that sudden wealth, by some mysterious decree of Providence, always seemed to come to the diggings on the other side of the hill.

One night Old Block and some fellow down-and-outers were huddled around a fire in a cold mining cabin, grumbling over the huge gap between the glowing stories of gold written up in the east coast newspapers, and the actual, raw-handed existence as it really was in placer country. Old Block vowed to set the record straight; and as soon as he reached San Francisco, he began publishing his humorous sketches of mining life and San Francisco.

Alas, an unhappy family life and an all-consuming business absorbed his energies more and more in later life, and he wrote less and less. Finally, in 1874, he passed away, and his nose was bronzed to serve for a monumental tombstone in his adopted home, Grass Valley.

Babel of San Francisco

All the world have read of Babylon, of the Tower of Babel—and the confusion of tongues. Had the event, recorded in Holy Writ, occurred in the present day, instead of locating it in the now wastes of Asia, I should have given it a local habitation of Central Wharf, Commercial Street, in San Francisco. Pass through Kearney Street, to the head of Commercial Street, and look down through a portion of the town, which appears going out to sea to meet the shipping, in a sort of compromise between the land and old ocean. What a sea of heads, what a moving mass of human beings meets the view!

Most have read the passage of Bonaparte over the bridge of Lodi, when the Austrian cannon disputed his progress, and pictured to their mind the rush of men, and the vast slaughter through that narrow passage, in that desperate attempt. Were a cannon to be placed on Montgomery Street to defend it from such an inroad, the slaughter could not be less, and the sacrifice of human life would equal that of the passage of Lodi. It is like the waving of a field of corn in the breeze, a crowded mass of flesh and blood, one of the main arteries of the city. A congregation of all nations, creeds and tongues—English and Spanish, German, French, Chinese, Sandwich Islands, Indian, &c., and in passing through, one hears their jargon at every corner, and sees the strange and peculiar costume of each nation—the flashy silk or muslin dresses of the embrowned Mexican senoritas—we can not call them pretty—bareheaded, or with a rich shawl carelessly thrown over their heads, which half hides a seeming Indian face; the sturdy German, with a heavy package nicely balanced on her head, or the neat, tidy French and American belle, tripping along with a light step and joyous countenance; or, perchance, the plain, honest, good-natured face of the Kanaka girl, dressed in petticoats after no peculiar fashion, meets the gaze, and excites the wonder where all these women came from and what brought them here. Handcarts, porters, drays, now and then a fine carriage, rattle over the plank pavement, adding confusion to the hub-bub, in a sound of thunder, while at points along the wharf, the thimble-rigger, the French monte dealer, and low gamblers are gathering crowds around them, to practice upon the credulity of the unsophisticated. The pickpocket, the thief, of all grades, are in the crowd, & often, for want of other opportunity, a fight or excitement is got up to order, so that these light-fingered gentry can practice their vocation upon the idle lovers of pugilistic fun.

At corners of Montgomery, and Leidesdorff, and Sansome Streets, are musical gambling halls, where your loose change can be fiddled away on the turning of a card, and where your losses can be drowned, for an addlepate, in the flowing bowl. Rows, fights, and robberies are the order of the day, aye, and night, too, and to see sin and depravity in its most glaring colors, the seeker after such *pleasures* has only to walk from one end of Long Wharf to the other. An excitement can be got up at any moment by pretending to examine a quartz specimen, and instantly a man becomes the center of a wondering crowd. Still as a pedestrian elbows his way, at open spaces along the dock, you see crowds of sail boats and lighters alongside, discharging vegetables—the produce of California—cattle and sheep for the market, wool, coal, hay, &c., while numerous wholesale and retail shops of various kinds, restaurant and cigar divans, fill up the sum of human operations on this Great Babel of San Francisco.

Near the end of the wharf is Whitehall, the haven of wherrys. If you are looking around, as if in search of something, a trim red shirt is at your side,

Published by T. C. BOYD, Wood Engraver. (Iron Building.) corner Washington and Montgomery sts., SAN FRANCISCO.

A Water Carrier.

and a voice enquires, "A boat, sir? Carry you out and back for two dollars." Here, on both sides, are ships, barks, schooners, steamboats, and propellers, just off the Gold Bluff, Panama, Sacramento, Marysville, or Stockton, as you please; in fact, one may go to China, or eternity, for about the same price. For the one take a ship; for the other a steamboat, and in due time the port of destination will be reached. Take out papers for the one from the Custom House, for the other at the monte table.

Among the incidents of Long Wharf life, deserving of notice, is a little hand-wagon with a tight box, labelled "Pure Water." This means just what it reads. There is no adulteration of salt, soda, soap, sulphur or suds. Get up at the peep of day, or look down at nine o'clock at night, in rain or shine, in hot or cold, and you will see that little cart of "pure water" moving along, drawn by a poor fellow with only one arm. Unobtrusive and modest in his demeanor, without a drop of hot water aristocracy in his veins, the maimed water carrier pursues his daily rounds, and supplies his customers with the water they want during the day. At home, I should have asked what could a man with only one arm do in the land of gold, to gain his bread? What folly for such a man to go where two hands and a pick and shovel were necessary, and hardly obtain a living with both! Undismayed at such prospects, he resolved to strive with fortune, and win her smile with one arm, and among the hardy adventurers he sought the golden shore, and is not only earning an honest living, but laying up money, in his humble calling of dispensing one of the best gifts of God to his fellow laborers in San Francisco. Always be ready with a bit for the honest water carrier.

Such is a faint picture of the "confusion worse confounded" which greets the visitor to Long Wharf. Every day is like its fellow; no change, no cessation of the varied scenes which attract, amuse or pain. It is one of *the* business places of San Francisco, and every one who has had occasion to visit it, will recognize the sketch I give above.

The Plaza

Did you ever study Natural Philosophy? When the grand burst up of creation occurred, and the hills of California first bade good morning to the sun from the "vasty deep," a sort of an inclined plane was formed from Montgomery up to Dupont Street, and from there a pretty considerable hill that was not all a plane, rose to take a peep at the world above water. Between Kearny & Dupont Streets, on this inclined plane, which will make one puff to walk up fast, and Clay and Washington, on the south and north sides, the Plaza lays spread out in all its glory. The green grass which does not grow, the tall shade trees that are not yet planted, the beautiful fountain playing in the center not yet voted for in the City Council, the wide gravel walks not yet made, bordered by lovely California flowers not yet cultivated, the easy seats not yet prepared for the weary, the invalid, or the quiet pedestrian, might make this the center of attraction in San Francisco, when city scrip, Aldermanic medals, and Colton grants are paid for, and the tax payers are expected to fill up a diarroeha treasury. As it is, the most attractive ornament of its bare and gray surface is the long narrow pathway made of old barrel staves, like a long ladder, which leads from the east side to Foley's Circus, so that his patrons can get there "o'nights," and not get over shoe in mud. On the west, and standing out a little from the line of buildings on that side, in meek and lowly dignity, apparently conscious of its own intrinsic merit, the old tiled roof adobe, appears gazing at the wonderful changes going on around it, without having a word to say; a remnant of semi-barbarism and a sample of primitive California City building.

Around the Plaza, however, buildings begin to appear, which, outwardly, are ornaments to it. As for the inside of some of them—why there are ornaments too. That large metallic building on the southwest corner of the Square, is ATWILL'S, where in the way of music you can make a selection from a jews harp to a piano forte; as for pictures, you can get anything from "La Belle Kanaka" to an astonished "Lumber Merchant" at home, receiving an account of sales from San Francisco. In the rear is the grand receptacle of joy and hope, of love and fear, disappointment and happiness, all mingled up in a general mass—the Post Office, where the grand rush is made for letters upon the arrival of every steamer. Miners, Mexicans, Chinese, Kanakas, Spaniards, French, Germans, English and Americans; loafers, lovers, lawyers, merchants, meddlers and mendicants, all dress by the right, form line and stand ready to take one step forward, when their turn come for saluting the boxkeeper with the usual "anything for me."

And how that *hombre,* who has charge of Box "A to E," can keep good natured at some of the silly questions we have heard asked him, we can't understand. But he does, day after day, and as he stands there clothed in a "little brief authority," he actually does give a civil reply to a multitude of tedious block-heads, who are enough to try the patience of Job.

One, two, three, four, five, six, seven, eight—a continuous line. Count 'em yourself, beginning at the corner of Clay—the Exchange, the Empire, the Union, Parker, the El Dorado, Verandah, Sociedad, and the Bella Union. Exactly eight of the principal buildings on the west and north of the Plaza, are gambling houses of the most extensive kind—where crowds assemble every night to drink, to chat, to smoke, to play. And these are no small affairs in their way, either. French monte and thimble-rig are voted ungentlemanly bores at these princely establishments. A man, to have the privilege of making himself a beggar here, must engage in the genteel games of old fashioned monte, lansquenet, rouge-et-noir, dice, lotteries, and the Lord knows what else, and if a loafer gets drunk, and becomes too noisy, he finds that his place is with other brutes, in the street.

Listen! Is not that fine band playing a beautiful air? and they are scientific players. From "Jim Crow" to "Hail Columbia," from "Yankee Doodle" to "Sweet Home," they delight our ears and ravish our senses. You say you are willing to pay a quarter to hear it, eh! It will cost you half a dollar, for if you drink I shall, and it costs two bits a drink, and—you pay the shot. Now take a cigar, to be in fashion, but I'll save you a bit, for I'll simply take a chew of fine cut, and we'll elbow through the crowd, and see the gorgeous paintings on the walls. Over the bar of the "Exchange" you see an American shield for every State, with a coat of arms in the center, the eagle holding an inscription of the two first letters of California in its beak, as if it was just entering into the file of the Union. On the left are Masonic emblems: an eye peering out between the square and compass. On the right are Odd Fellows' emblems.

In some of the other saloons you see Venuses, Ledas, Junos, Graces and Greek Slaves, in the most approved styles of voluptuousness, as naked as they were born, a credit to the artist, a credit to the taste of the visiting community, a credit to public morals—especially of young boys—a credit to decency, a credit to the women who throw dice or twirl the "elephant" ball. How would the reader like to see his wife, or sister, or sweetheart, lounging

Portsmouth Plaza, the heart of San Francisco, in the 1850s.

around, gazing at these "credits," as *he* does of an evening. [*Old Block*—Poh! it's no place for ladies.] Granted—and the ladies say it's no place for *gentlemen*. Where did you say the masked balls were held, and both ladies and gentlemen attended them? I didn't say anything about that, but the pictures are beyond.

Pacific Street

THERE, take my arm, and we'll have a peep at high life below stairs, as such things do exist in San Francisco. You will know more about them if you see it; well, it is not more than three minutes' walk from the Plaza, north, to that large building on the corner of Kearney and Pacific Streets.

Just look at that pale sided, piazzed, beporched, and well-worn three-story building which looks for the world "as if it tried to and couldn't't," with wooden gratings ranged like a row of bricks along the basement story, on Pacific Street; why that is the City Hall, where the Criminal Courts are held, where "City Justice" is administered "according to law and wisdom," where thieves, robbers, burglars, incendiaries & murderers go through the farce of being tried, and either acquitted by "alibis," or condemned to be locked up in an old shell of an apology for a prison, to which they complacently submit for the pleasure of breaking out immediately. You stare, eh? well it is a God's truth. Show me the first man who has been hung in San Francisco for murder. Then look at the many villains, who, condemned to imprisonment, have escaped from that old shell. The majesty of the law, forsooth! That majesty is stripped of its dignity, and its power is perverted to protect the man who fires your dwelling in the dead hour of night, who puts a pistol to your breast in a public street, who breaks your doors, who insults your wife, who commits every crime that is known on the criminal record, and yet the administrators of the law strive to do their duty. The magistrates, the police are indefatigable, yet the gold of the felon will secure counsel, who for dollars and cents will lend his aid to shield the villain by technicalities and false witnesses, from justice, and render the law nugatory, a dead letter, in spite of all that judge or police can do. He struts at large, a gentleman, and is as ready to pick your pocket, or burn your house, as he was before the trial.

What's to be done? Why, unless you would have California resolve itself into the primitive elements of society, where protection of the weak is gained by the price of vassalage to the strong—where castles and towns, men at arms, serfs and bondsmen, shall be held at the arbitrary command of some powerful lord; the people must rise in their might, and protect themselves from the tyranny of the law as administered, from the tyranny of these prowling midnight villains, and like the glorious fathers of the revolution, who resisted the tyranny of English law and English rules, break the law to make a new and a more effective one, which shall protect the mass from that band of assassins who would gorge themselves with innocent blood. Alas! there is but one resource left, desperate as it is, and six months will not pass before sanguinary scenes of a terrible character will be enacted in the streets of San Francisco. Goaded on to desperation, the people will rise in their might, and do what the law cannot do—protect themselves. One more fire, and the tocsin will be sounded. The fire will come, the alarm bell will toll, and the long smothered flame of popular indignation will break forth. It may come even before the fire shall again lay the city in ruins.

[*Old Block*—Why, my Pen-Knife, you are prophetic.] As surely so, as a bright morning sun predicts a fair day.

And this is Pacific Street; named, no doubt, from the peaceful character of its denizens. Exactly so; for like the great Pacific, or Peaceful Ocean, it is now and then subject to the most infernal squalls. Below Dupont, you see the children of Israel worshipping the golden calf in a variety of ways, from an "old clo' " to a crockery store; the long-tailed Chinaman, with the bright-eyed princess Atoy, from the flowery vale of Magdalen—no, some Po-Whang vale of the moon, dispensing stewed rats and mutton chops to the western barbarian; the dark-haired, swarthy Mexican, in his many-colored serape; the graceful madame of "la belle France" presiding with a smile over the "liquor rendezvous" at the "cafe," and lansquenet saloons, when you are attracted by the sweet sounds of music, and drop a quarter at the bar in spite of yourself; the d—d Yankee, the chivalric Southerner, the long bearded miner, Jew and Gentile, are mixed in the throng, giving a peculiar life & style to that portion of unburned San Francisco. Here, on the corner of Dupont, is the Polka; but we can't get in there. It is crammed to overflowing; its tables are surrounded by a throng, who watch the turning of a card with anxious eyes; its bar is freely dispensing the bane of man in a variety of forms, and mixing in the motley crowd you may see the glittering star of a policeman, as he fixes his gaze upon the full-fledged Sydney-bird, the escaped felon, the thief, the murderer, who prowls among the throng in search of a victim, for the practice of his infernal arts.

Cast your eyes on the quaint names of the restaurants and drinking houses: "The Welcome," to all you will pay for, no doubt; "The Rising Sun," that shines in your pockets if you enter; the "Harmony House," where harmony and peace are destroyed if you don't fork over the *"quid pro quo."* Above Dupont there is one honest sign, "The Green Devil," and any man who goes in there does so with his eyes wide open. The gates of Pandemonium are generally hid from view; but "give the devil his due," for here he stands over the door flat-footed. The proprietor of that house must be an honest man, for he "takes his customers in" with their full knowledge that the image of Satan is staring them in the face before they enter. I deem it simply a "sign of the time."—I say, shipmate, do you hear that, in the house across the way?

"O sweet Kitty Clover, you bother me so—oh—oh!
Did you ever hear of Kate Kearney before?
Jolly lads and pretty lasses, here they go,
There's luck in odd numbers, says Rory O'More!"

Let's take a peep. Jack on shore, with his blue shirt and broad trousers, is having a spree. Music murdered, or run mad, is squeaking out from an old fiddle, the scientific operator with his head twisted around, as if in agony at his own performance, in doubling his elbow in all shapes; or on one side is seated the moustachied Spaniard, half enveloped in his black cloak and thrumming a sprightly waltz on his "light guitar," or a harper, leaning on his harp, ekeing out a mazurka; while the floor is crowded with rollicking boys and flaunting senoras, Irish belles, or Sydney ladies, cutting it down shuffle or waltz, as if Nero was fiddling, and San Francisco burning. Go it boys while you're young, if you are not hung you'll die in the gutter. And lounging around the door, or sauntering through the street, the deep-dyed villain from the sinks of Sydney, the scum of England, the vicious and dissolute from all nations, are watching you with wary steps, ready to pounce upon and take your life for a dollar. Have your pistol loaded, and keep the middle of the street by night. [*Old Block*—Why, what a commentary on the times, my Pen-Knife.] It's true, nevertheless, and you know it.

 **VIII**

From *Prentice Mulford's Story*
by Prentice Mulford

Prentice Mulford's San Francisco adventure was one minor interlude in an eventful, if disappointing, life. He shipped out to San Francisco after his hotel business in New York went bankrupt. The captain of the ship discharged him in San Francisco, where he decided to let the days go by for a while. He happened to arrive at the time when the Vigilance Committee was garrisoned at "Fort Gunnybags," a makeshift barricade thrown up by the Committee against the possible attacks of either honest or dishonest men. Since most of the accounts of the Vigilance Committee are terrible, serious things, it is refreshing to come across a writer like Mulford who could find a kind of bizarre humor in the affair.

Mulford's later life is, except for his writing, a series of misfortunes and failures. He tried his hand at cooking for a ship's crew, mining for gold, mining for copper, teaching—all with indifferent success. Only when Joe Lawrence of the *Golden Era* discovered his talents did he thrive. Finally, though, he returned to the east coast where he had grown up. When his marriage broke up, he retreated to a New Jersey swamp and wrote spiritualist pamphlets. He was found dead in a small boat drifting back towards his birthplace, Sag Harbor.

San Francisco in 1856

The *Wizard* sailed through a great bank of fog one August morning and all at once the headlands of the Golden Gate came in sight. It was the first land we had seen for four months. We sailed into the harbor, anchored, and the San Francisco of 1856 lay before us.

The ship was tied up to the warf. All but the officers and "boys" left her. She seemed deserted, almost dead. We missed the ocean life of the set sails, the ship bowing to the waves and all the stir of the elements in the open ocean.

The captain called me one day into the cabin, paid me my scanty wages and told me he did not think I "was cut out for a sailor," I was not handy enough about decks.

Considering that for two months I had been crippled by a felon on the

139

middle finger of my right hand, which on healing had left that finger curved inward, with no power to straighten it, I thought the charge of awkwardness somewhat unjust.

However, I accepted the Captain's opinion regarding my maritime capacities, as well as the hint that I was a superfluity on board.

I left the *Wizard*—left her for sixteen years of varied life in California.

I had no plans, nor aims, nor purpose, save to exist from day to day and take what the day might give me.

Let me say here never accept any person's opinion of your qualifications or capacities for any calling. If you feel that you are "cut out" for any calling or that you desire to follow it, abide by that feeling, and trust to it. It will carry you through in time.

I believe that thousands on thousands of lives have been blasted and crippled through the discouragement thrown on them by relation, friend, parent, or employer's saying continually (or if not saying it verbally, thinking it) "You are a dunce. You are stupid. You can't do this or that. It's ridiculous for you to think of becoming this or that."

The boy or girl goes off with this thought thrown on them by others. It remains with them, becomes a part of them and chokes off aspiration and effort.

Years afterward, I determined to find out for myself whether I was "cut out for a sailor" or not. As a result I made myself master of a small craft in all winds and weathers and proved to myself that if occasion required, I could manage a bigger one.

San Francisco seemed to me then mostly fog in the morning, dust and wind in the afternoon, and Vigilance Committee the remainder of the time.

San Francisco was then in the throes of the great "Vigilanteeism" of 1856. Companies of armed men were drilling in the streets at night. In the city's commercial centre stood "Fort Gunnybags"—the strong hold of the Vigilantes—made, as its name implied, of sand-filled gunny sacks. Carronades protruded from its port holes, sentinels paced the ramparts. There was a constant surging of men in and out of the building behind the fort,— the headquarters and barracks of the Vigilantes. From its windows a few days before our arrival they had hung Casey for the killing of James King—one of the editors of the *Bulletin*. I saw two others hung there on the sixth of August. Vigilanteeism was then the business and talk of the town. The jail had just been captured from the "Law and Order" men, who were not "orderly" at all, but who had captured the city's entire governmental and legal machinery and ran it to suit their own purposes.

The local Munchausens of that era were busy; one day the U.S. ship of war, *St. Mary's*, was to open fire on Fort Gunnybags: the next, Governor Johnson, backed by twenty thousand stalwart men, was to fall upon the city and crush out the insurrection.

The Sharpshooters of the Vigilance Committee, 1856.

The up-country counties were arming or thought of arming to put down this "rebellion." The "Rebellion" was conducted by the respectability and solidity of San Francisco, which had for a few years been so busily engaged in money making as to allow their city government to drift into rather irresponsible hands; many of the streets were unbridged, many not lighted at night. Cause—lack of money to bridge and light. The money in the hands of the city officials had gone more for private pleasure than public good.

I speak of the streets being unbridged because at that time a large portion of the streets were virtually bridges. One-fourth of the city at least, was built over the water. You could row a boat far under the town, and for miles in some directions. This amphibious part of the city "bilged" like a ship's hold, and white paint put on one day would be lead colored the next, from the action on it of the gases let loose from the ooze at low tide.

There were frequent holes in these bridges into which men frequently tumbled, and occasionally a team and wagon. They were large enough for either, and their only use was to show what the city officials had not done with the city's money.

Then Commercial street between Leidesdorff and Battery was full of Cheap John auction stores, with all their clamor and attendant crowds at night. Then the old Railroad Restaurant was in its prime, and the

St. Nicholas, on Sansome, was the crack hotel. Then, one saw sand-hills at the further end of Montgomery street. To go to Long Bridge was a weary, body-exhausting tramp. The Mission was reached by omnibus. Rows of old hulks were moored off Market street wharf, maritime relics of " '49." That was "Rotten Row." One by one they fell victims to Hare. Hare purchased them, set Chinamen to picking their bones, broke them up, put the shattered timbers in one pile, the iron bolts in another, the copper in another, the cordage in another, and so in a short all time that remained of these bluff-bowed, old-fashioned ships and brigs, that had so often doubled the stormy corner of Cape Horn or smoked their try-pots in the Artic ocean was so many ghastly heaps of marine débris.

I had seen the *Niantic,* now entombed just below Clay street, leave my native seaport, bound for the South Pacific to cruise for whale, years ere the bars and gulches of California were turned up by pick and shovel. The *Cadmus,* the vessel which brought Lafayette over in 1824, was another of our "blubber hunters," and afterward made her last voyage with the rest to San Francisco.

Manners and customs still retained much of the old "49" flavor. Women were still scarce. Every river boat brought a shoal of miners in gray shirts from "upcountry." "Steamer Day," twice a month, was an event. A great crowd assembled on the wharf to witness the departure of those "going East" and a lively orange bombardment from wharf to boat and *vice versa* was an inevitable feature of these occasions.

The Plaza was a bare, barren, unfenced spot. They fired salutes there on Independence Day, and occasionally Chief Burke exhibited on its area gangs of sneak thieves, tied two and two by their wrists to a rope—like a string of onions.

There was a long low garret in my Commercial street lodgings. It was filled with dust-covered sea-chests, trunks, valises, boxes, packages, and bundles, many of which had been there unclaimed for years and whose owners were quite forgotten. They were the belongings of lost and strayed Long Islanders, ex-whaling captains, mates and others. For the "Market" was the chief rendezvous. Every Long Islander coming from the "States" made first for the "Market." Storage then was very expensive. It would soon "eat a trunk's head off." So on the score of old acquaintance all this baggage accumulated in the Market loft and the owners wandered off to the mines, to Oregon, to Arizona, to Nevada—to all parts of the great territory lying east, north and south, both in and out of California, and many never came back and some were never heard of more. This baggage had been accumulating for years.

I used occasionally to go and wander about that garret alone. It was like groping around your family vault. The shades of the forgotten dead came there in the evening twilight and sat each one on his chest, his trunk, his valise, his roll of blankets. In those dusty packages were some of the closest ties, binding them to earth, Bibles, mother's gifts, tiny baby shoes, bits of blue ribbon, which years by-gone fluttered in the tresses of some Long Island girl.

It was a sad, yet not a gloomy place. I could feel that the presence of one, whose soul in sad memory met theirs, one who then and there recalled familiar scenes, events and faces, one who again in memory lived over their busy preparations for departure, their last adieux and their bright anticipations of fortune, I could feel that even my presence in that lone, seldom-visited garret, was for them a solace, a comfort. Imagination? Yes, if you will. Even imagination, dreamy, unprofitable imagination, may be a tangible and valuable something to those who dwell in a world of thought.

One night—or, rather, one morning—I came home very late—or, rather, very early. The doors of the Long Island House were locked. I wanted rest. One of the window-panes in front, and a large window-pane at that, was broken out. All the belated Long Islanders stopping at the place, when locked out at night, used to crawl through that window-pane. So, I crawled through it. Now, the sentinel on the ramparts of Fort Gunnybags, having nothing better to do, had been watching me, and putting me up as a suspicious midnight loiterer. And so, as he looked, he saw me by degrees lose my physical identity, and vanish into the front of that building; first, head, then shoulders, then chest, then diaphragm, then legs, until naught but a pair of boot-soles were for a moment upturned to his gaze, and they vanished, and darkness reigned supreme. The sentinel deemed that the time for action had come. I had just got into bed, congratulating myself on having thus entered that house without disturbing the inmates, when there came loud and peremptory rappings at the lower door. Luther and John, the proprietors, put their heads out of the chamber windows. There was a squad of armed Vigilantes on the sidewalk below; and, cried out one of them, "There's a man just entered your house!" Now I heard this, and said to myself, "Thou art the man!" but it was so annoying to have to announce myself as the cause of all this disturbance, that I concluded to wait and see how things would turn out. John and Luther jumped from their beds, lit each a candle and seized each a pistol; down-stairs they went and let the Vigilantes in. All the Long Island Captains, mates, coopers, cooks, and stewards then resident in the house also turned out, lit each his candle, seized each a pistol or a butcher-knife, of which there were plenty on the meat-blocks below. John came rushing into my room where I lay, pretending to be asleep. He shook me and exclaimed, "Get up! get up! there's a robber in the house secreted somewhere!" Then I arose, lit a candle, seized a butcher-knife, and so all the Vigilantes with muskets, and all the Long Island butchers, captains, mates, cooks, coopers, and stewards went poking around, without any trousers on, and thrusting their candles and knives and pistols into dark corners, and under beds and behind beef barrels, after the robber. So did I; for the disturbance had now assumed such immense proportions that I would not have revealed myself for a hundred dollars. I never hunted for myself so long before, and I did wish they would give up the search. I saw no use in it; and besides, the night air felt raw and chill in our slim attire. They kept it up for two hours.

Fort Gunnybags was on Sacramento Street; I slept directly opposite under the deserted baggage referred to. The block between us and the fort was vacant. About every fourth night a report would be circulated through that house that an attack on Fort Gunnybags would be made by the Law and Order men. Now, the guns of Fort Gunnybags bore directly on us, and as they were loaded with hard iron balls, and as these balls, notwithstanding whatever human Law and Order impediments they might meet with while crossing the vacant block in front, were ultimately certain to smash into our house, as well as into whatever stray Long Island captains, mates, boat-steerers, cooks, and coopers might be lying in their path, these reports resulted in great uneasiness to us, and both watches used frequently to remain up all night, playing seven-up and drinking rum and gum in Jo. Holland's saloon below.

I became tired at last of assisting in this hunt for myself. I gave myself up. I said, "I am the man, I am the bogus burglar, I did it." Then the crowd put up their knives and pistols, blew out their candles, drew their tongues and fired reproaches at me. I felt that I deserved them; I replied to none of their taunts, conducted myself like a Christian, and went to bed weighted down with their reproof and invective. The sentinel went back to his post and possibly slept. So did I.

The Letters of Dame Shirley

The most vivid picture of life in the gold fields was written by a blonde-curled New England lady named Louise Clappe. "Dame Shirley," as Louise called herself, had come to San Francisco, and thence to the Mother Lode, with her husband, Doctor Fayette Clappe. Her letters to her sister back east were composed with meticulous attention to "epistolary style"—that is, composed with studied elegance and the hope that they would be read by the public. Both the *Marysville Herald* and the celebrated *Pioneer* published her letters in the 1850s. Since then, her 23 letters have been collected and republished many times.

Dame Shirley's letters cover only the years from September, 1851, to November, 1852. But in the course of her correspondence, she paints a convincing picture of the bizarre life style that emerged in the Gold Rush country. Much that she saw there shocked and horrified her—three-week drunken sprees, hunger, vigilante lynchings. She had "seen the elephant" in all its huge absurdity. But when her husband decided to return to San Francisco, Dame Shirley left with regret. "My heart is heavy," she wrote in her last letter from the gold fields, "at the thought of departing forever from this place. I *like* this wild and barbarous life. . . . Here, at least, I have been contented."

I intend to-day, dear M., to be as disagreeably statistical and as praise-worthily matter-of-factish as the most dogged utilitarian could desire. I shall give you a full, true and particular account of the discovery, rise and progress of this place, with a religious adherence to *dates* which will rather astonish your unmathematical mind. But let me first describe the spot, as it looked to my wondering and unaccustomed eyes. Remember, I had never seen a mining district before; and had just left San Francisco, amid whose flashy-looking shops and showy houses the most of my time had been spent, since my arrival into the Golden State. Of course, to me, the *coup d'oeuil* of Rich Bar was charmingly fresh and original. Imagine a tiny valley, about eight hundred yards in length and, perhaps, thirty in width, [it was measured for my especial information,] apparently hemmed in by lofty hills, almost perpendicular, draperied to their very summits with beautiful fir trees; the blue-blossomed

"Plumas," or Feather River I suppose I must call it, undulating along their base, and you have as good an idea as I can give you of the *locale* of "Barra Rica," as the Spaniards so prettily term it.

In almost any of the numerous books written upon California, no doubt you will be able to find a most scientific description of the origin of these "Bars." I must acknowledge, with shame, that my ideas on the subject are distressingly vague. I could never appreciate the poetry or the humor, of making one's wrists ache by knocking to pieces gloomy looking stones, or in dirtying one's fingers by analysing soils, in a vain attempt to fathom the osteology, or anatomy of our beloved earth; though my heart is thrillingly alive to the faintest shade of color and the infinite variety of styles in which she delights to robe her ever-changeful and ever-beautiful *surface*. In my unscientific mind the *formations* are without form and void; and you might as well talk Chinese to me, as to embroider your conversation with the terms "horn-blende," "mica," "limestone," "slate," "granite" and "quartz," in a hopeless attempt to enlighten me as to their merits. The dutiful diligence with which I attend course after course of lectures on Geology by America's greatest illustrator of that subject, arose rather from my affectionate reverence for our beloved Dr. H., and the fascinating charm which his glorious mind throws round every subject which it condescends to illuminate, than to any interest in the dry science itself. It is, therefore, with a most humiliating consciousness of my geological deficiencies, that I offer you the only explanation which I have been able to obtain from those most learned in such matters here. I gather from their remarks, that these bars are formed by deposits of earth, rolling down from the mountains, crowding the river aside and occupying a portion of its deserted bed. If my definition is unsatisfactory, I can but refer you to some of the aforesaid works upon California.

Through the middle of Rich Bar runs the street, thickly planted with about forty tenements; among which figure round tents, square tents, plank hovels, log cabins, &c.,—the residences, varying in elegance and convenience from the palatial splendor of "The Empire," down to a "local habitation," formed of pine boughs, and covered with old calico shirts.

To-day I visited the "Office"—the only one on the river. I had heard so much about it from others, as well as from F., that I really *did* expect something extra. When I entered this imposing place, the shock to my optic nerves was so great that I sank, helplessly, upon one of the benches which ran, divan-like, the whole length (ten feet!) of the building, and laughed till I cried. There was, of course, no floor; a rude nondescript in one corner, on which was ranged the medical library, consisting of half a dozen volumes, did duty as a table. The shelves, which looked like sticks snatched hastily from the wood-pile and nailed up without the least alteration, contained quite a respectable array of medicines. The white canvas window stared everybody in the face, with the interesting information painted on it, in perfect grenadiers of capitals, that this was Dr.———'s office.

At my loud laugh, (which, it must be confessed, was noisy enough to give the whole street assurance of the presence of a woman,) F. looked shocked, and his partner looked prussic acid. To him, (the partner, I mean, he hadn't been out of the mines for years)—the "Office" was a thing sacred and set apart for an almost admiring worship. It was a beautiful, architectural ideal, embodied in pine shingles and cotton cloth. Here, he literally "lived, and moved, and had his being," his bed and his board. With an admiration of the fine arts, truly praiseworthy, he had fondly decorated the walls thereof with sundry pictures from Godey, Graham and Sartain's Magazines, among which, fashion plates with imaginary monsters, sporting miraculous waists, impossible wrists and fabulous feet, largely predominated.

During my call at the office, I was introduced to one of the *finders* of Rich Bar—a young Georgian, who afterwards gave me a full description of all the facts connected with its discovery. This unfortunate had not spoken to a woman for two years; and in the elation of his heart at the joyful event, he rushed out and invested capital in some excellent champagne, which I, on Willie's principle of "doing in Turkey as the Turkies do," assisted the company in drinking to the honor of my own arrival. I mentioned this, as an instance, that nothing can be done in California without the sanctifying influence of the *spirit;* and it generally appears in much more "questionable shape" than that of sparkling wine. Mr. H. informed me, that on the twentieth of July, 1850, it was rumored at Nelson's Creek—a mining station situated at the Middle Fork of the Feather River, about eighty miles from Marysville—that one of those vague "Somebodies"—a near relation of the "They Says"—had discovered mines of a remarkable richness in a north-easterly direction, and about forty miles from the first-mentioned place. Anxious and immediate search was made for "Somebody," but, as our western brethren say, he "wasn't thar!" But his absence could not deter the miners when once the golden rumor had been set afloat. A large company packed up their goods and chattels, generally consisting of a pair of blankets, a frying-pan, some flour, salt pork, brandy, pickaxe and shovel, and started for the new Dorado. They "traveled, and traveled, and traveled," as we used to say in the fairy stories, for nearly a week in every possible direction, when one evening, weary and discouraged, about one hundred of the party found themselves at the top of that famous hill, which figures so largely in my letters, whence the river can be distinctly seen. Half of the number concluded to descend the mountain that night, the remainder stopping on the summit until the next morning. On arriving at Rich Bar, part of the adventurers camped there, but many went a few miles further down the river. The next morning two men turned over a large stone, beneath which they found quite a sizable piece of gold. They washed a small panful of the dirt, and obtained from it *two hundred and fifty-six dollars.* Encouraged by this success, they commenced staking off the legal amount of ground allowed to each person for mining purposes; and, the remainder of the party having descended the hill, before night the entire bar was "claimed." In a fortnight from that time, the two men who found the first bit of gold had each taken out six thousand dollars. Two others took out thirty-three pounds of gold in eight hours; which is the best day's work that has been done on this branch of the river; the largest amount ever taken from one panful of dirt was fifteen hundred dollars. In little more than a week after its discovery, five hundred men had settled upon the bar for the summer.—Such is the wonderful alacrity with which a mining town is built. Soon after was discovered on the same side of the river—about half a mile apart, and at nearly the same distance from this place—the two bars, "Smith" and "Indian," both very rich; also another, lying across the river, just opposite Indian, called "Missouri Bar." There are several more, all within a few miles of here, called "Frenchman's," "Taylor's," "Brown's," "The Junction," "Wyandott" and "Muggin's." But they are at present of little importance as mining stations.

Those who worked in these mines during the fall of 1850 were extremely fortunate; but, alas! the Monte fiend ruined hundreds! Shall I tell you the fate of two of the most successful of these gold hunters? From poor men, they found themselves at the end of a few weeks, absolutely rich. Elated with their good fortune, seized with a mania for Monte, in less than a year, these unfortunates,—so lately respectable and intelligent,—became a pair of drunken gamblers. One of them at this present writing, works for five dollars a day and boards himself out of that; the other actually suffers for the necessaries of life,—a too common result of scenes in the mines.

There were but a few that dared to remain in the mountains during the winter for fear of being buried in the snow; of which at that time they had a most vague idea. I have been told that in these sheltered valleys it seldom falls to the depth of more than a foot, and disappears almost invariably within a day or two. Perhaps there were three hundred that concluded to stay; of which number, two-thirds stopped on Smith's Bar, as the labor of mining there is much easier than it is here. Contrary to the general expectation, the weather was delightful until about the middle of March; it then commenced storming, and continued to snow and rain incessantly for nearly three weeks. Supposing that the rainy season had passed, hundreds had arrived on the river during the previous month. The snow, which fell several feet in depth on the mountains, rendered the trail impassable and entirely stopped the pack trains; provisions soon became scarce, and the sufferings of these unhappy men were, indeed, extreme. Some adventurous spirits, with true Yankee hardihood, forced their way through the snow to the Frenchman's ranch, and packed flour *on their backs,* for more than forty miles! The first meal that arrived sold for three dollars a pound. Many subsisted for days on nothing but barley, which is kept here to feed the pack-mules on. One unhappy individual who could not obtain even a little barley, for love or money, and had eaten nothing for three days, forced his way out to the Spanish rancho fourteen miles distant, and in less than an hour after his arrival, had devoured *twenty-seven* biscuit and a corresponding quantity of other eatables, and, of course, drinkables to match. Don't let this account alarm you. There is no danger of another famine here. They tell me that there is hardly a building in the place that has not food enough in it to last its occupants for the next two years; besides, there are two or three well-filled groceries in town.

Letter Eleventh

A Trip into the Mines

From Our Log Cabin, Indian Bar,
December 15, 1851

I little thought, dear M., that here, with the "green watching hills" as witnesses, amid a solitude so grand and lofty that it seems as if the faintest whisper of passion must be hushed by its holy stillness, I should have to relate the perpetration of one of those fearful deeds, which, were it for no other peculiarity than its startling suddenness—so utterly at variance with all *civilized* law—must make our beautiful California appear to strangers rather as a hideous phantom, than the flower-wreathed reality which she is.

Whether the life, which a few men, in the impertinent intoxication of power, have dared to crush out, was worth that of a fly, I do not know,—perhaps not; though God alone, methinks, can judge of the value of the soul upon which he has breathed. But certainly the effect upon the hearts of those who played the principal parts in the revolting scene referred to—a tragedy, in my simple judgment, so utterly useless—must be demoralizing in the extreme.

The facts in this sad case are as follows: Last fall, two men were arrested by their partners, on suspicion of having stolen from them eighteen hundred dollars in gold dust. The evidence was not sufficient to convict them, and they were acquitted. They were tried before a meeting of the miners—as at that time the law did not even *pretend* to wave its scepter over this place.

The prosecutors still believed them guilty, and fancied that the gold was hidden in a "coyote hole," near the camp from which it had been taken. They therefore watched the place narrowly while the suspected men remained on the Bar. They made no discoveries, however; and soon after the trial, the acquitted persons left the mountains for Marysville.

A few weeks ago, one of these men returned, and has spent most of the time since his arrival in loafing about the different bar-rooms upon the river.

He is said to have been constantly intoxicated. As soon as the losers of the gold heard of his return, they bethought themselves of the "coyote hole," and placed about its entrance some brushwood and stones, in such a manner that no one could go into it without disturbing the arrangement of them. In the meanwhile the thief settled at Rich Bar, and pretended that he was in search of some gravel ground for mining purposes.

A few mornings ago, he returned to his boarding place—which he had left some hour earlier—with a spade in his hand, and as he laid it down, carelessly observed that he had "been out prospecting." The losers of the gold went, immediately after breakfast, as they had been in the habit of doing, to see if all was right at the "coyote hole." On this fatal day, they saw that the entrance had been disturbed, and going in, they found upon the ground, a money belt which had apparently just been cut open. Armed with this evidence of guilt, they confronted the suspected person and sternly accused him of having the gold in his possession. Singularly enough, he did not attempt a denial, but said that if they would not bring him to a trial, (which of course they promised) he would give it up immediately. He then informed them that they would find it beneath the blankets of his *bunk,*—as those queer shelves on which miners sleep, ranged one above another, somewhat like the berths of the ship, are generally called. There, sure enough, were six hundred dollars of the missing money, and the unfortunate wretch declared that his partner had taken the remainder to the States.

By this time the exciting news had spread all over the Bar. A meeting of the miners was immediately convened, the unhappy man taken into custody, a jury chosen, and a judge, lawyer, etc., appointed. Whether the men, who had just regained a portion of their missing property, made any objections to the proceedings which followed, I know not; if they had done so, however, it would have made no difference, as the *people* had taken the matter entirely out of their hands.

At one o'clock, so rapidly was the trial conducted, the judge charged the jury, and gently insinuated that they could do no less than to bring in with their verdict of guilty, a sentence of *death!* Perhaps you know that when a trial is conducted without the majesty of the law, the jury are compelled to decide, not only upon the guilt of the prisoner, but the mode of his punishment also. After a few minutes' absence, the twelve men who had consented to burden their souls with a responsibility so fearful, returned, and the foreman handed to the judge a paper, from which he read the will of the *people,* as follows: "That William Brown, convicted of stealing, etc., should, in *one hour* from that time, be hung by the neck until he was dead."

By the persuasions of some men more mildly disposed, they granted him a respite of *three hours,* to prepare for his sudden entrance into eternity. He employed the time in writing in his native language (he is a Swede) to some friends in Stockholm; God help them when that fatal post shall arrive; for no doubt *he,* also, although a criminal, was fondly garnered in many a loving heart.

He had exhibited during the trial, the utmost recklessness and *nonchalance,* had drank many times in the course of the day, and when the rope was placed about his neck, was evidently much intoxicated. All at once, however, he seemed startled into a consciousness of the awful reality of his position, and requested a few moments for prayer.

The execution was conducted by the jury, and was performed by throwing the cord, one end of which was attached to the neck of the prisoner, across the limb of a tree standing outside of the Rich Bar grave-yard; when all, who felt disposed to engage in so revolting a task, lifted the poor wretch from the ground, in the most awkward manner possible. The whole affair, indeed, was a piece of cruel butchery, though *that* was not intentional, but arose from the ignorance of those who made the preparations. In truth, life was only crushed out of him, by hauling the writhing body up and down several times in succession, by the rope which was wound round a large bough of his green-leafed gallows. Almost everybody was surprised at the severity of the sentence; and many, with their hands on the cord, did not believe even *then,* that it would be carried into effect, but thought that at the last moment, the jury would release the prisoner and substitute a milder punishment.

It is said that the crowd generally, seemed to feel the solemnity of the occasion; but many of the drunkards, who form a large part of the community on these Bars, laughed and shouted, as if it were a spectacle got up for their particular amusement. A disgusting specimen of intoxicated humanity, struck with one of those luminous ideas peculiar to his class, staggered up to the victim, who was praying at the moment, and crowding a dirty rag into his almost unconscious hand, in a voice broken by a drunken hiccough, tearfully implored him to take his "hankercher," and if he were *innocent,* (the man had not denied his guilt since first accused), to drop it as soon as he was drawn up into the air, but if *guilty,* not to let it fall on any account.

The body of the criminal was allowed to hang for some hours after the execution. It had commenced storming in the earlier part of the evening; and when those, whose business it was to inter the remains, arrived at the spot, they found them enwrapped in a soft, white shroud of feathery snow-flakes, as if pitying Nature had tried to hide from the offended face of heaven, the cruel deed which her mountain children had committed.

I have heard no one approve of this affair. It seems to have been carried on entirely by the more reckless part of the community. There is no doubt, however, that they seriously *thought* they were doing right, for many of them are kind and sensible men. They firmly believed that such an example was absolutely necessary for the protection of this community. Probably the recent case of "Little John," rendered his last sentence more severe than it otherwise would have been. The "Squire," of course, could do nothing (as in criminal cases the *people* utterly refuse to acknowledge his authority) but protest against the whole of the proceedings, which he did, in the usual legal manner.

If William Brown had committed a murder, or had even attacked a man for his money,—if he had been a quarrelsome, fighting character, endangering lives in his excitement, it would have been a very different affair. But with the exception of the crime for which he perished, (he *said* it was his first, and there is no reason to doubt the truth of his assertion), he was a harmless, quiet, inoffensive person.

You must not confound this miner's judgment with the doings of the noble *Vigilance Committee* of San Francisco. They are almost totally different in their organization and manner of proceeding. The Vigilance Committee had become absolutely necessary for the protection of society. It was composed of the best and wisest men in the city. They used their powers with a moderation unexampled in history, and they laid it down with a calm and quiet readiness which was absolutely sublime, when they found that legal justice had again resumed that course of stern, unflinching duty which should always be its characteristic. They took ample time for a thorough investigation of all the circumstances relating to the criminals who fell into their hands; and in *no* case have they hung a man, who had not been proved beyond the shadow of a doubt, to have committed at least *one* robbery in which life had been endangered, if not absolutely taken.

Bret Harte.

X

"The Luck of Roaring Camp," "To the Cliff House," and "San Francisco from the Sea" by Bret Harte

Never was anyone so unfitted for the rough life of the gold era as Bret Harte. A dapper dresser, usually cautious with his words, reserved in bearing, a family man at heart—it is one of the ironies of Western American literature that Bret Harte is best known for his tales of gamblers, drunkards, prostitutes, and the sensational stories of the gold country.

Harte would never have advanced beyond the saccharine poetry or clever style-imitations of his early writing had it not been for the nuts and bolts apprenticeship he served on newspapers. The breathless style of his early writing slowly gave way to a style that blended realistic detail with a born romantic's flair for heartrending goodness. "The Luck of Roaring Camp," the best example of Harte's talent for imaginative local color, started the fashion among California writers for moral tales of the reformed gambler, the prostitute with the heart of gold, and a whole world of semi-legendary types that continue in full force today on television shows like "Gunsmoke" and "Bonanza."

In 1864, Harte and Charles Webb started *The Californian,* an ambitious literary journal that planned to outshine its predecessor and rival, *The Golden Era.* Like most other West Coast journals, it was heavily dependent on "borrowed" writing (strict copyright laws were non-existent). But some of its best work came from the local talent—Ina Coolbrith, Ambrose Bierce, Mark Twain, and Bret Harte himself.

We have included here a short sketch from *The Californian* by Harte on his visit to the Cliff House. To get an excellent idea of the contrast between the styles of San Francisco's two greatest writers in the last century, compare Harte's romantic "To the Cliff House" with Twain's earthier "Early Rising As Regards to Excursions to the Cliff House." Small wonder that their friendship always bordered on enmity.

The concluding Harte piece, "San Francisco from the Sea," is one of the two best poems yet written to the City (the other being George Sterling's "Cool Grey City of Love"). The poem moves from pride in the City as a focus of natural and human forces, to a condemnation of her (San Francisco has always been a lady) moral depravity, then to an expression of hope in the future, a dream that Art and Culture can redeem the sin of her youth. But the poem concludes not with a confident hope in salvation for the City's people, but with a recognition that the acts of his people and his time will pass into oblivion. At the poem's close, "San Francisco from the Sea" becomes a worthy elegy to the unremembered multitudes who toiled fairly or meanly in their place in those early years.

"The Luck of Roaring Camp"

There was commotion in Roaring Camp. It could not have been a fight, for in 1850 that was not novel enough to have called together the entire settlement. The ditches and claims were not only deserted, but "Tuttle's grocery" had contributed its gamblers, who, it will be remembered, calmly continued their game the day that French Pete and Kanaka Joe shot each other to death over the bar in the front room. The whole camp was collected before a rude cabin on the outer edge of the clearing. Conversation was carried on in a low tone, but the name of a woman was frequently repeated. It was a name familiar enough in the camp,—"Cherokee Sal."

Perhaps the less of her the better. She was a coarse, and, it is to be feared, a very sinful woman. But at that time she was the only woman in Roaring Camp, and was just then lying in sore extremity, when she most needed the ministration of her own sex. Dissolute, abandoned, and irreclaimable, she was yet suffering a martyrdom hard enough to bear even when veiled by sympathizing womanhood, but now terrible in her loneliness. The primal curse had come to her in that original isolation which must have made the punishment of the first transgression so dreadful. It was, perhaps, part of the expiation of her sin, that, at a moment when she most lacked her sex's intuitive tenderness and care, she met only the half-contemptuous faces of her masculine associates. Yet a few of the spectators were, I think, touched by her sufferings. Sandy Tipton thought it was "rough on Sal," and, in the contemplation of her condition, for a moment rose superior to the fact that he had an ace and two bowers* in his sleeve.

It will be seen, also, that the situation was novel. Deaths were by no means uncommon in Roaring Camp, but a birth was a new thing. People had been dismissed from the camp effectively, finally, and with no possibility of return; but this was the first time that anybody had been introduced *ab initio*. Hence the excitement.

"You go in there, Stumpy," said a prominent citizen known as "Kentuck," addressing one of the loungers. "Go in there, and see what you kin do. You've had experience in them things."

Perhaps there was a fitness in the selection. Stumpy, in other climes, had been the putative head of two families; in fact, it was owing to some legal informality in these preceedings that Roaring Camp—a city of refuge—was indebted to his company. The crowd approved the choice, and Stumpy was wise enough to bow to the majority. The door closed on the extempore surgeon and midwife, and Roaring Camp sat down outside, smoked its pipe, and awaited the issue.

The assemblage numbered about a hundred men. One or two of these

*jacks

were actual fugitives from justice, some were criminal, and all were reckless. Physically, they exhibited no indication of their past lives and character. The greatest scamp had a Raphael face, with a profusion of blond hair; Oakhurst, a gambler, had the melancholy air and intellectual abstraction of a Hamlet; the coolest and most courageous man was scarcely over five feet in height, with a soft voice and an embarrassed, timid manner. The term "roughs" applied to them was a distinction rather than a definition. Perhaps in the minor details of fingers, toes, ears, &c., the camp may have been deficient; but these slight omissions did not detract from their aggregate force. The strongest man had but three fingers on his right hand; the best shot had but one eye.

Such was the physical aspect of the men that were dispersed around the cabin. The camp lay in a triangular valley, between two hills and a river. The only outlet was a steep trail over the summit of a hill that faced the cabin, now illuminated by the rising moon. The suffering woman might have seen it from the rude bunk whereon she lay,—seen it winding like a silver thread until it was lost in the stars above.

A fire of withered pine-boughs added sociability to the gathering. By degrees the natural levity of Roaring Camp returned. Bets were freely offered and taken regarding the result. Three to five that "Sal would get through with"; even that the child would survive; side bets as to the sex and complexion of the coming stranger. In the midst of an excited discussion an exclamation came from those nearest the door, and the camp stopped to listen. Above the swaying and moaning of the pines, the swift rush of the river, and the crackling of the fire, rose a sharp, querulous cry—a cry unlike anything heard before in the camp. The pines stopped moaning, the river ceased to rush, and the fire to crackle. It seemed as if Nature had stopped to listen too.

The camp rose to its feet as one man! It was proposed to explode a barrel of gunpowder, but, in consideration of the situation of the mother, better counsels prevailed, and only a few revolvers were discharged; for, whether owing to the rude surgery of the camp, or some other reason, Cherokee Sal was sinking fast. Within an hour she had climbed, as it were, that rugged road that led to the stars, and so passed out of Roaring Camp, its sin and shame, forever. I do not think that the announcement disturbed them much, except in speculation as to the fate of the child. "Can he live now?" was asked of Stumpy. The answer was doubtful. The only other being of Cherokee Sal's sex and maternal condition in the settlement was an ass. There was some conjecture as to fitness, but the experiment was tried. It was less problematical than the ancient treatment of Romulus and Remus, and apparently as successful.

When these details were completed, which exhausted another hour, the door was opened, and the anxious crowd of men who had already formed themselves into a queue, entered in single file. Beside the low bunk or shelf, on which the figure of the mother was starkly outlined below the blankets, stood a pine table. On this a candle-box was placed, and within it, swathed in staring red flannel, lay the last arrival at Roaring Camp. Beside the candle-box was placed a hat. Its use was soon indicated. "Gentlemen," said Stumpy, with a singular mixture of authority and *ex officio* complacency,— "Gentlemen will please pass in at the front door, round the table, and out at the back door. Them as wishes to contribute anything toward the orphan will find a hat handy." The first man entered with his hat on; he uncovered, however, as he looked about him, and so, unconsciously, set an example to the next. In such communities good and bad actions are catching. As the procession filed in, comments were audible,—criticisms addressed, perhaps, rather to Stumpy, in the character of showman,—"Is that him?" "mighty small specimen"; "hasn't mor'n got the colour" "ain't bigger nor a derringer." The contributions were as characteristic: A silver tobacco-box; a doubloon; a navy revolver, silver mounted; a gold specimen; a very beautifully embroidered lady's handkerchief from Oakhurst, the gambler; a diamond breastpin; a diamond ring (suggested by the pin, with the remark from the giver that he "saw that pin and went two diamonds better"); a slung shot; a Bible (contributor not detected); a golden spur; a silver tea-spoon (the initials, I regret to say, were not the giver's); a pair of surgeon's shears; a lancet; a Bank of England note for 5 pounds; and about $200 in loose gold and silver coin. During these proceedings Stumpy maintained a silence as impassive as the dead on his left, a gravity as inscrutable as that of the newly born on his right. Only one incident occurred to break the monotony of the curious procession. As Kentuck bent over the candle-box half curiously, the child turned, and, in a spasm of pain, caught at his grop-ing finger, and held it fast for a moment. Kentuck looked foolish and em-barrassed. Something like a blush tried to assert itself in his weather-beaten cheek. "The d—d little cuss!" he said, as he extricated his finger, with, perhaps, more tenderness and care than he might have been deemed capable of showing. He held that finger a little apart from its fellows as he went out, and examined it curiously. The examination provoked the same original remark in regard to the child. In fact, he seemed to enjoy repeating it. "He rastled with my finger," he remarked to Tipton, holding up the member, "the d—d little cuss!"

It was four o'clock before the camp sought repose. A light burnt in the cabin where the watchers sat, for Stumpy did not go to bed that night. Nor did Kentuck. He drank quite freely, and related with great gusto his ex-perience, invariably ending with his characteristic condemnation of the new-comer. It seemed to relieve him of any unjust implication of sentiment, and Kentuck had the weaknesses of the nobler sex. When everybody else had gone to bed, he walked down to the river, and whistled reflectingly.

Then he walked up the gulch, past the cabin, still whistling with demonstrative unconcern. At a large red-wood tree he paused and retraced his steps, and again passed the cabin. Half-way down the river's bank he again paused, and then returned and knocked at the door. It was opened by Stumpy. "How goes it?" said Kentuck, looking past Stumpy toward the candle-box. "All serene," replied Stumpy. "Anything up?" "Nothing." There was a pause—an embarrassing one—Stumpy still holding the door. Then Kentuck had recourse to his finger, which he held up to Stumpy. "Rastled with it,—the d—d little cuss," he said, and retired.

The next day Cherokee Sal had such rude sepulcher as Roaring Camp afforded. After her body had been committed to the hill-side, there was a formal meeting of the camp to discuss what should be done with her infant. A resolution to adopt it was unanimous and enthusiastic. But an animated discussion in regard to the manner and feasibility of providing for its wants at once sprang up. It was remarkable that the argument partook of none of those fierce personalities with which discussions were usually conducted at Roaring Camp. Tipton proposed that they should send the child to Red Dog,—a distance of forty miles,—where female attention could be procured. But the unlucky suggestion met with fierce and unanimous opposition. It was evident that no plan which entailed parting from their new acquisition would for a moment be entertained. "Besides said Tom Ryder, "them fellows at Red Dog would swap it, and ring in somebody else on us." A disbelief in the honesty of other camps prevailed at Roaring Camp as in other places.

The introduction of a female nurse in the camp also met with objection. It was argued that no decent woman could be prevailed to accept Roaring Camp as her home, and the speaker urged that "they didn't want any more of the other kind." This unkind allusion to the defunct mother, harsh as it may seem, was the first spasm of propriety,—the first symptom of the camp's regeneration. Stumpy advanced nothing. Perhaps he felt a certain delicacy in interfering with the selection of a possible successor in office. But when questioned, he averred stoutly that he and "Jinny"—the mammal before alluded to—could manage to rear the child. There was something original, independent, and heroic about the plan that pleased the camp. Stumpy was retained. Certain articles were sent for to Sacramento. "Mind," said the treasurer, as he pressed a bag of gold-dust into the expressman's hand, "the best that can be got,—lace, you know, and filigree-work and frills—d—n the cost!"

Strange to say, the child thrived. Perhaps the invigorating climate of the mountain camp was compensation for material deficiencies. Nature took the fondling to her broader breast. In that rare atmosphere of the Sierra foothills,—that air pungent with balsamic odour, that ethereal cordial at once bracing and exhilarating,—he may have found food and nourishment, or a subtle chemistry that transmuted asses' milk to lime and phosphorus. Stumpy inclined to the belief that it was the latter, and good nursing. "Me and that ass," he would say, "has been father and mother to him! Don't you," he would add, apostrophizing the helpless bundle before him, "never go back on us."

By the time he was a month old, the necessity of giving him a name became apparent. He had generally been known as "the Kid," "Stumpy's boy," "the Cayote" (an allusion to his vocal powers), and even by Kentuck's endearing diminutive of "the d—d little cuss." But these were felt to be vague and unsatisfactory, and were at last dismissed under another influence. Gamblers and adventurers are generally superstitious, and Oakhurst one day declared that the baby had brought "the luck" to Roaring Camp. It was certain that of late they had been successful. "Luck" was the name agreed upon, with the prefix of Tommy for greater convenience. No allusion was made to the mother, and the father was unknown. "It's better," said the philosophical Oakhurst, "to take a fresh deal all round. Call him Luck, and start him fair." A day was accordingly set apart for the christening. What was meant by this ceremony the reader may imagine, who has already gathered some idea of the reckless irreverence of Roaring Camp. The master of ceremonies was one "Boston," a noted wag, and the occasion seemed to promise the greatest facetiousness. This ingenious satirist had spent two days in preparing a burlesque of the church service, with pointed local allusions. The choir was properly trained, and Sandy Tipton was to stand godfather. But after the procession had marched to the grove with music and banners, and the child had been deposited before a mock altar, Stumpy stepped before the expectant crowd. "It ain't my style to spoil fun, boys," said the little man, stoutly, eyeing the faces around him, "but it strikes me that this thing ain't exactly on the squar. It's playing it pretty low down on this yer baby to ring in fun on him that he ain't going to understand. And ef there's going to be any godfathers round, I'd like to see who's got any better rights than me." A silence followed Stumpy's speech. To the credit of all humorists be it said, that the first man to acknowledge its justice was the satirist, thus stopped of his fun. "But," said Stumpy, quickly, following up his advantage, "we're here for a christening, and we'll have it. I proclaim you Thomas Luck, according to the laws of the United States and the State of California, so help me God." It was the first time that the name of the Deity had been uttered otherwise than profanely in the camp. The form of christening was perhaps even more ludicrous than the satirist had conceived; but, strangely enough, nobody saw it, and nobody laughed. "Tommy" was christened as seriously as he would have been under a Christian roof, and cried and was comforted in as orthodox fashion.

And so the work of regeneration began in Roaring Camp. Almost imperceptibly a change came over the settlement. The cabin assigned to "Tommy Luck"—or "The Luck," as he was more frequently called—first showed signs of improvement. It was kept scrupulously clean and whitewashed. Then it was boarded, clothed, and papered. The rosewood cradle—packed eighty miles by mule—had, in Stumpy's way of putting it, "sorter killed the rest of the furniture." So the rehabilitation of the cabin became a necessity. The men who were in the habit of lounging in at Stumpy's to see "how the Luck got on" seemed to appreciate the change, and, in self-defence, the rival establishment of "Tuttle's grocery" bestirred itself, and imported a carpet and mirrors. The reflections of the latter on the appearance of Roaring Camp tended to produce stricter habits of personal cleanliness. Again, Stumpy imposed a kind of quarantine upon those who aspired to the honour and privilege of holding "The Luck." It was a cruel mortification to Kentuck—who, in the carelessness of a large nature and the habits of frontier life, had begun to regard all garments as a second cuticle, which, like a snake's, only sloughed off through decay—to be debarred this privilege from certain prudential reasons. Yet such was the subtle influence of innovation that he thereafter appeared regularly every afternoon in a clean shirt, and face still shining from his ablutions. Nor were moral and social sanitary laws neglected. "Tommy," who was supposed to spend his whole existence in a persistent attempt to repose, must not be disturbed by noise. The shouting and yelling which had gained the camp its infelicitous title were not permitted within hearing distance of Stumpy's. The men conversed in whispers, or smoked with Indian gravity. Profanity was tacitly given up in these sacred precincts, and throughout the camp a popular form of expletive, known as "D—n the luck!" and "Curse the luck!" was abandoned, as having a new personal bearing. Vocal music was not interdicted, being supposed to have a soothing, tranquillizing quality, and one song, sung by "Man-o'-war Jack," an English sailor, from her Majesty's Australian colonies, was quite popular as a lullaby. It was a lugubrious recital of the exploits of "the Arethusa, Seventy-four," in a muffled minor, ending with a prolonged dying fall at the burden of each verse, "On b-o-o-ard of the Arethusa." It was a fine sight to see Jack holding The Luck, rocking from side to side as if with the motion of a ship, and crooning forth this naval ditty. Either through the peculiar rocking of Jack or the length of his song—it contained ninety stanzas, and was continued with conscientious deliberation to the bitter end—the lullaby generally had the desired effect. At such times the men would lie at full length under the trees, in the soft summer twilight, smoking their pipes and drinking in the melodious utterances. An indistinct idea that this was pastoral happiness pervaded the camp. "This 'ere kind o' think," said the Cockney Simmons, meditatively reclining on his elbow, "is 'evingly." It reminded him of Greenwich.

On the long summer days The Luck was usually carried to the gulch, from whence the golden store of Roaring Camp was taken. There, on a blanket spread over pine-boughs, he would lie while the men were working in the ditches below. Latterly there was a rude attempt to decorate this bower with flowers and sweet-smelling shrubs, and generally some one would bring him a cluster of wild honeysuckles, azaleas, or the painted blossoms of Las Mariposas. The men had suddenly awakened to the fact that there were beauty and significance in these trifles, which they had so long trodden carelessly beneath their feet. A flake of glittering mica, a fragment of variegated quartz, a bright pebble from the bed of the creek, became beautiful to eyes thus cleared and strengthened, and were invariably put aside for "The Luck." It was wonderful how many treasures the woods and hillsides yielded that "would do for Tommy." Surrounded by playthings such as never child out of fairy-land had before, it is to be hoped that Tommy was content. He appeared to be securely happy, albeit there was an infantine gravity about him, a contemplative light in his round gray eyes, that sometimes worried Stumpy. He was always tractable and quiet, and it is recorded that once, having crept beyond his "corral,"—a hedge of tessellated pine-boughs, which surrounded his bed,—he dropped over the bank on his head in the soft earth, and remained with his mottled legs in the air in that position for at least five minutes with unflinching gravity. He was extricated without a murmur. I hesitate to record the many other instances of his sagacity, which rest, unfortunately, upon the statements of prejudiced friends. Some of them were not without a tinge of superstition. "I crep' up the bank just now," said Kentuck, one day, in a breathless state of excitement, "and dern my skin if he wasn't a talking to a jay-bird as was a sittin' on his lap. There they was, just as free and sociable as anything you please, a jawin' at each other just like two cherry-bums." Howbeit, whether creeping over the pine-boughs or lying lazily on his back blinking at the leaves above him, to him the birds sang, the squirrels chattered, and the flowers bloomed. Nature was his nurse and playfellow. For him she would let slip between the leaves golden shafts of sunlight that fell just within his grasp; she would send wandering breezes to visit him with the balm of bay and resinous gums; to him the tall redwoods nodded familiarly and sleepily, the bumble-bees buzzed, and the rooks cawed a slumbrous accompaniment.

Such was the golden summer of Roaring Camp. They were "flush times,"—and the luck was with them. The claims had yielded enormously. The camp was jealous of its privileges, and looked suspiciously on strangers. No encouragement was given to immigration, and, to make their seclusion more perfect, the land on either side of the mountain-wall that surrounded the camp they duly pre-empted. This, and a reputation for singular proficiency with the revolver, kept the reserve of Roaring Camp inviolate. The expressman—their only connecting link with the surrounding world—sometimes told wonderful stories of the camp. He would say, "They've a street up there in 'Roaring' that would lay over any street in Red Dog. They've got vines and flowers round their houses, and they wash themselves twice a day. But they're mighty rough on strangers, and they worship an Ingin baby."

With the prosperity of the camp came a desire for further improvement. It was proposed to build a hotel in the following spring, and to invite one or two decent families to reside there for the sake of "The Luck,"—who might perhaps profit by female companionship. The sacrifice that this concession to the sex cost these men, who were fiercely sceptical in regard to its general virtue and usefulness, can only be accounted for by their affection for Tommy. A few still held out. But the resolve could not be carried into effect for three months, and the minority meekly yielded in the hope that something might turn up to prevent it. And it did.

The winter of 1851 will long be remembered in the foothills. The snow lay deep on the Sierras, and every mountain creek became a river, and every river a lake. Each gorge and gulch was transformed into a tumultuous watercourse, that descended the hill-sides, tearing down giant trees, and scattering its drift and debris along the plain. Red Dog had been twice under water, and Roaring Camp had been forewarned. "Water put the gold into them gulches," said Stumpy; "it's been here once and will be here again!" And that night the North Fork suddenly leaped over its banks, and swept up the triangular valley of Roaring Camp.

In the confusion of rushing water, crushing trees, and crackling timber, and the darkness which seemed to flow with the water and blot out the fair valley, but little could be done to collect the scattered camp. When the morning broke, the cabin of Stumpy nearest the river-bank was gone. Higher up the gulch they found the body of its unlucky owner; but the pride, the hope, the joy, the Luck of Roaring Camp had disappeared. They were returning with sad hearts, when a shout from the bank recalled them.

It was a relief-boat from down the river. They had picked up, they said, a man and an infant, nearly exhausted, about two miles below. Did anybody know them, and did they belong here?

It needed but a glance to show them Kentuck lying there, cruelly crushed and bruised, but still holding the Luck of Roaring Camp in his arms. As they bent over the strangely assorted pair, they saw that the child was cold and pulseless. "He is dead," said one. Kentuck opened his eyes. "Dead?" he repeated, feebly. "Yes, my man, and you are dying too." A smile lit the eyes of the expiring Kentuck. "Dying," he repeated, "he's a taking me with him,—tell the boys I've got the Luck with me now;" and the strong man, clinging to the frail babe as a drowning man is said to cling to a straw, drifted away into the shadowy river that flows for ever to the unknown sea.

"To the Cliff House"

When the fierce southwester of the past week was at its height, and the Oakland ferry-boat failed to make a landing at its accumstomed wharf; when tall ships dragged their anchors, and umbrellas flew from the excited grasp of pedestrians; when signboards were loosed, tin roofs stripped off, and the "storm-wind Euroclydon" swept resistlessly through the deserted streets of San Francisco, two travellers in a buggy might have been seen breasting the blast on the desolate sandhills toward the ocean beach. But as at this point all resemblance to the opening chapters of a once popular novel ceased, I may as well admit that the two mysterious travellers were the present writer, and a companion, on their way to the Cliff House. The style of conveyance—whoever heard of a hero in a buggy?—the style of garment— India-rubber overcoats—were alone sufficient to unfit them for that romantic narrative which aims rather at the picturesque than the comfortable.

As we crept along, at times making scarcely any headway against the gale, which tore furioulsy across the road, charged with spray, that left upon our lips an ominous foretaste of the ocean, miles away, we noticed that the roar of the surf, at first quite perceptible, seemed to decrease as we approached the shore. The rain, mixed with flying particles of sand from the adjacent hills, stung our faces like the Lilliputian arrows discharged at Gulliver, and our "waterproofs"—alas! for the ingenuity of man— succumbed at last to the incessant beating of the storm. We finally sat in a douche bath, while from every angle of our garments the water poured in gentle rivulets, or from our hats dropped in a continuous "waterfall" behind. Our horse, the dauntless "Macadamizer"—albeit he had his own suspicions of the sanity of the two occupants of the buggy—butted away the storm from his broad shoulders, and, at last, "in the very tempest and whirlwind" of this elemental passion, we stood upon the balcony of the Cliff House.

Far as the eye could reach, or where the southerly trend of the beach mingled with the storm, and sky and shore line were blotted out by the driving scud, the whole vast expanse seemed to undulate with yawning caverns and toppling cliffs of water. Although the "yeasty surges" swept far up the beach, there was but little foam to seaward; the level gale sheared their white plumes almost as quickly as they heaved into sight, and drove them inland like the scattered down from some wild sea bird. The sand was covered with clinging patches of viscid spume thrown from the racing waves, as the foam is cast from the tossing bit of a thoroughbred. The lesser rocks, where the sea-lions were wont to bask in the sunlight, were scarcely ever free from the surging of tumultuous seas that boiled, hissed and seethed around them. At times a wave, larger than its fellows, charging upon the single peak known as "Seal Rock," and breaking halfway up its summit, would fling half its volume in snowy foam twenty feet above the crest, to fall and fill with a leaping torrent each ravine in the rocky flanks of the lonely peak. Far out to sea, wave after wave heaved their huge leaden sides like the dull scales of some undulating monster. Nearer in shore the billows were cleanly cut, but the fierce breeze dulled their edges, and they broke unevenly upon the sand.

The view was unsurpassed in grandeur. Whether from the windows of the parlor of the Cliff House, where but a single piece of plate-glass seemed to separate the comforts and refinements of civilization and peace from the rude jarring of elemental discord, and Nature in her rudest aspect, beyond. Whether from the cliff above, where we leaned against the wind, and looked down upon the gathering surf beneath our feet and the rollers hastening with impatient strides toward the Golden Gate, or whether from the beach itself, where huge trunks of spars were rolled and tossed like straws upon the sand, and where the waves raced like ravenous wolves, and it was perilous to venture. It was with a feeling of regret that we at last turned our faces—our cheeks buffeted by the elements into a healthy glow—once more toward the city, and exchanged the rough but hearty welcome of sea and shore for the blazing "sea-coal" and close windows of the town.

San Francisco from the Sea

Bret Harte

Serene, indifferent of Fate,
Thou sittest at the Western Gate;
Upon thy heights so lately won
Still slant the banners of the sun;
Thou seest the white seas strike their tents,
O Warder of two Continents!
And scornful of the peace that flies
Thy angry winds and sullen skies,
Thou drawest all things, small or great,
To thee, beside the Western Gate.

O, lion's whelp, that hidest fast
In jungle growth of spire and mast,
I know thy cunning and thy greed,

Thy hard high lust and wilful deed,
And all thy glory loves to tell
Of specious gifts material.
Drop down, O fleecy Fog, and hide
Her skeptic sneer, and all her pride!
Wrap her, O Fog, in gown and hood
Of her Franciscan Brotherhood.
Hide me her faults, her sin and blame,
With thy grey mantle cloak her shame!
So shall she, cowled, sit and pray
Till morning bears her sins away.
Then rise, O fleecy Fog, and raise
The glory of her coming days;
Be as the cloud that flecks the seas
Above her smoky argosies.
When forms familiar shall give place
To stranger speech and newer face;
When all her throes and anxious fears
Lie hushed in the repose of years;
When Art shall raise and Culture lift
The sensual joys and meaner thrift,
And all fulfilled the vision, we
Who watch and wait shall never see—
Who, in the morning of her race,
Toiled fair or meanly in our place—
But, yielding to the common lot,
Lie unrecorded and forgot.

The Cliff House at the time when Twain and Harte visited it.

The Cliff House, built by Mayor Sutro in 1896, destroyed by fire in 1907.

XI

Five Sketches by Mark Twain

Mark Twain came out to California in 1861 primarily to get away from the Civil War. His brief service in a Confederate home guard unit convinced him that he wanted no part of the hostilities. He tried silver mining and speculating in silver stocks in Nevada, both with no success. But between loafing and hoping something would turn up, he published some humorous sketches in the Virginia City *Territorial Enterprise.* When he was chosen to fill the shoes of the famous journalist, Dan De Quille, while the latter vacationed in the States, Twain's writing career was on its way.

It was only a matter of time before a man of Twain's restlessness would graduate from the alkalai flats of Nevada to the high-stepping life of San Francisco. He worked for several papers in the City, with varying pleasure and success. But he found the near-perfect home for his brand of tall-tale humor in the *Golden Era,* San Francisco's version of a literary journal, a real general store of verse, sketches, columns, news, and miscellaneous whatevers. In the *Era,* Twain could say what he liked and be paid for it—surely the happiest of all worlds for any writer. Twain would, of course, write his masterpieces long after his San Francisco apprenticeship. But he would never again find the congenial friendships and the easy-going life of his years in San Francisco.

The Pioneers' Ball

It was estimated that four hundred persons were present at the ball. The gentlemen wore the orthodox costume for such occasions, and the ladies were dressed the best they knew how. N.B.—Most of these ladies were pretty, and some of them absolutely beautiful. Four out of every five ladies present were pretty. The ratio at the Colfax party was two out of every five. I always keep the run of these things. While upon this department of the subject, I may as well tarry a moment and furnish you with descriptions of some of the most noticeable costumes.

Mrs. W.M. was attired in an elegant *pate de foi gras,* made expressly for her, and was greatly admired.

Miss S. had her hair done up. She was the centre of attraction for the gentlemen, and the envy of all the ladies.

169

Miss G.W. was tastefully dressed in a tout ensemble, and was greeted with deafening applause wherever she went.

Miss C.N. was superbly arrayed in white kid gloves. Her modest and engaging manner accorded well with the unpretending simplicity of her costume, and caused her to be regarded with absorbing interest by everyone.

The charming Miss M.M.B. appeared in a thrilling waterfall, whose exceeding grace and volume compelled the homage of pioneers and emigrants alike. How beautiful she was!

The queenly Mrs. L.B. was attractively attired in her new and beautiful false teeth, and the *bon jour* effect they naturally produced was heightened by her enchanting and well-sustained smile. The manner of this lady is charmingly pensive and melancholy, and her troops of admirers desired no greater happiness than to get on the scent of her sozodont-sweetened sighs and track her through her sinuous course among the gay and restless multitude.

Miss R.P., with that repugnance to ostentation in dress which is so peculiar to her, was attired in a simple white lace collar, fastened with a neat pearl-button solitaire. The fine contrast between the sparkling vivacity of her natural optic and the steadfast attentiveness of her placid glass eye was the subject of general and enthusiastic remark.

The radiant and sylph-like Mrs. T., late of your state, wore hoops. She showed to good advantage, and created a sensation wherever she appeared. She was the gayest of the gay.

Miss C.L.B. had her fine nose elegantly enameled, and the easy grace with which she blew it from time to time, marked her as a cultivated and accomplished woman of the world; its exquisitely modulated tone excited the admiration of all who had the happiness to hear it.

Being offended with Miss X., and our acquaintance having ceased prematurely, I will take this opportunity of observing to her that it is of no use for her to be slopping off to every ball that takes place, and flourishing around with a brass oyster-knife skewered through her waterfall, and smiling her sickly smile through her decayed teeth, with her dismal pug nose in the air. There is no use in it—she don't fool anybody. Everybody knows that she is old; everybody knows she is repaired (you might almost say built) with artificial bones and hair and muscles and things, from the ground up—put together scrap by scrap—and everybody knows, also, that all one would have to do would be to pull out her key-pin and she would go to pieces like a Chinese puzzle. There, now, my faded flower, take that paragraph home with you and amuse yourself with it; and if ever you turn your wart of a nose up at me again I will sit down and write something that will just make you rise up and howl.

The Only True and Reliable Account of
The Great Prize Fight
for $100,000 at
Seal Rock Point, on Sunday Last,
between his Excellency Gov. Stanford and Hon. F.F. Low,
Governor Elect of California

For the past month the sporting world has been in a state of feverish excitement on account of the grand prize fight set for last Sunday between the two most distinguished citizens of California, for a purse of a hundred thousand dollars. The high social standing of the competitors, their exalted position in the arena of politics, together with the princely sum of money staked upon the issue of the combat, all conspired to render the proposed prize-fight a subject of extraordinary importance, and to give it an eclat never before vouchsafed to such a circumstance since the world began. Additional lustre was shed upon the coming contest by the lofty character of the seconds or bottle-holders chosen by the two champions, these being no other than Judge Field (on the part of Gov. Low), Associate Justice of the Supreme Court of the United States, and Hon. Wm. M. Stewart, (commonly called "Bill Stewart," or "Bullyragging Bill Stewart,") of the city of Virginia, the most popular as well as the most distinguished lawyer in Nevada Territory, member of the Constitutional Convention, and future U.S. Senator for the State of Washoe, as I hope and believe—on the part of Gov. Stanford. Principals and seconds together, it is fair to presume that such an array of talent was never entered for a combat of this description upon any previous occasion.

Stewart and Field had their men in constant training at the Mission during the six weeks preceding the contest, and such was the interest taken in the matter that thousands visited that sacred locality daily to pick up such morsels of information as they might, concerning the physical and scientific improvement being made by the gubernatorial acrobats. The anxiety manifested by the populace was intense. When it was learned that Stanford had smashed a barrel of flour to atoms with a single blow of his fist, the voice of the people was on his side. But when the news came that Low had caved in the head of a tubular boiler with one stroke of his powerful "mawley" (which term is in strict accordance with the language of the ring,) the tide of opinion changed again. These changes were frequent, and they kept the minds of the public in such a state of continual vibration that I fear the habit thus acquired is confirmed, and that they will never more cease to oscillate.

The fight was to take place on last Sunday morning at ten o'clock. By nine every wheeled vehicle and every species of animal capable of bearing burthens, were in active service, and the avenues leading to the Seal Rock swarmed with them in mighty processions whose numbers no man might hope to estimate.

I determined to be upon the ground at an early hour. Now I dislike to be exploded, as it were, out of my balmy slumbers, by a sudden, stormy assault upon my door, and an imperative order to "Get up!"—wherefore I requested one of the intelligent porters of the Lick House to call at my palatial apartments, and murmur gently through the keyhole the magic monosyllable "Hash!" That "fetched me."

The urbane livery-stable keeper furnished me with a solemn, short-bodied, long-legged animal—a sort of animated counting-house stool, as it were—which he called a "Morgan" horse. He told me who the brute was "sired" by, and was proceeding to tell me who he was "dammed" by, but I gave him to understand that I was competent to damn the horse myself, and should probably do it very effectually before I got to the battle-ground. I mentioned to him, however, that as I was not proposing to attend a funeral, it was hardly necessary to furnish me an animal gifted with such oppressive solemnity of bearing as distinguished his "Morgan." He said in reply, that Morgan was only pensive when in the stable, but that on the road I would find him one of the liveliest horses in the world.

He enunciated the truth.

The brute "bucked" with me from the foot of Montgomery street to the Occidental Hotel. The laughter which he provoked from the crowds of citizens along the side-walks, he took for applause, and honestly made every effort in his power to deserve it, regardless of consequences.

He was very playful, but so suddenly were the creations of his fancy conceived and executed, and so much ground did he take up with them, that it was safest to behold them from a distance. In the selfsame moment of time, he shot his heels through the side of a street-car, and then backed himself into Barry and Patten's and sat down on the free-lunch table.

Such was the length of this Morgan's legs.

Between the Occidental and the Lick House, having become thoroughly interested in his work, he planned and carried out a series of the most extraordinary maneuvers ever suggested by the brain of any horse. He arched his neck and went tripping daintily across the street sideways, "rairing up" on his hind legs occasionally, in a very disagreeable way, and looking into the second-story windows. He finally waltzed into the large ice cream saloon opposite the Lick House, and—

But the memory of that perilous voyage hath caused me to digress from the proper subject of this paper, which is the great prize-fight between Governor Low and Stanford. I will resume.

After an infinitude of fearful adventures, the history of which would fill many columns of this newspaper, I finally arrived at the Seal Rock Point at a quarter to ten—two hours and a half out from San Francisco, and not less gratified than surpised that I ever got there at all—and anchored my noble Morgan to a boulder on the hill-side. I had to swathe his head in blankets also, because, while my back was turned for a single moment, he developed another atrocious trait of his most remarkable character. He tried to eat little Augustus Maltravers Jackson, the "humbly" but interesting off-spring of Hon. J. Belvidere Jackson, a wealthy barber from San Jose. It would have been a comfort to me to leave the infant to his fate, but I did not feel able to pay for him.

When I reached the battle-ground, the great champions were already stripped and prepared for the "mill." Both were in splendid condition, and displayed a redundancy of muscle about the breast and arms which was delightful to the eye of the sportive connoisseur. They were well matched. Adepts said that Stanford's "heft" and tall stature were fairly offset by Low's superior litheness and activity. From their heads to the Union colors around their waists, their costumes were similar to that of the Greek Slave; from thence down they were clad in fresh-colored tights and grenadier boots.

The ring was formed upon the beautiful level sandy beach above the Cliff House, and within twenty paces of the snowy surf of the broad Pacific ocean, which was spotted here and there with monstrous sea-lions attracted shoreward by curiosity concerning the vast multitudes of people collected in the vicinity.

At five minutes past ten, Brigadier General Wright, the Referee, notified the seconds to bring their men "up to the scratch." They did so, amid the shouts of the populace, the noise whereof rose high above the roar of the sea.

FIRST ROUND.—The pugilists advanced to the centre of the ring, shook hands, retired to their respective corners, and at the call of the time-keeper, came forward and went at it. Low dashed out handsomely with his left and gave Stanford a paster in the eye, and at the same moment his adversary mashed him in the ear. [These singular phrases are entirely proper, Mr. Editor—I find them in the copy of "Bell's Life in London" now lying before me.] After some beautiful sparring, both parties went down—that is to say, they went down to the bottle-holder Stewart and Field, and took a drink.

SECOND ROUND.—Stanford launched out a well intended plunger, but Low parried it admirably and instantly busted him in the snoot. [Cries of "Bully for the Marysville Infant! "] After some lively fibbing (both of them are used to it in political life) the combatants went to grass. [See "Bell's Life."]

THIRD ROUND.—Both came up panting considerably. Low let go a terrific side-winder, but Stanford stopped it handsomely and replied with an earthquake on Low's bread-basket. [Enthusiastic shouts of "Sock it to him, my Sacramento Pet!"] More fibbing—both down.

FOURTH ROUND.—The men advanced and sparred warily for a few moments, when Stanford exposed his cocoanut an instant, and Low struck out from the shoulder and split him in the mug. [Cries of "Bully for the Fat Boy!"]

FIFTH ROUND.—Stanford came up looking wicked, and let drive a heavy blow with his larboard flipper which caved in the side of his adversary's head. [Exclamations of "Hi! at him again Old Rusty!"]

From this time until the end of the conflict, there was nothing regular in the proceedings. The two champions got furiously angry, and used up each other thus:

No sooner did Low realize that the side of his head was crushed in like a dent in a plug hat, than he "went after" Stanford in the most desperate manner. With one blow of his fist he mashed his nose so far into his face that a cavity was left in its place the size and shape of an ordinary soupbowl. It is scarcely necessary to mention that in making room for so much nose, Gov. Stanford's eyes were crowded to such a degree as to cause them to "bug out" like a grasshopper's. His face was so altered that he scarcely looked like himself at all.

I never saw such a murderous expression as Stanford's countenance now assumed; you see it was so concentrated—it had such a small number of features to spread around over. He let fly one of his battering rams and caved in the other side of Low's head. Ah me, the latter was a ghastly sight to contemplate after that—one of the boys said it looked "like a beet which somebody had trod on it."

Low was "grit" though. He dashed out with his right and stove Stanford's chin clear back even with his ears. Oh, what a horrible sight he was, gasping and reaching after his tobacco, which was away back among his under-jaw teeth.

Stanford was unsettled for a while, but he soon rallied, and watching his chance, aimed a tremendous blow at his favorite mark, which crushed in the rear of Gov. Low's head in such a way that the crown thereof projected over his spinal column like a shed.

He came up to the scratch like a man, though, and sent one of his ponderous fists crashing through his opponent's ribs, and in among his vitals, and instantly afterward he hauled out poor Stanford's left lung and smacked him in the face with it.

If ever I saw an angry man in my life it was Leland Stanford. He fairly raved. He jumped at his old speciality, Gov. Low's head; he tore it loose from his body and knocked him down with it. [Sensation in the crowd.]

Staggered by his extraordinary exertion, Gov. Stanford reeled, and before he could recover himself the headless but indomitable Low sprang forward, pulled one of his legs out by the roots, and dealt him a smashing paster over the eye with the end of it. The ever watchful Bill Stewart sallied out to the assistance of his crippled principal with a pair of crutches, and the battle went on again as fiercely as ever.

At this stage of the game the battle ground was strewn with a sufficiency of human remains to furnish material for the construction of three or four men of ordinary size, and good sound brains enough to stock a whole country like the one I came from in the noble old state of Missouri. And so dyed were the combatants in their own gore that they looked like shapeless, mutilated, red-shirted firemen.

The moment a chance offered, Low grabbed Stanford by the hair of the head, swung him thrice round and round in the air like a lasso, and then slammed him on the ground with such mighty force that he quivered all over, and squirmed painfully, like a worm; and behold, his body and such of his limbs as he had left, shortly assumed a swollen aspect like unto those of a rag doll-baby stuffed with saw-dust.

He rallied again, however, and the two desperadoes clinched and never let up until they had minced each other into such insignificant odds and ends that neither was able to distinguish his own remnants from those of his antagonist. It was awful.

Bill Stewart and Judge Field issued from their corners and gazed upon the sanguinary reminiscences in silence during several minutes. At the end of that time, having failed to discover that either champion had got the best of the fight, they threw up their sponges simultaneously, and Gen. Wright proclaimed in a loud voice that the battle was "drawn." May my ears never again be rent asunder with a burst of sound similar to that which greeted this announcement, from the multitude. Amen.

By order of Gen. Wright, baskets were procured, and Bill Stewart and Judge Field proceeded to gather up the fragments of their late principals, while I gathered up my notes and went after my infernal horse, who had slipped his blankets and was foraging among the neighboring children. I——.* * * *

P.S.—Messrs. Editors, I have been the victim of an infamous hoax. I have been imposed upon by that ponderous miscreant, Mr. Frank Lawler, of the Lick House. I left my room a moment ago, and the first man I met on the stairs was Gov. Stanford, alive and well, and as free from mutilation as you or I. I was speechless. Before I reached the street, I actually met Gov. Low also, with his own head on his own shoulders, his limbs intact, his inner mechanism in its proper place, and his cheeks blooming with gorgeous robustitude. I was amazed. But a word of explanation from him convinced me that I had been swindled by Mr. Lawler with a detailed account of a fight which had never occurred, and was never likely to occur; that I had believed him so implicitly as to sit down and write it out (as other reporters have done before me) in language calculated to deceive the public into the conviction that I was present at it myself, and to embellish it with a string of falsehoods intended to render that deception as plausible as possible. I ruminated upon my singular position for many minutes, arrived at no conclusion—that is to say, no satisfactory conclusion, except that Lawler was an accomplished knave and I was a consummate ass. I had suspected the first before, though, and been acquainted with the latter fact for nearly a quarter of a century.

In conclusion, permit me to apologize in the most abject manner to the present Governor of California, to Hon. Mr. Low, the Governor-elect, to Judge Field and to Hon. Wm. M. Stewart, for the great wrong which my natural imbecility has impelled me to do them in penning and publishing the foregoing sanguinary absurdity. If it were to do over again, I don't really know that I would do it. It is not possible for me to say how I ever managed to believe that refined and educated gentlemen like these could stoop to engage in the loathsome and degrading pastime of prize-fighting. It was just Lawler's work, you understand—the lubberly, swelled-up effigy of a nine-days drowned man! But I shall get even with him for this. The only excuse he offers is that he got the story from John B. Winters, and thought of course it must be just so—as if a future Congressman for the State of Washoe could by any possibility tell the truth! Do you know that if either of these miserable scoundrels were to cross my path while I am in this mood I would scalp him in a minute? That's me—that's my style.

"Early Rising" as Regards Excursions to the Cliff House

Early to bed, and early to rise,
Makes a man healthy, wealthy and wise.
                    —Benjamin Franklin.

I don't see it—George Washington.

Now both of these are high authorities—very high and respectable authorities—but I am with George Washington first, last, and all the time on this proposition.

Because I don't see it, either.

I have tried getting up early, and I have tried getting up late—and the latter agrees with me best. As for a man's growing any wiser, or any richer, or any healthier, by getting up early, I know it is not so; because I have got up early in the station-house many and many a time, and got poorer and poorer for the next half a day, in consequence, instead of richer and richer. And sometimes, on the same terms, I have seen the sun rise four times a week up there at Virginia, and so far from my growing healthier on account of it, I got to looking blue, and pulpy, and swelled, like a drowned man, and my relations grew alarmed and thought they were going to lose me. They entirely despaired of my recovery, at one time, and began to grieve for me as one whose days were numbered—whose fate was sealed—who was soon to pass away from them forever, and from the glad sunshine, and the birds, and the odorous flowers, and murmuring brooks, and whispering winds, and all the cheerful scenes of life, and go down into the dark and silent tomb—and they went forth sorrowing, and jumped a lot in the graveyard, and made up their minds to grin and bear it with that fortitude which is the true Christian's brightest ornament.

You observe that I have put a stronger test on the matter than even Benjamin Franklin contemplated, and yet it would not work. Therefore, how is a man to grow healthier, and wealthier, and wiser by going to bed early and getting up early, when he fails to accomplish these things even when he does not go to bed at all? And as far as becoming wiser is concerned, you might put all the wisdom I acquired in these experiments in your eye, without obstructing your vision any to speak of.

As I said before, my voice is with George Washington's on this question.

Another philosopher encourages the world to get up at sunrise because "it is the early bird that catches the worm."

It is a seductive proposition, and well calculated to trap the unsuspecting. But its attractions are all wasted on me, because I have no use for the worm. If I had, I would adopt the Unreliable's plan. He was much interested in this quaint proverb, and directed the powers of his great mind to its consideration for three or four consecutive hours. He was supposing a case. He was supposing, for instance, that he really wanted the worm—that the possession of the worm was actually necessary to his happiness—that he yearned for it and hankered after it, therefore, as much as a man could yearn for and hanker after a worm under such circumstances—and he was supposing, further, that he was opposed to getting up early in order to catch it (which was much the more plausible of the two suppositions). Well, at the end of three or four hours' profound meditation upon the subject, the Unreliable rose up and said: "If he were so anxious about the worm, and he couldn't get along without him, and he didn't want to get up early in the morning to catch him—why then, by George, he would just lay for him the night before." I never would have thought of that. I looked at the youth, and said to myself, he is malicious, and dishonest, and unhandsome, and does not smell good—yet how quickly do these trivial demerits disappear in the shadow, when the glare from this great intellect shines out above them!

I have always heard that the only time in the day that a trip to the Cliff House could be thoroughly enjoyed was early in the morning (and I suppose it might be as well to withhold an adverse impression while the flow-tide of public opinion continues to set in that direction.)

I tried it the other morning with Harry, the stockbroker, rising at 4 A.M., to delight in the following described things, to wit:

A road unencumbered by carriages, and free from wind and dust; a bracing atmosphere; the gorgeous spectacle of the sun in the dawn of his glory; the fresh perfume of flowers still damp with dew; a solitary drive on the beach while its smoothness was yet unmarred by wheel or hoof, and a vision of white sails glinting in the morning light far out at sea.

These were the considerations, and they seemed worthy a sacrifice of seven or eight hours' sleep.

We sat in the stable, and yawned, and gaped, and stretched, until the horse was hitched up, and then drove out into the bracing atmosphere. (When another early voyage is proposed to me, I want it understood that there is to be no bracing atmosphere in the programme. I can worry along without it.) In half an hour we were so thoroughly braced up with it that it was just a scratch that we were not frozen to death. Then the harness came unshipped, or got broken, or something, and I waxed colder and drowsier while Harry fixed it. I am not fastidious about clothes, but I am not used to wearing fragrant, sweaty horse-blankets, and not partial to them, either; I am not proud, though, when I am freezing, and I added the horse-blanket to my overcoats, and tried to wake up and feel warm and cheerful. It was useless, however—all my senses slumbered and continued to slumber, save the sense of smell.

When my friend drove past suburban gardens and said the flowers never exhaled so sweet an odor before, in his experience, I dreamily but honestly endeavored to think so too, but in my secret soul I was conscious that they only smelled like horse-blankets. When another early voyage is proposed to me, I want it understood that there is to be no "fresh perfume or flowers" in the programme, either. I do not enjoy it. (My senses are not attuned to the flavor—there is too much horse about it and not enough eau de cologne.)

The wind was cold and benumbing, and blew with such force that we could hardly make headway against it. It came straight from the ocean, and I think there are icebergs out there somewhere. True, there was not much dust, because the gale blew it all to Oregon in two minutes; and by good fortune, it blew no gravel-stones, to speak of—only one of any consequence, I believe—a three-cornered one—it struck me in the eye. I have it there yet. However, it does not matter—for the future I suppose I can manage to see tolerably well out of the other. (Still, when another early voyage is proposed to me, I want it understood that the dust is to be put in, and the gravel left out of the programme. I might want my other eye if I continue to hang on until my time comes; and besides, I shall not mind the dust much hereafter, because I have only got to shut one eye, now, when it is around.)

No, the road was not encumbered by carriages—we had it all to ourselves. I suppose the reason was, that most people do not like to enjoy themselves too much, and therefore do not go out to the Cliff House in the cold and the fog, and the dread silence and solitude of four o'clock in the morning. They are right. The impressive solemnity of such a pleasure trip is only equalled by an excursion to Lone Mountain in a hearse. Whatever of advantage there may be in having that Cliff House road all to yourself we had—but to my mind a greater advantage would be in dividing it up in small sections among the entire community; because, in consequence of the repairs in progress on it just now, it's as rough as a corduroy bridge—(in a good many places) and consequently the less you have of it, the happier you are likely to be and the less shaken up and disarranged on the inside. (Wherefore, when another early voyage is proposed to me, I want it understood that the road is not to be unencumbered with carriages, but just the reverse—so that the balance of the people shall be made to stand their share of the jolting and the desperate lonesomeness of the thing.)

From the moment we left the stable, almost, the fog was so thick that we could scarcely see fifty yards behind or before, or overhead; and for a while, as we approached the Cliff House, we could not see the horse at all, and were obliged to steer by his ears, which stood up dimly out of the dense white mist that enveloped him. But for those friendly beacons, we must have been cast away and lost.

I have no opinion of a six-mile ride in the clouds; but if I ever have to take another, I want to leave the horse in the stable and go in a balloon. I shall prefer to go in the afternoon, also, when it is warm, so that I may gape, and yawn, and stretch, if I am drowsy, without disarranging my horse-blanket and letting in a blast of cold wind.

We could scarcely see the supportive seals on the rocks, writhing and squirming like exaggerated maggots, and there was nothing soothing in their discordant barking, to a spirit so depressed as mine was.

Harry took a cocktail at the Cliff House, but I scorned such ineffectual stimulus; I yearned for fire, and there was none there; they were about to make one, but the bar-keeper looked altogether too cheerful for me—I could not bear his unnatural happiness in the midst of such a ghastly picture of fog, and damp, and frosty surf, and dreary solitude. I could not bear the sacrilegious presence of a pleasant face at such a time; it was too much like sprightliness at a funeral, and we fled from it down the smooth and vacant beach.

We had that all to ourselves, too, like the road—and I want it divided up, also, hereafter. We could not drive in the roaring surf and seem to float abroad on the foamy sea, as one is wont to do the sunny afternoon, because the very thought of any of that icy-looking water splashing on you was enough to congeal your blood, almost. We saw no white-winged ships sailing away on the billowy ocean, with the pearly light of morning descending upon them like a benediction—"because the fog had the bulge on the pearly light," as the Unreliable observed when I mentioned it to him afterwards; and we saw not the sun in the dawn of his glory, for the same reason. Hill and beach, and sea and sun were all wrapped in a ghostly mantle of mist, and hidden from our mortal vision. (When another early voyage is proposed to me, I want it understood that the sun in his glory, and the morning light, and the ships at sea, and all that sort of thing are to be left out of the programme, so that when we fail to see them, we shall not be so infernally disappointed.)

We were human icicles when we got the Ocean House, and there was no fire there, either. I banished all hope, then, and succumbed to despair; I went back on my religion, and sought surcease of sorrow in soothing blasphemy. I am sorry I did it, now, but it was a great comfort to me, then. We could have had breakfast at the Ocean House, but we did not want it; can statues of ice feel hunger? But we adjourned to a private room and ordered red-hot coffee, and it was a sort of balm to my troubled mind to observe that the man who brought it was as cold, and as silent, and as solemn as the grave itself. His gravity was so impressive, and so appropriate and becoming to the melancholy surroundings, that it won upon me and thawed out some of the better instincts of my nature, and I told him he might ask a blessing if he thought it would lighten him up any—because he looked as if he wanted to, very bad—but he only shook his head resignedly and sighed.

That coffee did the business for us. It was made by a master artist, and it had not a fault; and the cream that came with it was so rich and thick that you could hardly have strained it through a wire fence. As the generous beverage flowed down our frigid throats, our blood grew warm again, our muscles relaxed, our torpid bodies awoke to life and feeling, anger and uncharitableness departed from us and we were cheerful once more. We got good cigars, also, at the Ocean House, and drove into town over a smooth road, lighted by the sun and unclouded by fog.

Near the Jewish cemeteries we turned a corner too suddenly, and got upset, but sustained no damage, although the horse did what he honestly could to kick the buggy out of the State while we were grovelling in the sand. We went on down to the steamer and while we were on board, the buggy was upset again by some outlaw, and an axle broken.

However, these little accidents, and all the deviltry and misfortune that preceded them, were only just and natural consequences of the absurd experiment of getting up at an hour in the morning when all God-fearing Christians ought to be in bed. I consider that the man who leaves his pillow, deliberately, at sun-rise, is taking his life in his own hands, and he ought to feel proud if he don't have to put it down again at the coroner's office before dark.

Now, for that early trip, I am not any healthier or any wealthier than I was before, and only wiser in that I know a good deal better than to go and do it again. And as for all those notable advantages, such as the sun in the dawn of his glory, and the ships, and the perfume of the flowers, etc., etc., etc., I don't see them, any more than myself and Washington see the soundness of Benjamin Franklin's attractive little poem.

If you go to the Cliff House at any time after seven in the morning, you cannot fail to enjoy it—but never start out there before daylight, under the impression that you are going to have a pleasant time and come back insufferably healthier and wealthier and wiser than your betters on account of it. Because if you do you will miss your calculation, and it will keep you swearing about it right straight along for a week, to get even again.

Put no trust in the benefits to accrue from early rising, as set forth by the infatuated Franklin—but stake the last cent of your substance on the judgment of old George Washington, the Father of his Country, who said "he couldn't see it."

And you hear me endorsing that sentiment.

The Great Quake of '65

A month afterward I enjoyed my first earthquake. It was one which was long called the "great" earthquake, and is doubtless so distinguished till this day. It was just after noon, on a bright October day. I was coming down Third street. The only objects in motion anywhere in sight in that thickly built and populous quarter, were a man in a buggy behind me, and a street car wending slowly up the cross street. Otherwise, all was solitude and a Sabbath stillness. As I turned the corner, around a frame house, there was a great rattle and jar, and it occurred to me that here was an item!—no doubt a fight in that house. Before I could turn and seek the door, there came a really terrific shock; the ground seemed to roll under me in waves, interrupted by a violent joggling up and down, and there was a heavy grinding noise as of brick houses rubbing together. I fell up against the frame house and hurt my elbow. I knew what it was, now, and from mere reportorial instinct, nothing else, took out my watch and noted the time of day; at that moment a third and still severer shock came, and as I reeled about on the pavement trying to keep my footing, I saw a sight! The entire front of a tall four-story brick building in Third street sprung outward like a door and fell sprawling across the street, raising a dust like a great volume of smoke! And here came the buggy—overboard went the man, and in less time than I can tell it the vehicle was distributed in small fragments along three hundred yards of street. One could have fancied that somebody had fired a charge of chair-rounds and rags down the thoroughfare. The street car had stopped, the horses were rearing and plunging, the passengers were pouring out at both ends, and one fat man had crashed half way through a glass window on one side of the car, got wedged fast and was squirming and screaming like an impaled madman. Every door, of every house, as far as the eye could reach, was vomiting a stream of human beings; and almost before one could execute a wink and begin another, there was a massed multitude of people stretching in endless procession down every street my position commanded. Never was solemn solitude turned into teeming life quicker.

Of the wonders wrought by "the great earthquake," these were all that came under my eye; but the tricks it did, elsewhere, and far and wide over the town, made toothsome gossip for nine days. The destruction of property was trifling—the injury to it was wide-spread and somewhat serious.

The "curiosities of the earthquake were simply endless. Gentlemen and ladies who were sick, or were taking a siesta, or had dissipated till a late hour and were making up lost sleep, thronged into the public streets in all sorts of queer apparel, and some without any at all. One women who had been washing a naked child, ran down the street holding it by the ankles as if it were a dressed turkey. Prominent citizens who were supposed to keep the Sabbath strictly, rushed out of saloons in their shirt-sleeves, with billiard cues in their hands. Dozens of men with necks swathed in napkins, rushed from barbershops, lathered to the eyes or with one cheek clean shaved and the other still bearing a hairy stubble. Horses broke from stables, and a frightened dog rushed up a short attic ladder and out on to a roof, and when his scare was over had not the nerve to go down again the same way he had gone up. A prominent editor flew down stairs, in the principal hotel, with nothing on but one brief undergarment—met a chambermaid, and exclaimed.

"Oh, what *shall* I do! Where shall I go!"

She responded with naive serenity:

"If you have no choice, you might try a clothing-store!"

A certain foreign consul's lady was the acknowledged leader of fashion, and every time she appeared in anything new or extraordinary, the ladies in the vicinity made a raid on their husbands' purses and arrayed themselves similarly. One man who had suffered considerably and growled accordingly, was standing at the window when the shocks came, and the next instant the consul's wife, just out of the bath, fled by with no other apology for clothing than—a bath-towel! The sufferer rose superior to the terrors of the earthquake, and said to his wife:

"Now *that* is something *like!* Get out your towel my dear!"

The plastering that fell from ceilings in San Francisco that day, would have covered several acres of ground. For some days afterward, groups of eyeing and pointing men stood about many a building, looking at long zig-zag cracks that extended from the eaves to the ground. Four feet of the tops of three chimneys on one house were broken square off and turned around in such a way as to completely stop the draft. A crack a hundred feet long gaped open six inches wide in the middle of one street and then shut together again with such force, as to ridge up the meeting earth like a slender grave. A lady sitting in her rocking and quaking parlor, saw the wall part at the ceiling, open and shut twice, like a mouth, and then drop the end of a brick on the floor like a tooth. She was a woman easily disgusted with foolishness, and she arose and went out of there. One lady who was coming down stairs was astonished to see a bronze Hercules lean forward on its pedestal as if to strike her with its club. They both reached the bottom of the flight at the same time,—the woman insensible from the fright. Her child, born some little time afterward, was club-footed. However—on second thought,—if the reader sees any coincidence in this, he must do it at his own risk.

The first shock brought down two or three huge organ-pipes in one of the churches. The minister, with uplifted hands, was just closing the services. He glanced up, hesitated, and said:

"However, we will omit the benediction!"—and the next instant there was a vacancy in the atmosphere where he had stood.

After the first shock, an Oakland minister said:

"Keep your seats! There is no better place to die than this"—

And added, after the third:

"But outside is good enough!" He then skipped out at the back door.

Earthquake Almanac

At the instance of several friends who feel a boding anxiety to know beforehand what sort of phenomena we may expect the elements to exhibit during the next month or two, and who have lost all confidence in the various patent medicine almanacs, because of the unaccountable reticence of those works concerning the extraordinary event of the 8th inst., I have compiled the following almanac expressly for this latitude:

Oct. 17.—Weather hazy; atmosphere murky and dense. An expression of profound melancholy will be observable upon most countenances.

Oct. 18.—Slight earthquake. Countenances grow more melancholy.

Oct. 19.—Look out for rain. It would be absurd to look in for it. The general depression of spirits increased.

Oct. 20.—More weather.

Oct. 21.—Same.

Oct. 22.—Light winds, perhaps. If they blow, it will be from the "east'ard, or the nor'ard, or the west'ard, or the suth'ard," or from some general direction approximating more or less to these points of the compass or otherwise. Winds are uncertain—more especially when they blow from whence they cometh and whither they listeth. N. B.—Such is the nature of winds.

Oct. 23.—Mild, balmy earthquakes.

Oct. 24.—Shaky.

Oct. 25.—Occasional shakes, followed by light showers of bricks and plastering. N. B.—Stand from under.

Oct. 26.—Considerable phenomenal atmospheric foolishness. About this time expect more earthquakes, but do not look out for them, on account of the bricks.

Oct. 27.—Universal despondency, indicative of approaching disaster. Abstain from smiling, or indulgence in humorous conversation, or exasperating jokes.

Oct. 28.—Misery, dismal forebodings and despair. Beware of all light discourse—a joke uttered at this time would produce a popular outbreak.

Oct. 29.—Beware!

Oct. 30.—Keep dark!

Oct. 31.—Go slow!

Nov. 1.—Terrific earthquake. This is the great earthquake month. More stars fall and more worlds are slathered around carelessly and destroyed in November than in any other month of the twelve.

Nov. 2.—Spasmodic but exhilarating earthquakes, accompanied by occasional showers of rain, and churches and things.

Nov. 3.—Make your will.

Nov. 4.—Sell out.

Nov. 5.—Select your "last words." Those of John Quincy Adams will do, with the addition of a syllable, thus: "This is the last of earthquakes."

Nov. 6.—Prepare to shed this mortal coil.

Nov. 7.—Shed.

Nov. 8.—The sun will rise as usual, perhaps; but if he does he will doubtless be staggered some to find nothing but a large round hole eight thousand miles in diameter in the place where he saw this world serenely spinning the day before.

XII

The Proclamations of Emperor Norton

Like thousands of other adventurers, Joshua A. Norton came to San Francisco in 1849 to make his fortune. He was born in Great Britain of Jewish parents, and led a life of speculation and adventure before coming out to the great golden land of dreamers and schemers. Within four years, he had parlayed his original $40,000 capital into a quarter of a million dollars. Then, in 1853, he overreached himself. In an attempt to corner the rice market, he lost his entire fortune. The pressures of litigation, and the humiliation of sudden poverty snapped his sanity, and he dropped out of public life for several years. When he returned to San Francisco in 1857, though, he did not come back as a penitent failure. Joshua Norton, like his model the French Emperor Napoleon III, returned to triumph! In 1859, Norton publically proclaimed himself Emperor of the United States (he would later, like the French monarch, add "Protector of Mexico" to his titles and responsibilities). Until his death in 1880, Emperor Norton was the best known and best loved of all the eccentric characters who roamed the streets of San Francisco. Robert Louis Stevenson appreciated what Norton symbolized about the nature of the city that would support such a fantasy:

> In what other city would a harmless madman who supposed himself to be emperor of the two Americas have been so fostered and encouraged? Where else would even the people of the streets have respected the poor soul's illusion? Where else would bankers and merchants have received his visits, cashed his cheques, and submitted to his small assessments? Where else would he have been suffered to attend and address the exhibition days of schools and colleges? where else, in God's green earth, have taken his pick of restaurants, ransacked the bill of fare, and departed scathless? They tell me he was even an exacting patron, threatening to withdraw his custom when dissatisfied.

Emperor Norton formally began his imperial reign in San Francisco with this proclamation:

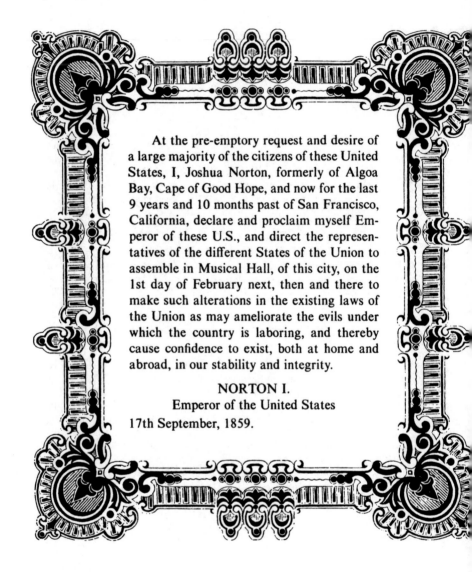

At the pre-emptory request and desire of a large majority of the citizens of these United States, I, Joshua Norton, formerly of Algoa Bay, Cape of Good Hope, and now for the last 9 years and 10 months past of San Francisco, California, declare and proclaim myself Emperor of these U.S., and direct the representatives of the different States of the Union to assemble in Musical Hall, of this city, on the 1st day of February next, then and there to make such alterations in the existing laws of the Union as may ameliorate the evils under which the country is laboring, and thereby cause confidence to exist, both at home and abroad, in our stability and integrity.

NORTON I.
Emperor of the United States
17th September, 1859.

In 1865, a New Yorker named D. Stellifer Moulton proclaimed himself "King, Reigning Prince of the house of David, and Guardian of Mexico." When Emperor Norton heard of this east coast pretender to his throne, he issued the following denunciation:

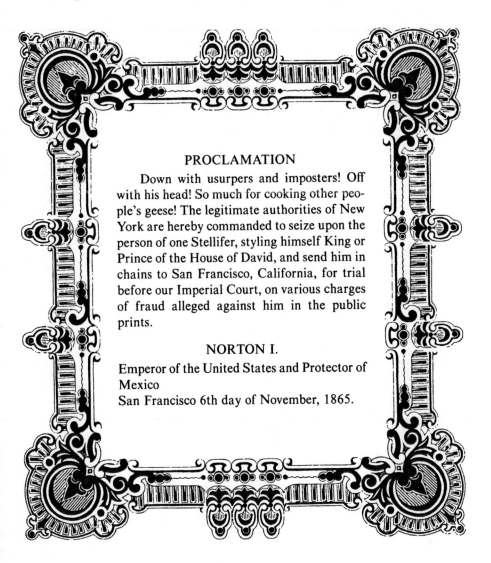

PROCLAMATION

Down with usurpers and imposters! Off with his head! So much for cooking other people's geese! The legitimate authorities of New York are hereby commanded to seize upon the person of one Stellifer, styling himself King or Prince of the House of David, and send him in chains to San Francisco, California, for trial before our Imperial Court, on various charges of fraud alleged against him in the public prints.

NORTON I.

Emperor of the United States and Protector of Mexico
San Francisco 6th day of November, 1865.

Emperor Norton was ahead of his time when he foresaw that the continued prosperity of San Francisco would depend on connecting the city by bridge to the north bay and east bay counties. His suggestion that a third bridge be built to link San Francisco to the Faralon Islands might strike us today as a bit extravagant.

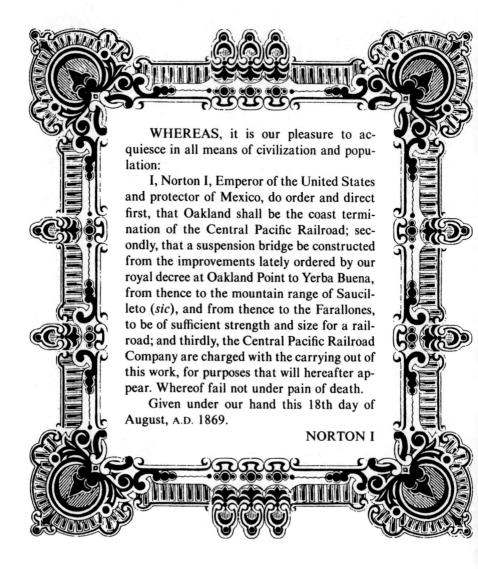

WHEREAS, it is our pleasure to acquiesce in all means of civilization and population:

I, Norton I, Emperor of the United States and protector of Mexico, do order and direct first, that Oakland shall be the coast termination of the Central Pacific Railroad; secondly, that a suspension bridge be constructed from the improvements lately ordered by our royal decree at Oakland Point to Yerba Buena, from thence to the mountain range of Saucilleto (*sic*), and from thence to the Farallones, to be of sufficient strength and size for a railroad; and thirdly, the Central Pacific Railroad Company are charged with the carrying out of this work, for purposes that will hereafter appear. Whereof fail not under pain of death.

Given under our hand this 18th day of August, A.D. 1869.

NORTON I

The Emperor maintained excellent relations with his fellow rulers in Japan and China, as these two imperial edicts demonstrate:

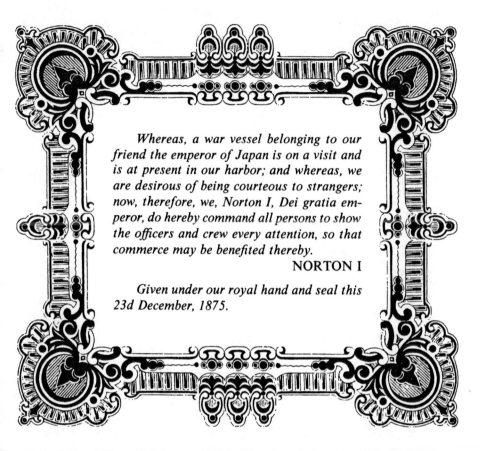

Whereas, a war vessel belonging to our friend the emperor of Japan is on a visit and is at present in our harbor; and whereas, we are desirous of being courteous to strangers; now, therefore, we, Norton I, Dei gratia emperor, do hereby command all persons to show the officers and crew every attention, so that commerce may be benefited thereby.

NORTON I

Given under our royal hand and seal this 23d December, 1875.

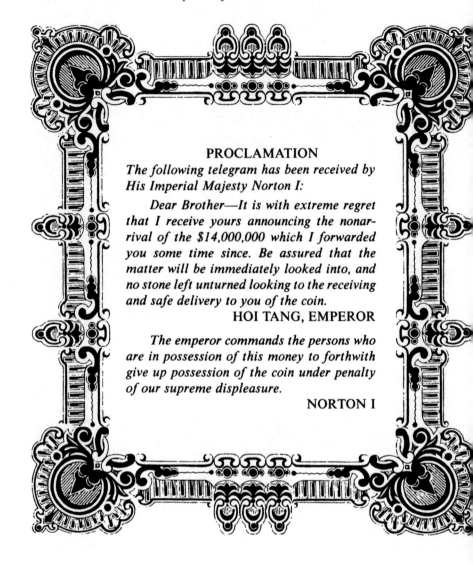

PROCLAMATION

The following telegram has been received by His Imperial Majesty Norton I:

Dear Brother—It is with extreme regret that I receive yours announcing the nonarrival of the $14,000,000 which I forwarded you some time since. Be assured that the matter will be immediately looked into, and no stone left unturned looking to the receiving and safe delivery to you of the coin.

HOI TANG, EMPEROR

The emperor commands the persons who are in possession of this money to forthwith give up possession of the coin under penalty of our supreme displeasure.

NORTON I

The Emperor was constantly outraged by politicians who presumed to make policy for the California portion of his domain without his consent—witness this call to action issued in 1879:

An Edict.

His Imperial Majesty, Norton I., has issued the following edict to Hall McAllister, Esq.:

H. McALLISTER, Esq.—You are hereby commanded to apply to the United States Supreme Court for a Writ of Error, so that we can legally proceed to the capitol, at Sacramento, and *burn up* the new Constitution.

Given under our hand and seal, this twenty-second day of May, A. D., 1879.   NORTON I. [SEAL.]

Dei Gratia Emperor of the United States, and Protector of Mexico.

Herb Caen wasn't the first person to scorn the nickname "Frisco":

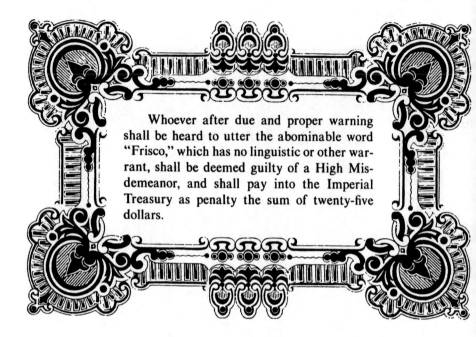

Whoever after due and proper warning shall be heard to utter the abominable word "Frisco," which has no linguistic or other warrant, shall be deemed guilty of a High Misdemeanor, and shall pay into the Imperial Treasury as penalty the sum of twenty-five dollars.

The Hopkins and Stanford mansions on Nob Hill.

PART THREE

From the Railroad
to the Earthquake

Introduction

In 1874, Walt Whitman conjured up a magnificent vision that evoked the quintessence of what California was supposed to be:

The flashing and golden pageant of California,
The sudden and gorgeous drama, the sunny and ample lands,
The long and varied stretch from Puget sound to Colorado south,
Lands bathed in sweeter, rarer, healthier air, valleys and mountain cliffs,
The fields of Nature long prepared and fallow, the silent, cyclic chemistry,
The slow and steady ages plodding, the unoccupied surface ripening, the rich ores forming beneath;
At last the New arriving, assuming, taking possession,
A swarming and busy race settling and organizing everywhere,
Ships coming in from the whole round world, and going out to the whole world,
To India and China and Australia and the thousand island paradises of the Pacific,
Populous cities, the latest inventions, the steamers on the rivers, the railroads, with many a thrifty farm, with machinery,
And wood and wheat and the grape, and diggings of yellow gold.

There is nothing in Whitman's song of anti-Chinese riots, labor depressions and bank failures, the exhaustion of the silver mines, and the countless other disasters and disappointments of the 1870s that led historian Oscar Lewis to christen this era "the discontented decade." And the following 25 years were replete with major difficulties of their own: graft and corruption in local government, machine politics and tong wars, and, overarching all major concerns of the time, the monstrous power of the railroads. San Francisco had become a full-fledged American metropolis, and the "flashing and golden pageant" had metamorphosed into the Cool Grey City.

The dominant theme in this chronicle of frustrated hopes was the railroad. Throughout the early years of San Francisco's life, everyone yearned for the iron rails that would put an end to the City's isolation and bind the continent into a truly United States. It was an inspiring dream; but it was destined to have a cruel, dollars-and-power ending. The railroads severely damaged San Francisco's shipping trade, virtually ended the river steamship business, provoked bloody encounters between imported Chinese railroad workers and displaced Americans, and brought an end to San Francisco's independence as the unrivaled financial and cultural center west of

197

the Rockies. In the City itself, the Big Four railroad magnates—Crocker, Standford, Huntington, and Hopkins—lorded it over the city, in symbol and in fact, from their expensive and dominating mansions poised at the crown of Snob Hill.

The coming of the railroad also brought to a close that unique kind of democracy that had taken root in the City of Gold. From 1870 until April 18, 1906, San Francisco became less and less a unique personality and more and more another American city—more beautiful than the others, certainly, and more tolerant to bizarre ways of believing and living, but more and more a colony of East Coast money and interests.

Even in the process of its assimilation into the American mainstream, though, San Francisco created some lasting symbols of a provincial (in the benign sense) style of its own. The luxuriant fantasies of Victorian architecture flourished here as elsewhere in the United States, but with some decisively local inflections. Eastlake detail—originally meant for furniture!—was nowhere so profuse as on the facades of San Francisco's victorians. And the bay window, though centuries old in its original English setting, came to be adopted as an especially San Franciscan hallmark, admirably suited for illuminating interiors of sun-hungry homes. And above all, the cable car stands out, at this point in the twentieth century, as the most serviceable historical landmark in the city. The cable cars were introduced in 1873 and became, by the sheer fact of their survival into an era of more "advanced" methods of public transportation, the outstanding symbol of San Francisco life: indoor/outdoor, easy-going, old fashioned, but not without drama (see Burgess' "The Ballad of Hyde Street Grip").

It was also during this era that the City attempted its magna opera in city planning: the civic center, and Golden Gate Park. The city hall project, hampered by graft and pork-barrel politics, was destined to finish its first life in ruins on April 18, 1906. But Golden Gate Park has remained the City's greatest public work. Deriving from the best tradition of the English romantic park, Golden Gate Park concentrates all the profusion of fruitfulness inherent in the California landscape and climate. Its use of tilted planes, clusters of dense flowers and foliage alternating stochastically with broad meadows and formal terraces, its museums and hideaways, and above all, the variety of human, animal, and plant life that it receives and nourishes make the Park a living creature, a huge green being with a life of its own, carefully guarded and nurtured by the City that created it. On any Sunday afternoon, Golden Gate Park *is* San Francisco.

The closing scene in this third chapter of San Francisco's biography is the fire and earthquake of 1906. The devastation brought in its wake both a tragic sense of loss of the old City, and a new, if short-lived, sense of community and brotherhood. An equality somewhat resembling the democracy of the Gold Rush (which was, after all, often united by destruction by fire and vandalism) returned to San Francisco for a brief time. Charles Field's "Barriers Burned" most aptly evokes this social leveling brought about by the tragedy. Society soon returned to its distinctions of class, of course. Lifestyles formed themselves along pre-earthquake lines, and San Francisco once again built itself into a major American metropolis (though there were some newspapers that speculated that Oakland would become the major city of the Bay!).

Locked inside the mind of every San Franciscan, though, is the latent premonition of another disaster. Picture this: a party on Russian Hill or in the Sunset—liquor, smoke, laughter and loud discussions, preludes to seduction, conclusions about the state of the world—then the floor rumbles, and everything loose starts to shake. It may only be a heavy truck going by, but at once every mind turns to the same thought.

The hopes for gold, the expectation of mild sunshine and cleansing fog, the subconscious fears of the Cataclysm—these are the peaks and chasms of the San Francisco experience, in whose valleys we cope with necessities of procreation and survival in the Cool Grey City of Love.

II

"California" by Ina Coolbrith

Ina Coolbrith did her best to conceal and forget her stormy past when she came to San Francisco in the early 1860s. As a child she had lived through the worst persecutions of the Mormons (her father was Joseph Smith's brother), and had survived a Sierra crossing that narrowly escaped turning into another Donner tragedy. As an adolescent in southern California, she had suffered through a brief, bitter marriage to an insanely jealous man, which ended in violence and divorce.

Once in San Francisco, however, her star began to rise. She was befriended—some say beloved—by Mark Twain, Bret Harte, and Charles Stoddard. Her poems appeared regularly in the journals, especially the *Overland Monthly,* and it was generally conceded that she wrote the best poetry in California. It is true, as Franklin Walker remarks, that "she piped but one silvery note, a wistful one in which unhappiness was temporarily submerged in pleasure over flowers, birds, and the wind." But her lyric talent was real, and her poems are still among the loveliest songs ever written in the land of the Golden Gate.

California

Was it the sigh and shiver of the leaves?
Was it the murmur of the meadow brook,
That in and out the reeds and water weeds
Slipped silverly, and on their tremulous keys
Uttered her many melodies? Or voice
Of the far sea, red with the sunset gold,
That sang within her shining shores, and sang
Within the Gate, that in the sunset shone
A gate of fire against the outer world?

For, ever as I turned the magic page
Of that old song the old, blind singer sang
Unto the world, when it and song were young—
The ripple of the reeds, or odorous,
Soft sigh of leaves, or voice of the far sea—

A mystical, low murmur, tremulous
Upon the wind, came in with musk of rose,
The salt breath of the waves, and far, faint smell
Of laurel up the slopes of Tamalpais. . . .

"Am I less fair, am I less fair than these,
    Daughters of far-off seas?
Daughters of far-off shores,—bleak, over-blown
With foam of fretful tides, with wail and moan
Of waves, that toss wild hands, that clasp and beat
Wild, desolate hands above the lonely sands,
Printed no more with pressure of their feet:
That chase no more the light feet flying swift
    Up golden sands, nor lift
Foam fingers white unto their garment hem,
    And flowing hair of them.

"For these are dead: the fair, great queens are dead!
The long hair's gold a dust the wind bloweth
    Wherever it may list;
    The curved lips, that kissed
Heroes and kings of men, a dust that breath,
Nor speech, nor laughter, ever quickeneth;
    And all the glory sped
From the large, marvelous eyes, the light whereof
Wrought wonder in their hearts,—desire, and love!
    And wrought not any good:
But strife, and curses of the gods, and flood,
    And fire and battle-death!
    Am I less fair, less fair,
    Because that my hands bear
Neither a sword, nor any flaming brand,
To blacken and make desolate my land,
But on my brows are leaves of olive boughs,
    And in mine arms a dove!

"Sea-born and goddess, blossom of the foam,
Pale Alphrodite shadowy as a mist
    Not any sun hath kissed!
    Tawny of limb *I* roam,
The dusks of forests dark within my hair;
    The far Yosemite,
For garment and for covering of me,
    Wove the white foam and mist,
The amber and the rose and amethyst

Of her wild fountains, shaken loose in air.
And I am of the hills and of the sea:
Strong with the strength of my great hills, and calm
With the calm of the fair sea, whose billowy gold
Girdles the land whose queen and Love I am!
   Lo! am I less than thou,
That with a sound of lyres, and harp-playing,
   Not any voice doth sing
The beauty of mine eyelids and my brow?
Nor hymm in all my fair and gracious ways,
   And lengths of golden days,
The measure and the music of my praise?

   "Ah, what indeed is this
Old land beyond the seas, that ye should miss
For her the grace and majesty of mine?
   Are not the fruit and vine
Fair on my hills, and in my vales the rose?
   The palm-tree and the pine
Strike hands together under the same skies
   In every wind that blows.
   What clearer heavens can shine
Above the land whereon the shadow lies
Of her dead glory, and her slaughtered kings,
   And lost, evanished gods?
   Upon my fresh green sods
No king has walked to curse and desolate:
But in the valleys Freedom sits and sings,
   And on the heights above;
Upon her brows the leaves of olive boughs,
   And in her arms a dove;
And the great hills are pure, undesecrate,
   White with their snows untrod,
And mighty with the presence of their God!

   "Hearken, how many years
I sat alone, I sat alone and heard
   Only the silence stirred
By wind and leaf, by clash of grassy spears,
And singing bird that called to singing bird.
   Heard but the savage tongue
Of my brown savage children, that among
The hills and valleys chased the buck and doe,
   And round the wigwam fires

Chanted wild songs of their wild savage sires,
And danced their wild, weird dances to and fro,
And wrought their beaded robes of buffalo.
    Day following upon day,
Saw but the panther crouched upon the limb,
    Smooth serpents, swift and slim,
Slip through the reeds and grasses, and the bear
    Crush through his tangled lair
Of chapparal, upon the startled prey!

    "Listen, how I have seen
Flash of strange fires in gorge and black ravine;
Heard the sharp clang of steel, that came to drain
    The mountain's golden vein—
And laughed and sang, and sang and laughed again,
Because that 'now,' I said, 'I shall be known!
    I shall not sit alone;
But reach my hands unto my sister lands!
    And they? Will they not turn
Old, wondering dim eyes to me, and yearn—
    Aye, they will yearn, in smooth,
To my glad beauty, and my glad fresh youth!'

    "What matters though the morn
Redden upon my singing fields of corn!
What matters though the wind's unresting feet
    Ripple the gold of wheat,
    And my vales run with wine,
    And on these hills of mine
The orchard boughs droop heavy with ripe fruit?
    When with nor sound of lute
Nor lyre, doth any singer chant and sing
    Me, in my life's fair spring:
The matin song of me in my young day?
But all my lays and legends fade away
From lake and mountain to the farther hem
Of sea, and there be none to gather them.

    "Lo! I have waited long!
How longer yet must my strung harp be dumb,
    Ere its great master come?
Till the fair singer comes to wake the strong
Rapt chords of it unto the new, glad song!
    Him a diviner speech

My song-birds wait to teach:
The secrets of the field
My blossoms will not yield
To other hands than his;
And, lingering for this,
My laurels lends the glory of their boughs
To crown no narrower brows.
For on his lips must wisdom sit with youth,
And in his eyes, and on the lids thereof,
The light of a great love—
And on his forehead, truth!" . . .

Was it the wind, or the soft sigh of leaves,
Or sound of singing waters? Lo, I looked,
And saw the silvery ripples of the brook,
The fruit upon the hills, the waving trees,
And mellow fields of harvest; saw the Gate
Burn in the sunset; the thin thread of mist
Creep white across the Saucelito hills;
Till the day darkened down the ocean rim,
The sunset purple slipped from Tamalpais,
And bay and sky were bright with sudden stars.

TEMPLE EMANU-EL

GERMAN HOSPITAL

UNION SQUARE

 **III**

"The Man and the Snake"
and "Prattle" by Ambrose Bierce

"Bitter Bierce," as he was called by friend and enemy alike, came to San Francisco shortly after the Civil War. He fought on the Union side, and was cited several times for bravery. But the war left Bierce without idealism, and replaced his earlier ideals with horrible images of shattered skulls and torn limbs. The horrors of the war, combined with his own saturnine temperament and chronic asthma, shaped and misshaped Bierce's talent into one of the most respected and feared talents on the West Coast.

Bierce served on the staff of several newspapers, but he was happiest—or, more precisely, least miserable—writing for the *News Letter* and *Wasp*. In issue after issue, year after year, Bierce lashed out at everything and everybody, from the stupidity of local politicians to the overrated benefits of California living. His journalism is the studied invective of a professional misanthrope; but with the distance of time, we can take a certain relish in his destruction of Oscar Wilde's dandyism, or his apparently sincere joy upon hearing that many of Bierstadt's paintings of the California landscape had been destroyed by fire.

The Wilde article is Bierce with a club instead of a rapier; but the blows are well placed, and the modern reader might even find a certain refreshment at reading unconcealed malignity. "The Man and the Snake" is a comparatively mild dose of Bierce, but a good, San Francisco-based story. For those with a stronger stomach, "My Favorite Murder" or "Oil of Dog" will bite the palate more sharply.

The Man and the Snake

It is of veritabyll report, and attested of so many that there be nowe of wyse and learned none to gaynsaye it, that ye serpente hys eye hath a magnetick propertie that whosoe falleth into its svasion is drawn forwards in despyte of his wille, and perisheth miserabyll by ye creature hys byte.

Stretched at ease upon a sofa, in gown and slippers, Harker Brayton smiled as he read the foregoing sentence in old Morryster's *Marvells of Science*. "The only marvel in the matter," he said to himself, "is that the wise and learned in Morryster's day should have believed such nonsense as is rejected by most of even the ignorant in ours."

A train of reflection followed—for Brayton was a man of thought—and he unconsciously lowered his book without altering the direction of his eyes. As soon as the volume had gone below the line of sight, something in an obscure corner of the room recalled his attention to his surroundings. What he saw, in the shadow under his bed, was two small points of light, apparently about an inch apart. They might have been reflections of the gas jet above him, in metal nail heads; he gave them but little thought and resumed his reading. A moment later something—some impulse which it did not occur to him to analyze—impelled him to lower the book again and seek for what he saw before. The points of light were still there. They seemed to have become brighter than before, shining with a greenish lustre that he had not at first observed. He thought, too, that they might have moved a trifle— were somewhat nearer. They were still too much in shadow, however, to reveal their nature and origin to an indolent attention, and again he resumed his reading. Suddenly something in the text suggested a thought that made him start and drop the book for the third time to the side of the sofa, whence, escaping from his hand, it fell sprawling to the floor, back upward. Brayton, half-risen, was staring intently into the obscurity beneath the bed, where the points of light shone with, it seemed to him, an added fire. His attention was now fully aroused, his gaze eager and imperative. It disclosed, almost directly under the foot-rail of the bed, the coils of a large serpent—the points of light were its eyes! Its horrible head, thrust flatly forth from the innermost coil and resting upon the outermost, was directed straight toward him, the definition of the wide, brutal jaw and the idiot-like forehead serving to show the direction of its malevolent gaze. The eyes were no longer merely luminous points; they looked into his own with a meaning, a malign significance.

II

A snake in a bedroom of a modern city dwelling of the better sort is, happily, not so common a phenomenon as to make explanation altogether needless. Harker Brayton, a bachelor of thirty-five, a scholar, idler and something of an athlete, rich, popular and of sound health, had returned to San Francisco from all manner of remote and unfamiliar countries. His tastes, always a trifle luxurious, had taken on an added exuberance from long privation; and the resources of even the Castle Hotel being inadequate to their perfect gratification, he had gladly accepted the hospitality of his friend, Dr. Druring, the distinguished scientist. Dr. Druring's house, a large, old-fashioned one in what is now an obscure quarter of the city, had an outer and visible aspect of proud reserve. It plainly would not associate with the contiguous elements of its altered environment, and appeared to have developed some of the eccentricities which come of isolation. One of these was a "wing," conspicuously irrelevant in point of architecture, and no less rebellious in matter of purpose; for it was a combination of laboratory, menagerie and museum. It was here that the doctor indulged the scientific side of his nature in the study of such forms of animal life as engaged his interest and comforted his taste—which, it must be confessed, ran rather to the lower types. For one of the higher nimbly and sweetly to recommend itself unto his gentle senses it had at least to retain certain rudimentary characteristics allying it to such "dragons of the prime" as toads and snakes. His scientific sympathies were distinctly reptilian; he loved nature's vulgarians and described himself as the Zola of zoology. His wife and daughters not having the advantage to share his enlightened curiosity regarding the works and ways of our ill-starred fellow-creatures, were with needless austerity excluded from what he called the Snakery and doomed to companionship with their own kind, though to soften the rigors of their lot he had permitted them out of his great wealth to outdo the reptiles in the gorgeousness of their surroundings and to shine with a superior splendor.

Architecturally and in point of "furnishing" the Snakery had a severe simplicity befitting the humble circumstances of its occupants, many of whom, indeed, could not safely have been intrusted with the liberty that is neccessary to the full enjoyment of luxury, for they had the troublesome peculiarity of being alive. In their own apartments, however, they were under as little personal restraint as was compatible with their protection from the baneful habit of swallowing one another; and, as Brayton had thoughtfully been apprised, it was more than a tradition that some of them had at divers times been found in parts of the premises where it would have embarrassed them to explain their presence. Despite the Snakery and its uncanny associations—to which, indeed, he gave little attention—Brayton found life at the Druring mansion very much to his mind.

III

Beyond a smart shock of surprise and a shudder of mere loathing Mr. Brayton was not greatly affected. His first thought was to ring the call bell and bring a servant; but although the bell cord dangled within easy reach he made no movement toward it; it had occurred to his mind that the act might subject him to the suspicion of fear, which he certainly did not feel. He was more keenly conscious of the incongruous nature of the situation than affected by its perils; it was revolting, but absurd.

The reptile was of species with which Brayton was unfamiliar. Its length he could only conjecture; the body at the largest visible part seemed about as thick as his forearm. In what way was it dangerous, if in any way? Was it venomous? Was it a constrictor? His knowledge of nature's danger signals did not enable him to say; he had never deciphered the code.

If not dangerous the creature was at least offensive. It was *de trop*—

"matter out of place"—an impertinence. The gem was unworthy of the setting. Even the barbarous taste of our time and country, which had loaded the walls of the room with pictures, the floor with furniture and the furniture with bric-a-brac, had not quite fitted the place for this bit of the savage life of the jungle. Besides—insupportable thought!—the exhalations of its breath mingled with the atmosphere which he himself was breathing.

These thoughts shaped themselves with greater or less definition in Brayton's mind and begot action. The process is what we call consideration and decision. It is thus that we are wise and unwise. It is thus that the withered leaf in an autumn breeze shows greater or less intelligence than its fellows, falling upon the land or upon the lake. The secret of human action is an open one: something contracts our muscles. Does it matter if we give to the preparatory molecular changes the name of will?

Brayton rose to his feet and prepared to back softly away from the snake, without disturbing it if possible, and through the door. Men retire so from the presence of the great, for greatness is power and power is a menace. He knew that he could walk backward without error. Should the monster follow, the taste which had plastered the walls with paintings had consistently supplied a rack of murderous Oriental weapons from which he could snatch one to suit the occasion. In the mean time the snake's eyes burned with a more pitiless malevolence than before.

Brayton lifted his right foot free of the floor to step backward. That moment he felt a strong aversion to doing so.

"I am accounted brave," he thought; "is bravery, then, no more than pride? Because there are none to witness the shame shall I retreat?"

He was steadying himself with his right hand upon the back of a chair, his foot suspended.

"Nonsense!" he said aloud; "I am not so great a coward as to fear to seem to myself afraid."

He lifted the foot a little higher by slightly bending the knee and thrust it sharply to the floor—an inch in front of the other! He could not think how that occurred. A trial with the left foot had the same result; it was again in advance of the right. The hand upon the chair back was grasping it; the arm was straight, reaching somewhat backward. One might have said that he was reluctant to lose his hold. The snake's malignant head was still thrust forth from the inner coil as before, the neck level. It had not moved, but its eyes were now electric sparks, radiating an infinity of luminous needles.

The man had an ashy pallor. Again he took a step forward, and another, partly dragging the chair, which when finally released fell upon the floor with a crash. The man groaned; the snake made neither sound nor motion, but its eyes were two dazzling suns. The reptile itself was wholly concealed by them. They gave off enlarging rings of rich and vivid colors, which at their greatest expansion successively vanished like soap-bubbles; they seemed to approach his very face, and anon were an immeasurable distance away. He heard, somewhere, the continuous throbbing of a great drum, with desultory bursts of far music, inconceivably sweet, like the tones of an aeolian harp. He knew it for the sunrise melody of Memnon's statue, and thought he stood in the Nileside reeds hearing with exalted sense that immortal anthem through the silence of the centuries.

The music ceased; rather, it became by insensible degrees the distant roll of a retreating thunder-storm. A landscape, glittering with sun and rain, stretched before him, arched with a vivid rainbow framing in its giant curve a hundred visible cities. In the middle distance a vast serpent, wearing a crown, reared its head out of its voluminous convolutions and looked at him with his dead mother's eyes. Suddenly this enchanting landscape seemed to rise swiftly upward like the drop scene at a theatre, and vanished in a blank. Something struck him a hard blow upon the face and breast. He had fallen to the floor; the blood ran from his broken nose and his bruised lips. For a time he was dazed and stunned, and lay with closed eyes, his face against the floor. In a few moments he had recovered, and then knew that this fall, by withdrawing his eyes, had broken the spell that held him. He felt that now, by keeping his gaze averted, he would be able to retreat. But the thought of the serpent within a few feet of his head, yet unseen— perhaps in the very act of springing upon him and throwing its coils about his throat—was too horrible! He lifted his head, stared again into those baleful eyes and was again in bondage.

The snake had not moved and appeared somewhat to have lost its power upon the imagination; the gorgeous illusions of a few moments before were not repeated. Beneath that flat and brainless brow its black, beady eyes simply glittered as at first with an expression unspeakably malignant. It was as if the creature, assured of its triumph, had determined to practise no more alluring wiles.

Now ensued a fearful scene. The man, prone upon the floor, within a yard of his enemy, raised the upper part of his body upon his elbows, his head thrown back, his legs extended to their full length. His face was white between its stains of blood; his eyes were strained open to their uttermost expansion. There was froth upon his lips; it dropped off in flakes. Strong convulsions ran through his body, making almost serpentile undulations. He bent himself at the waist, shifting his legs from side to side. And every movement left him a little nearer to the snake. He thrust his hands forward to brace himself back, yet constantly advanced upon his elbows.

IV

Dr. Druring and his wife sat in the library. The scientist was in rare good humor.

"I have just obtained by exchange with another collector," he said, "a splendid specimen of the *ophiophagus*."

"And what may that be?" the lady inquired with a somewhat languid interest.

"Why, bless my soul, what profound ignorance! My dear, a man who ascertains after marriage that his wife does not know Greek is entitled to a divorce. The *ophiophagus* is a snake that eats other snakes."

"I hope it will eat all yours," she said, absently shifting the lamp. "But how does it get the other snakes? By charming them, I suppose."

"That is just like you, dear," said the doctor, with an affectation of petulance. "You know how irritating to me is any allusion to that vulgar superstition about a snake's power of fascination."

The conversation was interrupted by a mighty cry, which rang through the silent house like a voice of a demon shouting in a tomb! Again and yet again it sounded, with terrible distinctness. They sprang to their feet, the man confused, the lady pale and speechless with fright. Almost before the echoes of the last cry had died away the doctor was out of the room, springing up the stairs two steps at a time. In the corridor in front of Brayton's chamber he met some servants who had come from the upper floor. Together they rushed at the door without knocking. It was unfastened and gave way. Brayton lay upon his stomach on the floor, dead. His head and arms were partly concealed under the foot rail of the bed. They pulled the body away, turning it upon the back. The face was daubed with blood and froth, the eyes were wide open, staring—a dreadful sight!

"Died in a fit," said the scientist, bending his knee and placing his hand upon the heart. While in that position he chanced to look under the bed. "Good God!" he added, "how did this thing get in here?"

He reached under the bed, pulled out the snake and flung it, still coiled, to the center of the room, whence with a harsh, shuffling sound it slid across the polished floor till stopped by the wall, where it lay without motion. It was a stuffed snake; its eyes were two shoe buttons.

"Prattle"

That sovereign of insufferables, Oscar Wilde, has ensued with his opulence of twaddle and his penury of sense. He has mounted his hind legs and blown crass vapidities through the bowel of his neck, to the capital edification of circumjacent fools and foolesses, fooling with their foolers. He has tossed off the top of his head and uttered himself in copious overflows of ghastly bosh. The ineffable dunce has nothing to say and says it—says it with a liberal embellishment of bad delivery, embroidering it with reasonless vulgarities of attitude, gesture and attire. There was never an imposter so hateful, a blockhead so stupid, a crank so variously and offensively daft. Therefore is the she-fool enamored of the feel of his tongue in her ear to tickle her understanding.

The limpid and spiritless vacuity of this intellectual jellyfish is in ludicrous contrast with the rude but robust mental activities he came to quicken and inspire. Not only has he no thoughts, but no thinker. His lecture is mere verbal ditch-water—meaningless, trite and without coherence. It lacks even the nastiness that exalts and refines his verse. Moreover, it is obviously his own; he had not even the energy and independence to steal it. And so, with a knowledge that would equip an idiot to dispute with a cast-iron dog, an eloquence to qualify him for the duties of caller on a hog-ranch, and imagination adequate to the conception of a tomcat when fired by contemplation of a fiddle-string, this consummate and star-like youth, missing everywhere his heaven-appointed functions and offices, wanders about, posing as a statue of himself, and, like the sun-smitten image of Memnon, emitting meaningless murmurs in the blaze of women's eyes. He makes me tired.

And this gawky gowk has the divine effrontery to link his name with those of Swinburne, Rossetti and Morris—this dunghill he-hen would fly with eagles. He dares to set his tongue to the honored name of Keats. He is the leader, quoth'a, of a *renaissance* in art, this man who cannot draw—of a revival in letters, this man who cannot write! This littlest and looniest of a brotherhood of simpletons, whom the wicked wits of London, haling him from his obscurity, have crowned and crucified as King of the Cranks, has accepted the distinction in stupid good faith and our foolish people take him at his word. Mr. Wilde is pinnacled upon a dazzling eminence, but the earth still trembles to the dull thunder of the kicks that set him up.

[This lyric appeared in the same issue of *The Wasp,* and was probably written by Bierce:]

There was a sweet infant named Wilde
A precious and crystaline child;
   While sucking his playthings,
   However he'd say things,
That proved that his mind was defiled.

PALACE HOTEL.

UPPER FLOOR, PALACE COURT.

PALACE COURT.

☷☷☷☷☷ **IV** ☷☷☷☷☷

From *American Notes*
by Rudyard Kipling

On his way to England from India, Kipling stopped for several days in San Francisco in the spring of 1889. Having spent so many years as an Anglo-Saxon in a nation of Indians, Kipling is constantly conscious of himself as a white man in a city of—predominantly—fellow Caucasians. But at the same time he feels like an outsider, an alien in the midst of barbarians who spit tobacco, gorge themselves at mealtime, and drink to undignified excesses.

Most revealing of all was his change in feelings toward Bret Harte. As long as Kipling could read from a safe distance about the heroic days in the gold camps, Harte was a master artist. But in the midst of unenglish voices and American grit, the frontier loomed too appallingly real for Kipling's upper class English sense of propriety. He would never again be able to read his wonderful Bret Harte stories without the annoying reality of his memories of San Francisco intruding on his imagination. Nearness lent repulsion to the view.

Rudyard Kipling at the Golden Gate

"Serene, indifferent to fate,
Thou sittest at the western gate,
Thou seest the white seas fold their tents,
Oh warder of two Continents.
Thou drawest all things small and great
To thee beside the Western Gate."

This is what Bret Harte has written of the great city of San Francisco, and for the past fortnight I have been wondering what made him do it.

There is neither serenity nor indifference to be found in these parts; and evil would it be for the Continent whose wardship were intrusted to so reckless a guardian.

Behold me pitched neck-and-crop from twenty days of the High Seas, into the whirl of California, deprived of any guidance, and left to draw my own conclusions. Protect me from the wrath of an outraged community if these letters be ever read by American eyes. San Francisco is a mad city—

215

inhabited for the most part by perfectly insane people whose women are of a remarkable beauty.

When the "City of Peking" steamed through the Golden Gate I saw with great joy that the block-house which guarded the mouth of the "finest harbour in the world, Sir," could be silenced by two gunboats from Hong Kong with safety, comfort and dispatch. Also, there was not a single American record of war in the harbor.

A Reporter

Then a reporter leaped aboard, and ere I could gasp held me in his toils. He pumped me exhaustively while I was getting ashore, demanding, of all things in the world, news about Indian journalism. It is an awful thing to enter a new land with a new lie on your lips. I spoke the truth to the evil-minded Custom-house man who turned my most sacred raiment on a floor composed of stable-refuse and pine-splinters; but the reporter over-whelmed me not so much by his poignant audacity as his beautiful ignorance. I am sorry now that I did not tell him more lies as I passed into a city of three hundred thousand white men! Think of it! Three hundred thousand white men and women gathered in one spot, walking upon real pavements in front of real plate-glass windowed shops, and talking something that was not very different from English. It was only when I had tangled myself up in a hopeless maze of small wooden houses, dust, street-refuse, and children who play with empty kerosene tins, that I discovered the difference of speech.

"You want to go to the Palace Hotel?" said an affable youth on a dray. "What in hell are you doing here, then? This is about the lowest place in the city. Go six blocks north to corner of Geary and Market; then walk around till you strike corner of Gutter and Sixteenth, and that brings you there."

I do not vouch for the literal accuracy of these directions, quoting but from a disordered memory.

"Amen," I said. "But who am I that I should strike the corners of such as you name? Peradventure they be gentlemen of repute, and might hit back. Bring it down to dots, my son."

I thought he would have smitten me, but he didn't. He explained that no one ever used the word "street," and that every one was supposed to know how the streets run; for sometimes the names were upon the lamps and sometimes they weren't. Fortified with these directions I proceeded till I found a mighty street full of sumptuous buildings four or five stories high, but paved with rude cobble stones in the fashion of the Year One.

The Cable Car

Here a tram-car without any visible means of support slid stealthily behind me and nearly struck me in the back. A hundred yards further there was a slight commotion in the street—a gathering together of three or four—and something that glittered as it moved very swiftly. A ponderous Irish gentleman with priest's cords in his hat and a small nickel-plated badge on his fat bosom emerged from the knot, supporting a Chinaman who had been stabbed in the eye and was bleeding like a pig. The bystanders went their ways, and the Chinaman, assisted by the policeman, his own. Of course this was none of my business, but I rather wanted to know what had happened to the gentleman who had dealt the stab. It said a great deal for the excellence of the municipal arrangements of the town that a surging crowd did not at once block the street to see what was going forward. I was the sixth man and the last who assisted at the performance, and my curiosity was six times the greatest. Indeed, I felt ashamed of showing it.

A Crack at the Hotel Clerk

There were no more incidents till I reached the Palace Hotel, a seven-storied warren of humanity with a thousand rooms in it. All the travel-books will tell you about hotel arrangements in this country. They should be seen to be appreciated. Understand clearly—and this letter is written after a thousand miles of experiences—that money will not buy you service in the West. When the hotel clerk—the man who awards your room to you and who is supposed to give you information—when that resplendent individual stoops to attend to your wants, he does so whistling or humming, or picking his teeth, or pauses to converse with someone he knows. These performances, I gather, are to impress upon you that he is a free man and your equal. From his general appearance and the size of his diamonds he ought to be your superior. There is no necessity for this swaggering, self-consciousness of freedom. Business is business, and the man who is paid to attend to a man might reasonably devote his whole attention to the job.

In a vast marble-paved hall under the glare of an electric light sat forty or fifty men; and for their use and amusement were provided spittoons of infinite capacity and generous gape. Most of the men wore frock-coats and top-hats,—the things that we in India put on at a wedding breakfast if we possessed them,—but they all spat. They spat on principle. The spittoons were on the staircases, in each bedroom—yea, and in chambers even more sacred than these. They chased one into retirement, but they blossomed in chiefest splendour round the Bar, and they were all used, every reeking one of 'em.

Answers Mendacious and Evasive

Just before I began to feel deathly sick, another reporter grappled me. What he wanted to know was the precise area of India in square miles. I referred him to Whittaker. He had never heard of Whittaker. He wanted it from my own mouth, and I would not tell him. Then he swerved off, like the other man, to details of journalism in our own country. I ventured to suggest that the interior economy of a paper most concerned people who worked it.

"That's the very thing that interests us," he said. "Have you got reporters anything like our reporters on Indian newspapers?"

"We have not," I said, and suppressed the "thank God" rising to my lips.

"Why haven't you?" said he.

"Because they would die," I said.

It was exactly like talking to a child—a very rude little child. He would begin almost every sentence with: "Now tell me something about India," and would turn aimlessly from one question to another without the least continuity. I was not angry, but keenly interested. The man was a revelation to me. To his questions I returned answers mendacious and evasive. After all, it really did not matter what I said. He could not understand. I can only hope and pray that none of the readers of the "Pioneer" will ever see that portentous interview. The man made me out to be an idiot several sizes more drivelling than my destiny intended, and the rankness of his ignorance managed to distort the few poor facts with which I supplied him into large and elaborate lies. Then thought I: "The matter of American journalism shall be looked into later on. At present I will enjoy myself."

About the City

No man rose to tell me what were the lions of the place. No one volunteered any sort of conveyance. I was absolutely alone in this big city of white folks. By instinct I sought refreshment and came upon a bar-room, full of bad Salon pictures, in which men with hats on the backs of their heads were wolfing food from a counter. It was the institution of the "Free Lunch" that I had struck. You paid for a drink and got as much as you wanted to eat. For something less than a rupee a day a man can feed himself sumptuously in San Francisco, even though he be bankrupt. Remember this if ever you are stranded in these parts.

Later, I began a vast but unsystematic exploration of the streets. I asked for no names. It was enough that the pavements were full of white men and women, the streets clanging with traffic, and that the restful roar of a great city rang in my ears. The cable-cars glided to all points of the compass. I took them one by one till I could go no further. San Francisco has been pitched down on the sand-bunkers of the Bikaneer desert. About one-fourth of it is ground reclaimed from the sea—any old-timer will tell you all about that. The remainder is ragged, unthrifty sand-hills, pegged down by houses.

Up and Down the Sand Hills

From an English point of view there has not been the least attempt at grading those hills, and indeed you might as well try to grade the hillocks of

Sind. The cable-cars have for all practical purposes made San Francisco a dead level. They take no count of rise or fall, but slide equably on their appointed courses from one end to the other of a six-mile street. They turn corners almost at right angles; cross other lines, and, for aught I know, may run up the sides of houses. There is no visible agency of their flight; but once in a while you shall pass a five-storied building, humming with machinery that winds up an everlasting wire-cable, and the initiated will tell you that here is the mechanism. I gave up asking questions. If it pleases Providence to make a car run up and down a slit in the ground for any miles, and if for two-pence-halfpenny I can ride in that car, why shall I seek the reasons of the miracle? Rather let me look out of the windows till the shops give place to thousands and thousands of little houses made of wood—each house just big enough for a man and his family. Let me watch the people in the cars, and try to find out in what manner they differ from us, their ancestors. They delude themselves into the belief that they talk English,—"the" English,—and I have already been pitied for speaking with "an English accent." The man who pitied me spoke, so far as I was concerned, the language of thieves. And they all do. Where we put the accent forward, they throw it back, and vice versa; where we use the long "a," they use the short; and words so simple as to be past mistaking, they pronounce somewhere up in the dome of their heads. How do these things happen?

No American Language

Oliver Wendell Holmes says that Yankee schoolmarms, the cider, and the salt codfish of the Eastern States are responsible for what he calls a nasal accent. I know better . . . a Hindoo is a Hindoo and a brother to the man who knows his vernacular; and a Frenchman is French because he speaks his own language; but the American has no language. He is dialect, slang, provincialism, accent, and so forth. Now that I have heard their voices, all the beauty of Bret Harte is being ruined for me, because I find myself catching through the roll of his rhythmical prose the cadence of his peculiar fatherland. Get an American lady to read to you "How Santa Claus came to Simpson's Bar," and see how much is, under her tongue, left of the beauty of the original.

But I am sorry for Bret Harte. It happened this way. A reporter asked me what I thought of the city, and I made answer sauvely that it was hallowed ground to me because of Bret Harte. That was true.

"Well," said the reporter, "Bret Harte claims California, but California don't claim Bret Harte. He's been so long in England that he's quite English. Have you seen our cracker-factories and the new offices of the *Examiner?*"

He could not understand that to the outside world the city was worth a great deal less than the man.

Jack London.

V

"A Raid on the Oyster Pirates"
by Jack London

A wharf rat, hobo, oyster pirate, prospector, sailor—Jack London was all these things as he grew into a novelist of importance. He lived in and around San Francisco and Oakland, but he unfortunately only rarely used his home base as a setting for his "realistic romances." He was a world-rover, and could never content himself with local color stories.

The story included here, though, is a happy exception to the rule. In "A Raid on the Oyster Pirates," London is drawing on his own youthful escapades in the San Francisco Bay—in the days when there were oysters and shrimp there in abundance. In a significant change of heart, though, London places himself on the side of the law in this work. We find few of the trademarks of London's mature writing in this story—no Nietzchean superheroes, no dignified proletaires—but we can still feel the pull of controlled excitement and crescendoing suspense that is always a part of London's best work.

A Raid on the Oyster Pirates

Of the fish patrolmen under whom we served at various times, Charley Le Grant and I were agreed, I think, that Neil Partington was the best. He was neither dishonest nor cowardly; and while he demanded strict obedience when we were under his orders, at the same time our relations were those of easy comradeship, and he permitted us a freedom to which we were ordinarily unaccustomed, as the present story will show.

Neil's family lived in Oakland, which is on the Lower Bay, not more than six miles across the water from San Francisco. One day, while scouting among the Chinese shrimp-catchers of Point Pedro, he received word that his wife was very ill; and within the hour the *Reindeer* was bowling along for Oakland, with a stiff northwest breeze astern. We ran up the Oakland Estuary and came to anchor, and in the days that followed, while Neil was ashore, we tightened up the *Reindeer's* rigging, overhauled the ballast, scraped down, and put the sloop into thorough shape.

This done, time hung heavy on our hands. Neil's wife was dangerously ill, and the outlook was a week's lie-over, awaiting the crisis. Charley and I

From *Tales of the Fish Patrol* by Jack London. Cleveland: 1905.

roamed the docks, wondering what we should do, and so came upon the oyster fleet lying at the Oakland City Wharf. In the main they were trim, natty boats, made for speed and bad weather, and we sat down on the stringer-piece of the dock to study them.

"A good catch, I guess," Charley said, pointing to the heaps of oysters, assorted in three sizes, which lay upon their decks.

Pedlers were backing their wagons to the edge of the wharf, and from the bargaining and chaffering that went on, I managed to learn the selling price of the oysters.

"That boat must have at least two hundred dollars' worth aboard," I calculated. "I wonder how long it took to get the load?"

"Three or four days," Charley answered. "Not bad wages for two men—twenty-five dollars a day apiece."

The boat we were discussing, the *Ghost,* lay directly beneath us. Two men composed its crew. One was a squat, broad-shouldered fellow with remarkably long and gorilla-like arms, while the other was tall and well proportioned, with clear blue eyes and a mat of straight black hair. So unusual and striking was this combination of hair and eyes that Charley and I remained somewhat longer than we intended.

And it was well that we did. A stout, elderly man, with the dress and carriage of a successful merchant, came up and stood beside us, looking down upon the deck of the *Ghost.* He appeared angry, and the longer he looked the angier he grew.

"Those are my oysters," he said at last. "I know they are my oysters. You raided my beds last night and robbed me of them."

The tall man and the short man on the *Ghost* looked up.

"Hello, Taft," the short man said, with insolent familiarity. (Among the bayfarers he had gained the nickname of "The Centipede" on account of his long arms.) "Hello, Taft," he repeated, with the same touch of insolence. "Wot 'r you growlin' about now?"

"Those are my oysters—that's what I said. You've stolen them from my beds."

"Yer mighty wise, ain't ye?" was the Centipede's sneering reply. "S'pose you can tell your oysters wherever you see 'em?"

"Now, in my experience," broke in the tall man, "oysters is oysters wherever you find 'em, an' they're pretty much alike all the Bay over, and the world over, too, for that matter. We're not wantin' to quarrel with you, Mr. Taft, but we jes' wish you wouldn't insinuate that them oysters is yours an' that we're thieves an' robbers till you can prove the goods."

"I know they're mine; I'd stake my life on it!" Mr. Taft snorted.

"Prove it," challenged the tall man, who we afterward learned was known as "The Porpoise" because of his wonderful swimming abilities.

Mr. Taft shrugged his shoulders helplessly. Of course he could not prove the oysters to be his, no matter how certain he might be.

"I'd give a thousand dollars to have you men behind the bars!" he cried. "I'll give fifty dollars a head for your arrest and conviction, all of you!"

A roar of laughter went up from the different boats, for the rest of the pirates had been listening to the discussion.

"There's more money in oysters," the Porpoise remarked dryly.

Mr. Taft turned impatiently on his heel and walked away. From out of the corner of his eye, Charley noted the way he went. Several minutes later, when he had disappeared around a corner, Charley rose lazily to his feet. I followed him, and we sauntered off in the opposite direction to that taken by Mr. Taft.

"Come on! Lively!" Charley whispered, when we passed from the view of the oyster fleet.

Our course was changed at once, and we dodged around corners and raced up and down side-streets till Mr. Taft's generous form loomed up ahead of us.

"I'm going to interview him about that reward," Charley explained, as we rapidly overhauled the oyster-bed owner. "Neil will be delayed here for a week, and you and I might as well be doing something in the meantime. What do you say?"

"Of course, of course," Mr. Taft said, when Charley had introduced himself and explained his errand. "Those thieves are robbing me of thousands of dollars every year, and I shall be glad to break them up at any price,—yes, sir, at any price. As I said, I'll give fifty dollars a head, and call it cheap at that. They've robbed my beds, torn down my signs, terrorized my watchmen, and last year killed one of them. Couldn't prove it. All done in the blackness of night. All I had was a dead watchman and no evidence. The detectives could do nothing. Nobody has been able to do anything with those men. We have never succeeded in arresting one of them. So I say, Mr.—What did you say your name was?"

"Le Grant," Charley answered.

"So I say, Mr. Le Grant, I am deeply obliged to you for the assistance you offer. And I shall be glad, most glad, sir, to cooperate with you in every way. My watchmen and boats are at your disposal. Come and see me at the San Francisco offices any time, or telephone at my expense. And don't be afraid of spending money. I'll foot your expenses, whatever they are, so long as they are within reason. The situation is growing desperate, and something must be done to determine whether I or that band of ruffians own those oyster beds."

"Now we'll see Neil," Charley said, when he had seen Mr. Taft upon his train to San Francisco.

Not only did Neil Partington interpose no obstacle to our adventure, but he proved to be of the greatest assistance. Charley and I knew nothing of the oyster industry, while his head was an encyclopaedia of facts concerning it. Also, within an hour or so, he was able to bring to us a Greek boy of seventeen or eighteen who knew thoroughly well the ins and outs of oyster piracy.

At this point I may as well explain that we of the fish patrol were free lances in a way. While Neil Partington, who was a patrolman proper, received a regular salary, Charley and I, being merely deputies, received only what we earned—that is to say, a certain percentage of the fines imposed on convicted violators of the fish laws. Also, any rewards that chanced our way were ours. We offered to share with Partington whatever we should get from Mr. Taft, but the patrolman would not hear of it. He was only too happy, he said, to do a good turn for us, who had done so many for him.

We held a long council of war, and mapped out the following line of action. Our faces were unfamiliar on the Lower Bay, but as the *Reindeer* was well known as a fish-patrol sloop, the Greek boy, whose name was Nicholas, and I were to sail some innocent-looking craft down to Asparagus Island and join the oyster pirates' fleet. Here, according to Nicholas's description of the beds and the manner of raiding, it was possible for us to catch the pirates in the act of stealing oysters, and at the same time to get them in our power. Charley was to be on the shore, with Mr. Taft's watchmen and a posse of constables, to help us at the right time.

"I know just the boat," Neil said, at the conclusion of the discussion, "a crazy old sloop that's lying over at Tiburon. You and Nicholas can go over by the ferry, charter it for a song, and sail direct for the beds."

"Good luck be with you, boys," he said at parting, two days later. "Remember, they are dangerous men, so be careful."

Nicholas and I succeeded in chartering the sloop very cheaply; and between laughs, while getting up sail, we agreed that she was even crazier and older than she had been described. She was a big, flat-bottomed, square-sterned craft, sloop-rigged, with a sprung mast, slack rigging, dilapidated sails, and rotten running-gear, clumsy to handle and uncertain in bringing about, and she smelled vilely of coal tar, with which strange stuff she had been smeared from stem to stern and from cabin-roof to centreboard. And to cap it all, *Coal Tar Maggie* was printed in great white letters the whole length of either side.

It was an uneventful though laughable run from Tiburon to Asparagus Island where we arrived in the afternoon of the following day. The oyster pirates, a fleet of a dozen sloops, were lying at anchor on what was known as the "Deserted Beds." The *Coal Tar Maggie* came sloshing into their midst with a light breeze astern, and they crowded on deck to see us. Nicholas and I had caught the spirit of the crazy craft, and we handled her in most lubberly fashion.

"Wot is it?" some one called.

"Name it 'n' ye kin have it!" called another.

"I swan naow, ef it ain't the old Ark itself!" mimicked the Centipede from the deck of the *Ghost.*

"Hey! Ahoy there, clipper ship!" another wag shouted. "Wot's yer port?"

We took no notice of the joking, but acted, after the manner of greenhorns, as though the *Coal Tar Maggie* required our undivided attention. I rounded her well to windward of the *Ghost,* and Nicholas ran for'ard to drop the anchor. To all appearances it was a bungle, the way the chain tangled and kept the anchor from reaching the bottom. And to all appearances Nicholas and I were terribly excited as we strove to clear it. At any rate, we quite decieved the pirates, who took huge delight in our predicament.

But the chain remained tangled, and amid all kinds of mocking advice we drifted down upon and fouled the *Ghost,* whose bowsprit poked square through our mainsail and ripped a hole in it as big as a barn door. The Centipede and the Porpoise doubled up on the cabin in paroxysms of laughter, and left us to get clear as best we could. This, with much unseamanliké performance, we succeeded in doing, and likewise in clearing the anchor-chain, of which we let out about three hundred feet. With only ten feet of water under us, this would permit the *Coal Tar Maggie* to swing in a circle six hundred feet in diameter, in which circle she would be able to foul at least half the fleet.

The oyster pirates lay snugly together at short hawsers, the weather being fine, and they protested loudly at our ignorance in putting out such an unwarranted length of anchor-chain. And not only did they protest, for they made us heave it in again, all but thirty feet.

Having sufficiently impressed them with our general lubberliness, Nicholas and I went below to congratulate ourselves and to cook supper. Hardly had we finished the meal and washed the dishes, when a skiff ground against the *Coal Tar Maggie's* side, and heavy feet trampled on deck. Then the Centipede's brutal face appeared in the companionway, and he descended into the cabin, followed by the Porpoise. Before they could seat themselves on a bunk, another skiff came alongside, and another, and another, till the whole fleet was represènted by the gathering in the cabin.

"Where'd you swipe the old tub?" asked a squat and hairy man, with cruel eyes and Mexican features.

"Didn't swipe it," Nicholas answered, meeting them on their own ground and encouraging the idea that we had stolen the *Coal Tar Maggie.* "And if we did, what of it?"

"Well, I don't admire your taste, that's all," sneered he of the Mexican features. "I'd rot on the beach first before I'd take a tub that couldn't get out of its own way."

"How were we to know till we tried her?" Nicholas asked, so innocently as to cause a laugh. "And how do you get the oysters?" he hurried on. "We want a load of them; that's what we came for, a load of oysters."

"What d'ye want 'em for?" demanded the Porpoise.

"Oh, to give away to our friends, of course," Nicholas retorted. "That's what you do with yours, I suppose."

This started another laugh, and as our visitors grew more genial we could see that they had not the slightest suspicion of our identity or purpose.

"Didn't I see you on the dock in Oakland the other day?" the Centipede asked suddenly of me.

"Yep," I answered boldly, taking the bull by the horns. "I was watching you fellows and figuring out whether we'd go oystering or not. It's a pretty good business, I calculate, and so we're going in for it. That is," I hastened to add, "if you fellows don't mind."

"I'll tell you one thing, which ain't two things," he replied, "and that is you'll have to hump yerself an' get a better boat. We won't stand to be disgraced by any such box as this. Understand?"

"Sure," I said. "Soon as we sell some oysters we'll outfit in style."

"And if you show yerself square an' the right sort," he went on, "why, you kin run with us. But if you don't" (here his voice became stern and menacing), "why, it'll be the sickest day of yer life. Understand?"

"Sure," I said.

After that and more warning and advice of similar nature, the conversation became general, and we learned that the beds were to be raided that very night. As they got into their boats, after an hour's stay, we were invited to join them in the raid with the assurance of "the more the merrier."

"Did you notice that short, Mexican-looking chap?" Nicholas asked, when they had departed to their various sloops. "He's Barchi, of the Sporting Life Gang, and the fellow that came with him is Skilling. They're both out now on five thousand dollars' bail."

I had heard of the Sporting Life Gang before, a crowd of hoodlums and criminals that terrorized the lower quarters of Oakland, and two-thirds of which were usually to be found in state's prison for crimes that ranged from perjury and ballot-box stuffing to murder.

"They are not regular oyster pirates," Nicholas continued. "They've just come down for the lark and to make a few dollars. But we'll have to watch out for them."

We sat in the cockpit and discussed the details of our plan till eleven o'clock had passed, when we heard the rattle of an oar in a boat from the direction of the *Ghost*. We hauled up our own skiff, tossed in a few sacks, and rowed over. There we found all the skiffs assembling, it being the intention to raid the beds in a body.

To my surprise, I found barely a foot of water where we had dropped anchor in ten feet. It was the big June run-out of the full moon, and as the ebb had yet an hour and a half to run, I knew that our anchorage would be dry ground before slack water.

Mr. Taft's beds were three miles away, and for a long time we rowed silently in the wake of the other boats, once in a while grounding and our oar blades constantly striking bottom. At last we came upon soft mud covered with not more than two inches of water—not enough to float the boats. But the pirates at once were over the side, and by pushing and pulling on the flat-bottomed skiffs, we moved steadily along.

The full moon was partly obscured by high-flying clouds, but the pirates went their way with the familiarity born of long practice. After half a mile of the mud, we came upon a deep channel, up which we rowed, with dead oyster shoals looming high and dry on either side. At last we reached the picking grounds. Two men, on one of the shoals, hailed us and warned us off. But the Centipede, the Porpoise, Barchi, and Skilling took the lead, and followed by the rest of us, at least thirty men in half as many boats, rowed right up to the watchmen.

"You'd better slide outa this here," Barchi said threateningly, "or we'll fill you so full of holes you wouldn't float in molasses."

The watchmen wisely retreated before so overwhelming a force, and rowed their boat along the channel toward where the shore should be. Besides, it was in the plan for them to retreat.

We hauled the noses of the boats up on the shore side of a big shoal, and all hands, with sacks, spread out and began picking. Every now and again the clouds thinned before the face of the moon, and we could see the big oysters quite distinctly. In almost no time sacks were filled and carried back to the boats, where fresh ones were obtained. Nicholas and I returned often and anxiously to the boats with our little loads, but always found some one of the pirates coming or going.

"Never mind," he said; "no hurry. As they pick farther and farther away, it will take too long to carry to the boats. Then they'll stand the full sacks on end and pick them up when the tide comes in and the skiffs will float to them."

Fully half an hour went by, and the tide had begun to flood, when this came to pass. Leaving the pirates at their work, we stole back to the boats. One by one, and noiselessly, we shoved them off and made them fast in an awkward flotilla. Just as we were shoving off the last skiff, our own, one of the men came upon us. It was Barchi. His quick eye took in the situation at a glance, and he sprang for us; but we went clear with a mighty shove, and he was left floundering in the water over his head. As soon as he got back to the shoal he raised his voice and gave the alarm.

We rowed with all our strength, but it was slow going with so many boats in tow. A pistol cracked from the shoal, a second, and a third; then a regular fusillade began. The bullets spat and spat all about us; but thick clouds had covered the moon, and in the dim darkness it was no more than random firing. It was only by chance that we could be hit.

"Wish we had a little steam launch," I panted.

"I'd just as soon the moon stayed hidden," Nicholas panted back.

It was slow work, but every stroke carried us farther away from the shoal and nearer the shore, till at last the shooting died down, and when the moon did come out we were too far away to be in danger. Not long afterward we answered a shoreward hail, and two Whitehall boats, each pulled by three pairs of oars, darted up to us. Charley's welcome face bent over to us, and he gripped us by the hands while he cried, "Oh, you joys! You joys! Both of you!"

When the flotilla had been landed, Nicholas and I and a watchman rowed out in one of the Whitehalls, with Charley in the stern-sheets. Two other Whitehalls followed us, and as the moon now shone brightly, we easily made out the oyster pirates on their lonely shoal. As we drew closer, they fired a rattling volley from their revolvers, and we promptly retreated beyond range.

"Lot of time," Charley said. "The flood is setting fast, and by the time it's up to their necks there won't be any fight left in them."

So we lay on our oars and waited for the tide to do its work. This was the predicament of the pirates: because of the big run-out, the tide was now rushing back like a mill-race, and it was impossible for the strongest swimmer in the world to make against it the three miles to the sloops. Between the pirates and the shore were we, precluding escape in that direction. On the other hand, the water was rising rapidly over the shoals, and it was only a question of a few hours when it would be over their heads.

It was beautifully calm, and in the brilliant white moonlight we watched them through our night glasses and told Charley of the voyage of the *Coal Tar Maggie.* One o'clock came, and two o'clock, and the pirates were clustering on the highest shoal, waist-deep in water.

"Now this illustrates the value of imagination," Charley was saying. "Taft has been trying for years to get them, but he went at it with bull strength and failed. Now we used our heads . . ."

Just then I heard a scarcely audible gurgle of water, and holding up my hand for silence, I turned and pointed to a ripple slowly widening out in a growing circle. It was not more than fifty feet from us. We kept perfectly quiet and waited. After a minute the water broke six feet away, and a black head and white shoulder showed in the moonlight. With a snort of surprise and of suddenly expelled breath, the head and shoulder went down.

We pulled ahead several strokes and drifted with the current. Four pairs of eyes searched the surface of the water, but never another ripple showed, and never another glimpse did we catch of the black head and white shoulder.

"It's the Porpoise," Nicholas said. "It would take broad daylight for us to catch him."

At a quarter to three the pirates gave their first sign of weakening. We heard cries for help, in the unmistakable voice of the Centipede, and this time, on rowing closer, we were not fired upon. The Centipede was in a truly perilous plight. Only the heads and shoulders of his fellow-marauders showed above the water as they braced themselves against the current, while his feet were off the bottom and they were supporting him.

"Now, lads," Charley said briskly, "we have got you, and you can't get away. If you cut up rough, we'll have to leave you alone and the water will finish you. But if you're good, we'll take you aboard, one man at a time, and you'll all be saved. What do you say?"

"Ay," they chorused hoarsely between their chattering teeth.

"Then one man at a time, and the short men first."

The Centipede was the first to be pulled aboard, and he came willingly, though he objected when the constable put the handcuffs on him. Barchi was next hauled in, quite meek and resigned from his soaking. When we had ten in our boat we drew back, and the second Whitehall was loaded. The third Whitehall received nine prisoners only—a catch of twenty-nine in all.

"You didn't get the Porpoise," the Centipede said exultantly, as though his escape materially diminished our success.

Charley laughed. "But we saw him just the same, a-snorting for shore like a puffing pig."

It was a mild and shivering band of pirates that we marched up the beach to the oyster house. In answer to Charley's knock, the door was flung open, and a pleasant wave of warm air rushed out upon us.

"You can dry your clothes here, lads, and get some hot coffee," Charley announced, as they filed in.

And there, sitting ruefully by the fire, with a steaming mug in his hand, was the Porpoise. With one accord Nicholas and I looked at Charley. He laughed gleefully.

"That comes of imagination," he said. "When you see a thing, you've got to see it all around, or what's the good of seeing it at all? I saw the beach, so I left a couple of constables behind to keep an eye on it. That's all."

Frank Norris.

VI

From "Polk Street," "The Passing of Little Pete" and "Among Cliff Dwellers" by Frank Norris

In 1884, at the age of fourteen, Frank Norris moved from Chicago to San Francisco. Thereafter he considered himself a native Californian, and he set the locale of his masterpieces, *McTeague* and *The Octopus,* in California. But his eye had been trained by his reading of the European Realists, especially Zola. The setting of his works might be California, but the form for his expression of them came from France.

Norris' twin gifts, over and above his mastery of the Realistic form, were sympathy and accuracy. His psychologically empathetic portraits of McTeague, Marcus, and Trina are at the same time touching and powerful. But it is Norris' second talent, the eye for accurate detail, that we find in the selection included here. Even out of context, the realistic vignettes depicting daily life on Polk Street in Victorian San Francisco have an almost cinematic quality. Better than any other writer in this volume, Norris gives us the *rhythm* of the life of the people. In his vivid human landscapes, Norris is doing for fiction what the San Francisco photographer did a few years earlier for image-making: minute accuracy in particulars, and the broad scope that embraces the whole society that surrounds the individuals.

"Polk Street"

It was Sunday, and, according to his custom on that day, McTeague took his dinner at two in the afternoon at the car conductor's coffee-joint on Polk Street. He had a thick gray soup; heavy, underdone meat, very hot, on a cold plate; two kinds of vegetables; and a sort of suet pudding, full of strong butter and sugar. On his way back to his office, one block above, he stopped at Joe Frenna's saloon and bought a pitcher of steam beer. It was his habit to leave the pitcher there on his way to dinner.

Once in his office, or, as he called it on his signboard, "Dental Parlors," he took off his coat and shoes, unbuttoned his vest, and having crammed his little stove full of coke, lay back in his operating chair at the bay window, reading the paper, drinking his beer, and smoking his huge porcelain pipe while his food digested; crop-full, stupid, and warm. By and by, gorged with steam beer, and overcome by the heat of the room, the cheap tobacco, and the effects of his heavy meal, he dropped off to sleep.

231

Late in the afternoon his canary bird, in its gilt cage just over his head, began to sing. He woke slowly, finished the rest of his beer—very flat and stale by this time—and taking down his concertina from the book-case, where in week days it kept the company of seven volumes of "Allen's Practical Dentist," played upon it some half-dozen very mournful airs.

McTeague looked forward to these Sunday afternoons as a period of relaxation and enjoyment. He invariably spent them in the same fashion. These were his only pleasures—to eat, to smoke, to sleep, and to play upon his concertina.

The six lugubrious airs that he knew always carried him back to the time when he was a car-boy at the Big Dipper Mine in Placer County, ten years before. He remembered the years he had spent there trundling the heavy cars of ore in and out of the tunnel under the direction of his father. For thirteen days of each fortnight his father was a steady, hard-working shift-boss of the mine. Every other Sunday he became an irresponsible animal, a beast, a brute, crazy with alcohol.

McTeague remembered his mother, too, who, with the help of the Chinaman, cooked for forty miners. She was an overworked drudge, fiery and energetic for all that, filled with the one idea of having her son rise in life and enter a profession. The chance had come at last when the father died, corroded with alcohol, collapsing in a few hours. Two or three years later a traveling dentist visited the mine and put up his tent near the bunkhouse. He was more or less of a charlatan, but he fired Mrs. McTeague's ambition, and young McTeague went away with him to learn his profession. He had learnt it after a fashion, mostly by watching the charlatan operate. He had read many of the necessary books, but he was too hopelessly stupid to get much benefit from them.

Then one day at San Francisco had come the news of his mother's death; she had left him some money—not much, but enough to set him up in business; so he had cut loose from the charlatan and had opened his "Dental Parlors" on Polk Street, an "accommodation street" of small shops in the residence quarter of the town. Here he had slowly collected a clientele of butcher boys, shop girls, drug clerks, and car conductors. He made but a few acquaintances. Polk Street called him the "Doctor" and spoke of his enormous strength. For McTeague was a young giant, carrying his huge shock of blond hair six feet three inches from the ground; moving his immense limbs, heavy with ropes of muscle, slowly, ponderously. His hands were enormous, red, and covered with a fell of stiff yellow hair; they were hard as wooden mallets, strong as vises, the hands of the old-time car-boy. Often he dispensed with forceps and extracted a refractory tooth with his thumb and finger. His head was square-cut, angular; the jaw salient, like that of the carnivora.

McTeague's mind was as his body, heavy, slow to act, sluggish. Yet there was nothing vicious about the man. Altogether he suggested the draught horse, immensely strong, stupid, docile, obedient.

When he opened his "Dental Parlors," he felt that his life was a success, that he could hope for nothing better. In spite of the name, there was but one room. It was a corner room on the second floor over the branch post-office, and faced the street. McTeague made it do for a bedroom as well, sleeping on the big bed-lounge against the wall opposite the window. There was a washstand behind the screen in the corner where he manufactured his moulds. In the round bay window were his operating chair, his dental engine, and the movable rack on which he laid out his instruments. Three chairs, a bargain at the second-hand store, ranged themselves against the wall with military precision underneath a steel engraving of the court of Lorenzo de' Medici, which he had bought because there were a great many figures in it for the money. Over the bed-lounge hung a rifle manufacturer's advertisement calendar which he never used. The other ornaments were a small marble-topped centre table covered with back numbers of "The American System of Dentistry," a stone pug dog sitting before the little stove, and a thermometer. A stand of shelves occupied one corner, filled with the seven volumes of "Allen's Practical Dentist." On the top shelf McTeague kept his concertina and a bag of bird seed for the canary. The whole place exhaled a mingled odor of bedding, cresote, and ether.

But for one thing, McTeague would have been perfectly contented. Just outside his window was his signboard—a modest affair—that read: "Doctor McTeague. Dental Parlors. Gas Given"; but that was all. It was his ambition, his dream, to have projecting from that corner window a huge gilded tooth, a molar with enormous prongs, something gorgeous and attractive. He would have it some day, on that he was resolved; but as yet such a thing was far beyond his means.

When he had finished the last of his beer, McTeague slowly wiped his lips and huge yellow mustache with the side of his hand. Bulllike, he heaved himself laboriously up, and, going to the window, stood looking down into the street.

The street never failed to interest him. It was one of those cross streets peculiar to Western cities, situated in the heart of the residence quarter, but occupied by small tradespeople who lived in the rooms above their shops. There were corner drug stores with huge jars of red, yellow, and green liquids in their windows, very brave and gay; stationers' stores, where illustrated weeklies were tacked upon bulletin boards; barber shops with cigar stands in their vestibules; sad-looking plumbers' offices; cheap restaurants, in whose windows one saw piles of unopened oysters weighted down by cubes of ice, and china pigs and cows knee deep in layers of white beans. At one end of the street McTeague could see the huge power-house of the cable line. Immediately opposite him was a great market; while farther on, over the chimney stacks of the intervening houses, the glass roof of some huge public baths glittered like crystal in the afternoon sun. Underneath him the branch post-office was opening its doors, as was its custom between two and three o'clock on Sunday afternoons. An acrid odor of ink rose upward to him. Occasionally a cable car passed, trundling heavily, with a strident whirring of jostled glass windows.

On week days the street was very lively. It woke to its work about seven o'clock, at the time when the newsboys made their appearance together with the day laborers. The laborers went trudging past in a straggling file— plumbers' apprentices, their pockets stuffed with sections of lead pipe, tweezers, and pliers; carpenters, carrying nothing but their little pasteboard lunch baskets painted to imitate leather; gangs of street workers, their overalls soiled with yellow clay, their picks and long-handled shovels over their shoulders; plasterers, spotted with lime from head to foot. This little army of workers, tramping steadily in one direction, met and mingled with other toilers of a different description—conductors and "swing men" of the cable company going on duty; heavy-eyed night clerks from the drug stores on their way home to sleep; roundsmen returning to the precinct police station to make their night report, and Chinese market gardeners teetering past under their heavy baskets. The cable cars began to fill up; all along the street could be seen the shop keepers taking down their shutters.

Between seven and eight the street breakfasted. Now and then a waiter from one of the cheap restaurants crossed from one sidewalk to the other, balancing on one palm a tray covered with a napkin. Everywhere was the smell of coffee and of frying steaks. A little later, following in the path of the day laborers, came the clerks and shop girls, dressed with a certain cheap smartness, always in a hurry, glancing apprehensively at the power-house clock. Their employers followed an hour or so later—on the cable cars for the most part—whiskered gentlemen with huge stomachs, reading the morning papers with great gravity; bank cashiers and insurance clerks with flowers in their buttonholes.

At the same time the school children invaded the street, filling the air with a clamor of shrill voices, stopping at the stationers' shops, or idling a moment in the doorways of the candy stores. For over half an hour they held possession of the sidewalks, then suddenly disappeared, leaving behind one or two stragglers who hurried along with great strides of their little thin legs, very anxious and preoccupied.

Towards eleven o'clock the ladies from the great avenue a block above Polk Street made their appearance, promenading the sidewalks leisurely, deliberately. They were at their morning's marketing. They were handsome women, beautifully dressed. They knew by name their butchers and grocers and vegetable men. From his window McTeague saw them in front of the stalls, gloved and veiled and daintily shod, the subservient provision-men at their elbows, scribbling hastily in the order books. They all seemed to know one another, these grand ladies from the fashionable avenue. Meetings took place here and there; a conversation was begun; others arrived; groups were formed; little impromptu receptions were held before the chopping blocks of butchers' stalls, or on the sidewalk, around boxes of berries and fruit.

From noon to evening the population of the street was of a mixed character. The street was busiest at that time; a vast and prolonged murmur arose—the mingled shuffling of feet, the rattle of wheels, the heavy trundling of cable cars. At four o'clock the school children once more swarmed the sidewalks, again disappearing with surprising suddenness. At six the great homeward march commenced; the cars were crowded, the laborers thronged the sidewalks, the newsboys chanted the evening papers. Then all at once the street fell quiet; hardly a soul was in sight; the sidewalks were deserted. It was supper hour. Evening began; and one by one a multitude of lights, from the demoniac glare of the druggists' windows to the dazzling blue whiteness of the electric globes, grew thick from street corner to street corner. Once more the street was crowded. Now there was no thought but for amusement. The cable cars were loaded with theatre-goers—men in high hats and young girls in furred opera cloaks. On the sidewalks were groups and couples—the plumbers' apprentices, the girls of the ribbon counters, the little families that lived on the second stories over their shops, the dressmakers, the small doctors, the harness makers—all the various inhabitants of the street were abroad, strolling idly from shop window to shop window, taking the air after the day's work. Groups of girls collected on the corners, talking and laughing very loud, making remarks upon the young men that passed them. The *tamale* men appeared. A band of Salvationists began to sing before a saloon.

Then, little by little, Polk Street dropped back to solitude. Eleven o'clock struck from the power-house clock. Lights were extinguished. At one o'clock the cable stopped, leaving an abrupt silence in the air. All at once it seemed very still. The only noises were the occasional footfalls of a policeman and the persistent calling of ducks and geese in the closed market. The street was asleep.

Day after day, McTeague saw the same panorama unroll itself. The bay window of his "Dental Parlors" was for him a point of vantage from which he watched the world go past.

On Sundays, however, all was changed. As he stood in the bay window, after finishing his beer, wiping his lips, and looking out into the street, McTeague was conscious of the difference. Nearly all the stores were closed. No wagons passed. A few people hurried up and down the sidewalks, dressed in cheap Sunday finery. A cable car went by; on the outside seats were a party of returning picnickers. The mother, the father, a young man, and a young girl, and three children. The two older people held empty lunch baskets in their laps, while the bands of the children's hats were stuck full of oak leaves. The girl carried a huge bunch of wilting poppies and wild flowers.

As the car approached McTeague's window the young man got up and swung himself off the platform, waving good-bye to the party. Suddenly McTeague recognized him.

"There's Marcus Schouler," he muttered behind his mustache.

Marcus Schouler was the dentist's one intimate friend. The acquaintance had begun at the car conductors' coffee-joint, where the two occupied the same table and met at every meal. Then they made the discovery that they both lived in the same flat, Marcus occupying a room on the floor above McTeague. On different occasions McTeague had treated Marcus for an ulcerated tooth and had refused to accept payment. Soon it came to be an understood thing between them. They were "pals."

McTeague, listening, heard Marcus go up-stairs to his room above. In a few minutes his door opened again. McTeague knew that he had come out into the hall and was leaning over the banisters.

"Oh, Mac!" he called. McTeague came to his door.

"Hullo! 's that you, Mark?"

"Sure," answered Marcus. "Come on up."

"You come on down."

"No, come on up."

"Oh, you come on down."

"Oh, you lazy duck!" retorted Marcus, coming down the stairs.

"Been out to the Cliff House on a picnic," he explained as he sat down on the bed-lounge, "with my uncle and his people—the Sieppes, you know. By damn! it was hot," he suddenly vociferated. "Just look at that! Just look at that!" he cried, dragging at his limp collar. "That's the third one since morning; it is—it is, for a fact—and you got your stove going." He began to tell about the picnic, talking very loud and fast, gesturing furiously, very excited over trivial details. Marcus could not talk without getting excited.

"You ought t'have seen, y'ought t'have seen. I tell you, it was outa sight. It was; it was, for a fact."

"Yes, yes," answered McTeague, bewildered, trying to follow. "Yes, that's so."

In recounting a certain dispute with an awkward bicyclist in which it appeared he had become involved Marcus quivered with rage. " 'Say that again', says I to um. 'Just say that once more, and' "—here a rolling explosion of oaths—" 'you'll go back to the city in the Morgue wagon. Ain't I got a right to cross a street even, I'd like to know, without being run down—what? I say it's outrageous. I'd a knifed him in another minute. It was an outrage. I say it was an *outrage*."

"Sure it was," McTeague hastened to reply. "Sure, sure."

"Oh, and we had an accident," shouted the other, suddenly off on another tack. "It was awful. Trina was in the swing there—that's my cousin Trina, you know who I mean—and she fell out. By damn! I thought she'd killed herself; struck her face on a rock and knocked out a front tooth. It's a wonder she didn't kill herself. It *is* a wonder; it is, for a fact. Ain't it, now? Huh? Ain't it? Y'ought t'have seen."

McTeague had a vague idea that Marcus Schouler was stuck on his cousin Trina. They "kept company" a good deal; Marcus took dinner with the Sieppes every Saturday evening at their home at B Street station, across the bay, and Sunday afternoons he and the family usually made little excursions into the suburbs. McTeague began to wonder dimly how it was that on this occasion Marcus had not gone home with his cousin. As sometimes happens, Marcus furnished the explanation upon the instant.

"I promised a duck up here on the avenue I'd call for his dog at four this afternoon."

Marcus was Old Grannis's assistant in a little dog hospital that the latter had opened in a sort of alley just off Polk Street, some four blocks above. Old Grannis lived in one of the back rooms of McTeague's flat. He was an Englishman and an expert dog surgeon, but Marcus Schouler was a bungler in the profession. His father had been a veterinary surgeon who had kept a livery stable near by, on California Street, and Marcus's knowledge of the diseases of domestic animals had been picked up in a haphazard way, much after the manner of McTeague's education. Somehow he managed to impress Old Grannis, a gentle, simple-minded old man, with a sense of his fitness, bewildering him with a torrent of empty phrases that he delivered with fierce gestures and with a manner of the greatest conviction.

"You'd better come along with me, Mac," observed Marcus. "We'll get the duck's dog, and then we'll take a little walk, huh? You got nothun to do. Come along."

McTeague went out with him, and the two friends proceeded up to the avenue to the house where the dog was to be found. It was a huge mansion-like place, set in an enormous garden that occupied a whole third of the block; and while Marcus tramped up the front steps and rang the doorbell boldly to show his independence, McTeague remained below on the sidewalk, gazing stupidly at the curtained windows, the marble steps, and the bronze griffins, troubled and a little confused by all this massive luxury.

After they had taken the dog to the hospital and had left him to whimper behind the wire netting, they returned to Polk Street and had a glass of beer in the back room of Joe Frenna's corner grocery.

Ever since they had left the huge mansion on the avenue, Marcus had been attacking the capitalists, a class which he pretended to execrate. It was a pose which he often assumed, certain of impressing the dentist. Marcus had picked up a few half-truths of political economy—it was impossible to say where—and as soon as the two had settled themselves to their beer in Frenna's back room he took up the theme of the labor question. He discussed it at the top of his voice, vociferating, shaking his fists, exciting himself with his own noise. He was continually making use of the stock phrases of the professional politician—phrases he had caught at some of the ward "rallies" and "ratification meetings." These rolled off his tongue with incredible emphasis, appearing at every turn of his conversation— "Outraged constituencies," "cause of labor," "wage earners," "opinions biased by personal interests," "eyes blinded by party prejudice." McTeague listened to him, awe-struck.

"There's where the evil lies," Marcus would cry. "The masses must learn self-control; it stands to reason. Look at the figures, look at the figures. Decrease the number of wage earners and you increase wages, don't you? don't you?"

Absolutely stupid, and understanding never a word, McTeague would answer:

"Yes, yes, that's it—self control—that's the word."

"It's the capitalists that's ruining the cause of labor," shouted Marcus, banging the table with his fist till the beer glasses danced; "white-livered drones, traitors, with their livers white as snow, eatun the bread of widows and orphuns; there's where the evil lies."

Stupefied with his clamor, McTeague answered, wagging his head:

"Yes, that's it; I think it's their livers."

Suddenly Marcus fell calm again, forgetting his pose all in an instant.

"Say, Mac, I told my cousin Trina to come around and see you about that tooth of hers. She'll be in to-morrow, I guess."

Passing of "Little Pete"*

When a man is vulgar he is vulgar according to fixed standards. He conforms to a certain common type of vulgarity; but every woman is vulgar in her own way. There is the brutally vulgar woman, the meanly vulgar, the self-consciously vulgar, the brazenly vulgar, and the modestly vulgar. There is the vulgar woman who knows that she allows herself to be vulgar and is ashamed of it, and there is the woman who is proud of her vulgarity, and calls it liberty and equality and fraternity and democracy and independence

---

*"Little Pete" was shot to death in a tong war. He was reputed to be very wealthy, and his funeral attracted widespread public interest.

and I don't know what, and who trumpets her vulgarity to the four winds of heaven, and is only ashamed when men fail to take notice.

That is the kind of woman who was most in evidence at the funeral ceremonies of a certain wealthy man, known by the name of L.F. Peters, who was shot to death this month of January, 1897.

Perhaps I have seen a more disgusting spectacle than that which took place at "Little Pete's" funeral ceremonies, but I cannot recall it now. A reckless, conscienceless mob of about two thousand, mostly women, crowded into the Chinese cemetery. There was but one policeman to control them, and they took advantage of the fact. The women thronged about the raised platform and looted everything they could lay their hands on: China bowls, punk, tissue paper ornaments, even the cooked chickens and bottles of gin. This, mind you, before the procession had as much as arrived.

The procession itself was rather disappointing—from a picturesque point of view. Perhaps one expected too much. There might possibly have been a greater display of colour and a greater number of bands. Nor were there any of the street ceremonies in front of Pete's Chinatown residence that you had been told to look for. The company of chief mourners, in blue and white cambric, was too suggestive of a campaign club to be very impressive, and the members of the carriage orchestras refused to take themselves very seriously, seeming more interested in the crowd of spectators than in the funeral cortege.

At the cemetery, however, things were different. There was a certain attempt here at rites and observances and customs that would have been picturesque and striking had it not been for the shamelessness, the unspeakable shamelessness of the civilized women of the crowd.

A few mandarins came first, heads, no doubt, of the Sam Yup, one of them in particular, with all the dignity and imposing carriage of a senator. He was really grand, this mandarin, calm, austere, unmoved amidst this red-faced, scrambling mob. A band of women followed, the female relatives of the deceased.

"Here comes his wife!" screamed half a dozen white women in chorus.

Pete's widow was wrapped from head to foot in what might have been the sackcloth of the Bible stories; certainly it had the look of jute. A vast hood of the stuff covered her whole face, and was tied about the neck. Two other women, similarly dressed, but without the hood, were supporting her. A mat was unrolled, and after the white women had been driven back from the platform by the main strength of two or three men, not yet lost to the sense of decency, the mourners kneeled upon it, forehead to the ground, and began a chant, or rather a series of lamentable cries and plaints. "Ai yah, ai-yah-yah."

A gong beat. A priest in robes and octagon cap persistently jingled a little bell and droned under his breath. There was a smell of punk and sandalwood in the air. The crouching women, mere bundles of clothes, rocked to and fro and wailed louder and louder.

Suddenly the coffin arrived, brought up by staggering hack drivers and assistants, a magnificent affair, heavy black cloth and heavy silver appointments. The white women of the crowd made the discovery that Little Pete's powder-marked face could be seen. They surged forward on the instant. The droning priest was hustled sharply; he dropped his little bell, which was promptly stolen. The mourners on the mat, almost under foot, were jostled and pushed from their place or bundled themselves out of the way hurriedly to escape trampling. Just what followed after this I do not know. A mob of red-faced, pushing women thronged about the coffin and interrupted everything that went on. There were confusion and cries in Cantonese and English; a mounted policeman appeared and was railed at. There can be no doubt that more ceremonies were to follow but that those in charge preferred to cut short the revolting scene. The coffin was carried back to the hearse, a passage at length being forced through the crowd, and the Chinese returned to the city. Then the civilized Americans, some thousand of them, descended upon the raised platform, where the funeral meats were placed—pigs and sheep roasted whole, and chickens and bowls of gin and rice. Four men seized a roast pig by either leg and made off with it; were pursued by the mounted police and made to return the loot. Then the crowd found amusement in throwing bowlfuls of gin at each other. The roast chickens were hurled back and forth in the air. The women scrambled for the China bowls for souvenirs of the occasion, as though the occasion were something to be remembered.

The single mounted police, red-faced and overworked, rode his horse into the crowd, and, after long effort, at last succeeded in thrusting it back from the plundered altar and in keeping it at a distance. But still it remained upon the spot; this throng, this crowd, this shameless mob, that was mostly of women. There was nothing more to happen, the ceremony was over, but still these people stayed and looked.

This was the last impression one received of Little Pete's funeral—a crowd of two thousand men and women, standing in a huge circle, stupidly staring at the remains of a roasted pig.

*

Among Cliff Dwellers

Of course one has heard of the strangeness of the neighbourhoods upon Telegraph Hill, and of course one has read a good deal in Bret Harte and Stevenson upon the subject, but the curiousness of the place cannot be altogether appreciated at second hand. You are told, for instance, that to enter this locality is to be transported to another country—to Italy, to France, or to Spain, as the case may be. This is quite true, but it is not all. The foreignness of, let us say, Ohio Street, is complete, and yet one fancies that one would recognize San Francisco in the place if one should suddenly drop into it out of the blue, as it were. They are a queer, extraordinary mingling of peoples, these Cliff Dwellers, for they are isolated enough to have begun already to lose their national characteristics and to develop into a new race. There are children romping about after hens perilously near that tremendous precipice that overhangs the extension of Sansome Street, of an origin so composite that not even the college of heralds could straighten the tangle. Here, for instance, is a child of an Italian woman and a Spanish half-breed. Think of that, now! The descendant of a Compagnian peasant, a Pueblo Indian and a water carrier of Andalusia, squattering up and down a San Francisco sidewalk, shrieking after an hysterical chicken. But there are queerer combinations than that. I have seen in a wine shop in this same Ohio Street a child who was half Jew, half Chinese, and its hair was red. I have heard of—may I yet live to see him!—a man who washes glasses in a Portuguese wine shop on the other side of the hill, whose father was a Negro and whose mother a Chinese slave girl. As I say, I have not yet set eyes on this particular Cliff Dweller. I can form no guess as to what his appearance should be. Can you? Imagine the Mongolian and African types merged into one. He should have the flat nose, and yet the almond eye; the thick lip, and yet the high cheek bone; but how as to his hair? Should it be short and crinkly, or long and straight, or merely wavy? But the ideas of the man, his bias, his prejudices, his conception of things, his thoughts—what a jumble, what an amorphous, formless mist!

But there is still another kind of Cliff Dweller—him I know and have talked with. He was watching a man paint a bunch of grapes upon the sign of a wine shop (there are neither bars, nor saloons, nor "resorts" in the country of the Cliff Dwellers, only wine shops), and on pretense of asking a direction I had some little speech with him. He was a very, very old Spaniard, and rather feeble. Do you know that this man has never—but from a distance—seen the Emporium, nor the Mills Building, nor the "Call" Building, nor the dome of the City Hall; that he would be lost on Kearny or Market Street, that he hears or reads in the papers of plays given at the Baldwin or California or Columbia as we hear or read of a new Massenet opera in Paris or a piece at the Comedie Francaise or a successful ballet at La Scala? For eight years this old man has never been down into the city. Old age has trapped him on the top of that sheer hill, and lays siege to him there. Once up here he must stay, or if possibly he should get down, never could he climb those ladderlike sidewalks. No cable cars run over the hill, and the horses of the market carts pause on a corner one third of the way up, blowing till the cart rattles, while their drivers make the delivery on foot. This old man will never come down but feet first. The world rolls by beneath him, under his eyes and in reach of his ears; Kearny Street, like the dried bed of a canon overrun with beetles, hums and lives beneath his back windows, and ships from the Horn and the Cape and the Archipelago shift and slide below the seaward streets, and he sees it all and hears it all and is yet as out of it, as exiled from it as if marooned on a South Pacific atoll. Perched on that hill of the heart of the city, he is a hermit, a Simeon Stylites on a huge scale.

The houses are as indeterminate as the inhabitants. But while the Cliff Dwellers themselves are busily at the work of race forming, new and vigorous, the buildings are rapidly going to wrack—plaster is crumbling, brick walls disintegrating, wooden rails, worn to a rosewood polish, trembling and reeling drunkenly over the steep slopes. You may see them by the score, these collapsing buildings, the frailer and feebler ones invariably clinging to the very edge of the precipitous banks of the hill, like weaker things pushed to the wall. They are patched up indiscriminately, on stilts and beams, as if upon false legs or crutches, and the wind shoulders them grudgingly toward the brink, and their old bones rattle and quake with every blast from the excavations that are going forward halfway down the hill. My old man, the hermit, the castaway, told me of an ancient lady who lives in one of the shanties that are clawing and clutching at the verge of the cliff, who, with her house, will some day be quite literally blown over the ledge. At night, when the west wind blows (you may imagine for yourselves how strong can be this wind coming in from the Farallones to the cliffs at a single hungry leap), this ancient lady sits up till dawn quaking with the quaking of the house, ready to make a wild scramble to the door as soon as the stilts begin to go.

The houses of these people are of no particular style. Some are of plaster over brick, with a second-story piazza, Mexican fashion; some with flat faces and false fronts, and some with bays that are all glass in little frames somehow suggestive of the sea. There are even some with the blunt gable and green blinds that recall New England, and now and then one comes across a miserable, senile, decrepit rabbit warren of an old villa, the cupola turned into a bedroom, a wretched green fountain sunken into the hard-beaten earth of what was once a lawn, a goat or two looking through the crazy pickets, and a litter of kittens on a sunny corner of the porch roof. Thus they have their being, the Cliff Dwellers of this San Francisco of ours; mountaineers, if you will; race formers. The hill is swarming and boiling with the life of them. Here on this wartlike protuberance bulging above the city's roof a great milling is going on, and a fusing of peoples, and in a few more generations the Celt and the Italian, the Mexican and the Chinaman, the Negro and the Portuguese, and the Levantines and the "scatter-mouches" will be merged into one type. And a curious type it will be.

VII

From *Lights and Shades of San Francisco* by B. E. Lloyd

Lights and Shades is the *Annals of San Francisco* for the 1870s. The book opens with a brief historical section, but soon gets down to its real business: a graphic, highly moralistic picture of San Francisco life. Since the book was intended primarily for an East Coast audience, Lloyd spends a good deal of time on the more bizarre and sensational aspects of the city: hoodlums, the Barbary Coast, street preaching and opium dens. But *Lights and Shades* also shows the other side of San Francisco: the writers, the religious leaders, the schoolteachers, Golden Gate Park and local business concerns. Lloyd's concerns are as wonderfully eclectic as the Victorian houses that were beginning to sprout up along the hills and avenues of the city.

Lloyd makes no attempt to be objective in his assessment of San Francisco. The Wicked draw down his wrath, and the Good win lavish praise. Readers today might find his outbursts of indignation merely quaint at best, or arrogant and offensive at worst. But we should remember that he cared passionately about this youthful city, and felt the nineteenth-century moralist's obligation to encourage virtue and scorn vice. Even when we smile at the starched morality, we should respect the conviction and concern at its core.

The Paris of America

San Francisco has been denominated the Paris of America. This certainly should not be looked upon by her citizens as a disparagement. It is true that there are many manners and customs obtaining in Paris that are to be condemned; but what city can be named that surpasses her in the attainments that are the boast of modern civilization? If it be the good qualities of the French capital that San Francisco emulates so as to be yclept "Our Paris," then may she well be proud of the christening.

But we fear that the "fastness" of her inhabitants, their apparent disregard of the Sabbath, together with other naughty Parisian ways, is the cause of her having received that appellation.

Barbary Coast: The Curse-Mark on San Francisco's Brow

"Barbary Coast" proper, is in the northerly part of the city, comprising both sides of Broadway and Pacific streets, and the cross streets between them, from Stockton street to the water front. Nearly the whole length of Dupont street, running south from Broadway, and many of its intersecting by-ways, might be called the highlands to this region, as most of the dwellers therein are perhaps not a whit less immoral and vicious; and only for the distinction that rich apparel and some of the refining accomplishments bestow, would be classed in the same social grade. Like the malaria arising from a stagnant swamp and poisoning the air for miles around, does this stagnant pool of human immorality and crime spread its contaminating vapors over the surrounding blocks on either side. Nay, it does not stop here, for even the remotest parts of the city do not entirely escape its polluting influence.

It is true that inside the limits of Barbary Coast, even among its foulest dens, are some who witness from day to day the lowest phases of human depravity and yet remain undefiled. These are not there by choice; but by force of circumstances are compelled to abide in the unhallowed precincts. But the great number of those who dwell there have chosen the locality as the most fitting place wherein to pursue their respective callings.

In the early days of San Francisco, Barbary Coast was the place of refuge and security for the hundreds of criminals that infested the city. When they had passed within its boundary, they were strongly fortified against any assault that the officers of the law might lead against them. It was, in those days, an easy matter for a stranger to enter this fortress of vice, but when once behind the walls he was exceedingly fortunate who had the opportunity to depart, taking with him his life. Then villains of every nationality held high carnival there. The jabber of the Orient, the soft-flowing tone of the South Sea Islander, the guttural gabbing of the Dutch, the Gallic accent, the round full tone of the son of Africa, the melodious voice of the Mexicano, and the harsh, sharp utterances of the Yankee, all mingled in the boisterous revels.

It was a grand theatre of crime. The glittering stiletto, the long blade bowie knife, the bottle containing the deadly drug, and the audacious navy revolver, were much-used implements in the plays that were there enacted. There was no need of mimic dying groans, and crimson water, for the drawing of warm heart-blood and the ringing of real agonizing moans of death only, would be recognized as the true style of enacting tragedy.

Were the restraining power of the law and public sentiment removed, Barbary Coast to-day could soon develop the same kind of outlawry that made it notorious in the primitive days. The material is ready at all times, and should the favorable circumstances transpire to kindle it into destructive activity, scenes as startling as those that won for the locality its christening, would be re-enacted. Even in the presence of a strong police force, and in the face of frowning cells and dungeons, it is unsafe to ramble through many of the streets and lanes in this quarter. Almost nightly there are drunken carousals and broils, frequently terminating in dangerous violence; men are often garroted and robbed, and it is not by any means a rare occurrence for foul murder to be committed. "Murderers' Corner" and "Deadman's Alley" have been rebaptized with blood over and over again, and yet call for other sacrifices.

Barbary Coast is the haunt of the low and vile of every kind. The petty thief, the house burglar, the tramp, the whoremonger, lewd women, cut-throats and murderers, all are found there. Dance-houses and concert saloons, where blear-eyed men and faded women drink vile liquor, smoke offensive tobacco, engage in vulgar conduct, sing obscene songs, and say and do everything to heap upon themselves more degradation, unrest and misery, are numerous. Low gambling houses thronged with riot-loving rowdies in all stages of intoxication are there. Opium dens, where heathen Chinese and God-forsaken women and men are sprawled in miscellaneous confusion, disgustingly drowsy, or completely overcome by inhaling the vapors of the naseous narcotic, are there. Licentiousness, debauchery, pollution, loathsome disease, insanity from dissipation, misery, poverty, wealth, profanity, blasphemy and death, are there. And Hell, yawning to receive the putrid mass, is there also.

The Hoodlum

Who Is He?—Where Is He?—Problems

Who Is He?

The Hoodlum had his origin in San Francisco. He is the offspring of San Francisco society. What particular phase in social life possesses the necessary fertility to produce such fruit is not obvious. It is certain, however, that the seed has been sown in productive soil, for the harvest is abundant.

The hoodlum has been called "a ruffian in embryo." It would be a better definition to call him simply a *ruffian*. He has all the essential qualities of the villain. He is acquainted with crime in all its forms. The records of vice are his textbooks. He is a free-born American in its widest sense. He knows no restraint and obeys no superior. He is too large for the parents' lash and too small for the cudgel of outraged citizens. He is at that critical period in life that forms an epoch in the history of most persons—neither boy nor man. Hitherto he has had no defined road to travel. His course has led over broad undulating meadows. He could scamper over the level plain, follow the tortuous hill-road, or labor through the sloughs and marshes, as his disposition prompted. Now there are two roads, and he is at the point of divergence. One leads to honor and usefulness, the other to dishonor and ruin. He is of that class who follow the latter. This is the full-grown hoodlum. There are smaller members of the same family; there are also female hoodlums. It is really wonderful—this growth of hoodlumism. A few years ago it was unknown; now it is met in every department of social life. "Young America" was a wayward prodigy; the hoodlum is the youthful graduate in vice and crime.

He is of no particular nationality; but if he is not American born, he is Americanized. His parentage may be noble and of high repute, or he may be a bastard. The millionaire, whose home is a mansion, contributes a son to the ranks, as well as the poor wretch who inhabits a hovel.

Where Is He?

The hoodlum is met more commonly on dimly-lighted street corners; in front of the "corner grocery" (in fact, he is a fixture here); on vacant lots; in dark alley-ways and nooks; at the entrance to suburbun public halls, and on public conveyances, during excursions and picnics. While the sun shines, he withdraws from public highways, and is found in isolated streets, sunning himself by a wall and planning with his associates the mischief of the coming night. At such times he is mopish and apparently inoffensive. A passing Chinaman might be made aware of his presence by a whizzing missile, but even this amusement he generally foregoes until the curtain of night has fallen. On holidays, however, and on Sundays, his daylight deeds sometimes surpass his most daring midnight crimes. But at night he is in his glory. He was reared in the darkness and he acknowledges its friendliness and protection.

So numerous and bold are the hoodlums in San Francisco that it is dangerous for a single individual to travel a quiet street late at night. They congregate on street corners, drop insulting remarks at passers-by, ogle the ladies and stone or beat the peaceful Chinese. They swagger up and down the streets, frightening from their pathway any belated citizen, ringing door-bells, unhinging gates, yelling and singing obscene songs, uttering horrid oaths—striking terror to the hearts of all would-be sleepers for blocks away. They rifle the pockets, and make footballs of any inebriated straggler that happens in their way; not unfrequently clubbing and robbing business men as they return from their stores or offices. Street cars are boarded by them, the driver "brained," and the passengers put to flight. Working-girls and women, returning late from the factory or workshop, are insulted and sometimes outraged. Policemen are overpowered and beaten by them. They are the dread of all peacefully-disposed persons.

The hoodlum is the sworn enemy of the Chinamen. Striking them down with their fists, jerking their queues, belaboring them with clubs and hurling cobble-stones at them, is their most favorite pastime.

Problems

The social mechanism lacks a moral cog, that produces such results. Parental authority is a rare virtue in San Francisco. The "home circle" has become a myth. Home attractions do not exist; or where they do exist, have lost the wonted charm. That sacred word, *home* is fast losing its significance. Many families have no home. They live in hotels and boarding houses, or dwell in lodging houses and eat at restaurants, and as a consequence the family never meets around the home hearthstone.

Children must have amusement, and if the home-folk do not provide for them in this regard, they go elsewhere to find it. "They are allowed to run wild on the streets." They grow bold from necessity. Cast, as they are upon their own resources for amusement, they must needs make their way through the world. And they do it, unguided by experienced and wiser persons. Hence they become "fast" and uncontrollable ere they have outgrown their baby lispings. "Now I lay me down to sleep," coming in soft and loving accents from a mother's lips, as she bends low over the couch of her child, would be strange and startling words in many family chambers in this "city by the Golden Gate." The name of God is oftener heard by the little prattlers while at play on the street than at their mother's knee. They know not of reverence. They are profane from infancy; they have quick ears to catch the floating slang, and where parental restraint is not felt, they soon learn to commit petty misdeeds.

This, perhaps, partly solves the problem, whence this hoodlumism?

How to check hoodlumism is a problem that sorely puzzles the brain of the moralist. We do not propose to try to solve it. It might, however, be well to draw the legal reins a little tighter. Reclaim the little wanderers (who would do harm but cannot) by removing from their presence the larger, whose example they aspire to follow. Treat with severity the criminals in the well-grown ranks. Make the law a terror to them. Should ordinary penalties fail to have the desired effect, establish a whipping-post, as has been suggested, and let the lash be freely applied. This would produce a wondrous change in the morals of some "young bloods."

The Public Schools

Liberality

San Francisco expends more, in proportion, upon her public schools, than any city in the Union. No matter how much opposed to taxation for municipal purposes her people may be; how they will frown upon any attempt to make them bear the expense of a street extension; to experiment with a new pavement; or to enrich private corporations at public cost—they will vote money for educational purposes without stint. To afford their children unexcelled school advantages, they are really profuse in their liberality.

Management and Classification

The public schools of San Francisco are divided for the purpose of classification, into three divisions: The Primary Department, the Grammar Department, and the High Schools. To complete the entire course of study under this system, requires eleven years—three years for the senior, middle, and junior classes of the high schools, and eight years for the light grades of the grammar and primary departments. Annual examinations in each grade determine whether the pupil shall be advanced in the regular order, or remain another year.

A class of schools, known as Cosmopolitan Schools, are in operation, where pupils are instructed altogether in German and French. During ten months of the school year, evening schools are in operation, where competent teachers give free instruction to all who attend. The evening schools accomplish a vast deal of good, by educating those whose circumstances in life compel them to labor during the day. The pupils are of all nationalities, and of all ages—the boy of twelve, and gray-haired men and women, here take their first lessons in reading and writing.

The city has heretofore supported separate schools for the colored population, but now the distinction is removed, and they sit together in the same schoolroom, and pursue the same studies, with the children of white parents.

The Teachers

It is a matter of pride with San Franciscans, that the teachers of their public schools stand in the very front rank, in regard to culture and literary attainments. The gentlemen are polished in manner, and proficient in all the departments of learning.

The ladies are well bred, well educated, and many of them possessed of rare personal accomplishments. In fact, the San Francisco "school marms," as a class, are the blue stockings of the Pacific coast. Many of the most charming sketches, the sagest home advice, and the sweetest poetry, that have graced the pages of our magazines and newspapers, were written in intervals of school work, by the lady teachers in the public schools of the city.

The salaries paid teachers are liberal, and by some might be deemed magnificent. The Principal of the Boys' High School receives an annual salary of $4,000. The Principal of the Girls' High School, $3,000. Special teachers of Latin and Greek, $2,400. Special teachers of French and German, $2,100. Special teachers of Natural Science, $2,400. Principals of the Grammar Schools, from $2,400 to $2,700. The salaries of teachers in the Primary Schools range from $600, for those holding second grade certificates and having no experience in teaching, to $1,800.

The Bohemian Club

The Bohemian Club is perhaps the most interesting organization of all. It was organized April 1, 1872. Its membership numbers over two hundred and fifty persons. The badge or motto of this club is very suggestive. It consists of a shield, upon which an "owl-eyed" owl, perched upon a grinning, brainless skull, stares ominously around; across his breast is traced the apt inscription, "Weaving spiders come not here." The inference might be drawn—it were better to have no brains at all, than to have webby brains.

The first article of the constitution says: "The organization shall be known as the Bohemian Club. It is instituted for the association of gentlemen connected professionally with literature, art, music, the drama, and also those who, by reason of their love or appreciation of these objects, may be deemed eligible." So, therefore, its members are necessarily journalists, authors, artists, actors, and musicians—professions requiring intellectual advancement. Their intercourse is very pleasant and instructive. The entertainments given monthly (which the club terms "High Jinks,") are exceedingly interesting, and sometimes develop into real intellectual brilliancy. A subject is chosen, and socially discussed—the members of the histrionic art, employing their professional talents and acquirements in their style of argument; the orator, his flights of eloquence; the writer, his finished rhetoric; the artist, his crayon and brush; and the musician, restoring harmony to the whole by touching his sweetest chords. Most of the artists, actors, and writers in the city are members, besides many amateurs, and persons of other professions who have an appreciation of, and taste for, art and literature.

The Press of San Francisco

The Press

Did the "power of the press" consist in the number of public journals and periodicals that are regularly issued, San Francisco would present a most formidable front. Whatever principle, party or person it should attack, would do well to surrender at once, as the numerical force that could be marshaled out is sufficient to overcome and crush anything antagonistic, however powerful, unless perchance it should be a railroad corporation or Chinese immigration.

There are eighty distinct periodicals thrown out to the public, at intervals—some quarterly and monthly, but the greater number issuing daily and weekly. These all are (or at least profess to be) published in the interest of humanity, each having a particular object in view aside from the great general aim of money-getting. It is furthermore true that each of these periodicals claims to labor, in *its own especial* and *peculiar* way, for the *betterment* of mankind in general and the inhabitants of San Francisco and California in particular.

It would therefore follow, as a natural sequence, that the individuals composing the community in which these publications most do circulate, would be, and are, the nearest approach to perfect intelligent mortals that claim a habitation on this terrestrial sphere. However desirable that condition may be, it is evident from the volume wherein you now read that, with all the advantages pointing to moral, intellectual, physical, and social perfection, San Franciscans are still "prone to err."

Yet San Francisco is not too boastful of her public journals. The height she has attained as a city, commercially and socially, she has also reached intellectually. The press has been the leader, is yet in advance, and to it is due the unparalleled progress San Francisco and California have made in the past quarter of a century. The history of journalism on the Pacific Coast, although extending over so brief a period, would abound in interesting and exciting narrative, and would reveal the fact that the standard of excellence it has reached has been literally through fire and tribulation.

But these very circumstances have tended to develop the real legitimate journalistic pursuit, and therefore when, by accident or otherwise, unfit persons have drifted into the channel, the current of public sentiment has generally washed them upon the rocks, and they have disappeared from view.

The West has developed independent journalism. There is manifest in the abler Western newspapers a blunt boldness, not hampered by palliative phrases, that is discovered in but few Eastern journals. Any new country, possessing similar attractions to California, is, in its earlier history, overrun by a desperate and dangerous class of adventurers; and hence, in the West, it required not only literary ability to establish a newspaper that would exert a power for the good of the country and society, but courageous hearts withal.

Thus it is that the very nature of the circumstances through which Western journalism has grown up, compelled an independent course that—though, perhaps, in its crudeness, was audacious and insolent—has developed into a power, the proper exercise of which is the true mission of the newspaper in these latter years of the nineteenth century.

The California public look upon the press as a power, whose strength it were better not to test; with a sort of reverential awe. To this fact, is possibly due, the restrictions that have been attempted to be placed upon it—by the recent State Legislature. It is difficult to understand why this feeling should obtain among the people—especially those whose lives, hitherto, have been as they should, free from tarnish, upright and honorable.

It has been observed, however, that when the secular journals have exposed any great evil, whether of a social, business, or official nature, and earnestly agitated the subject, they have almost universally succeeded in uprooting it, and have guided the hand of justice to deal the merited blow upon the perpetrators. When the city of San Francisco had become as a house of refuge to criminals of all classes, and dishonesty and vice knew no limit beyond which they could not with impunity pass, it was the press, that awakened the dormant principle of right, and aroused the people to action. The press urged them onward, until they had purged the city of its most vicious inhabitants.

Only let one of the standard San Francisco journals express distrust in the financial condition of a banking house, or prominent business firm, and the impulsive populace at once sees impending, a financial stringency that cannot but result in great disaster; and ten times in twelve it will, by its hasty action; precipitate a real panic. A reverse feeling will be induced by the press coming out strongly in favor of an institution, that may be tottering from its own weight, so that the slightest disturbance would cause it to fall; a few well-timed editorials, based upon reason and expressing confidence, sets the public mind at rest, and the chasm may be bridged.

Yet in the face of this dreaded power and independence, wealthy corporations have grown thrifty, and, to-day, threaten to rise in their strength and dictate to the masses what they shall or shall not do. There has been no country more prolific of monopolies than California, and unless they are held in check by legislation, the oppression that results from their tyrannical power when given unbridled sway, will become intolerable. The spirit of communism, that is occasionally manifest among the laboring classes, is enkindled and fed by the blighting influence the monopolies exert, and will develop into a power that will, by sheer force, establish an equilibrium, even though a period of anarchy should result, unless some protection be extended to the working-men.

The press of California, has therefore much to contend with. It is essential, then, that the leading journals possess and maintain a true independence, such as gold will not neutralize nor influence bend, for the masses accept them as leaders, and have faith that they will lead aright.

In San Francisco, there are twenty periodicals, published in different foreign languages, which, more certainly indicate the extent of the foreign population, than anything short of an actual enumeration. The whole number of daily papers is twelve, and of dailies and weeklies together there are fifty-five.

VIII

From "Love Sonnets of a Hoodlum" by Wallace Irwin

Wallace Irwin's *Love Sonnets of a Hoodlum* have long deserved a reprinting. The radical incongruity between the delicate, sophisticated form of the Petrarchan sonnet and the low-class slang of the narrator is the perfect counterpart to San Francisco' Victorian architecture, which could show forth a beaux-arts style mansion designed in the best of Continental taste, and crown it with a redwood statue of the great grizzly bear of California. It depends solely on our own taste whether we regard the final product as a deft marriage or a forcible rape.

The poems comprise a sonnet sequence, written in underworld slang, about the love of a guy named Willie for a gal named Mame. Willie woos and loses her to a "dark rival" named Murphy, whose superior social position as the night clerk in McCann's drug store wins him the hand of the fickle Mame. But, as with Renaissance sonnet sequences (on which the *Hoodlum* sonnets are based), the poems are more than love songs. They reveal the psychology of the speaker even more completely than the character of the beloved.

The portrait of the hard-drinking, swearing, rough-but-lovable hoodlum who loves more with his pride than with his heart is, of course, more revealing of what Irwin himself felt about the past than of the past itself. The original hoodlums were gangs of troublemakers that roamed the streets of the City in the 1860s and 1870s. They dressed in flashy clothes (see sonnet #3), hung out in the dives of the Barbary coast, and loafed around the streets looking for action. According to the newspapers of the time, the hoodlums were always an annoyance and sometimes a menace to the upstanding citizens and were feared and despised by all who wrote of them in print. But by 1901, when *Love Sonnets of a Hoodlum* was written, the hoodlums themselves had long since vanished (as a recognizable and blameable type), and could be safely romanticized as a "colorful" episode in San Francisco's turbulent, irrecoverable past.

The Love Sonnets of a Hoodlum

I

Say, will she treat me white, or throw me down,
Give me the glassy glare, or welcome hand,

Shovel me dirt, or treat me on the grand,
Knife me, or make me think I own the town?
Will she be on the level, do me brown,
Or will she jolt me lightly on the sand,
Leaving poor Willie froze to beat the band,
Limp as your grandma's Mother Hubbard gown?

I do not know, nor do I give a whoop,
But this I know: if she is so inclined
She can come play with me on our back stoop,
Even in office hours, I do not mind—
In fact I know I'm nice and good and ready
To get an option on her as my steady.

III

As follows is the make-up I shall buy,
Next week, when from the boss I pull my pay:—
A white and yellow zig-zag cutaway,
A sunset-colored vest and purple tie,
A shirt for vaudeville and something fly
In gunboat shoes and half-hose on the gay.
I'll get some green shoe-laces, by the way,
And a straw lid to set 'em stepping high.

Then shall I shine and be the great main squeeze,
The warm gazook, the only on the bunch,
The Oklahoma wonder, the whole cheese,
The baby with the Honolulu hunch—
That will bring Mame to time—I should say yes!
Ain't my dough good as Murphy's? Well, I guess!

V

Last night—ah, yesternight—I flagged my queen
Steering for Grunsky's ice-cream joint full sail!
I up and braced her, breezy as a gale,
And she was the all-rightest ever seen.
Just then Brick Murphy butted in between,
Rushing my funny song-and-dance to jail,
My syncopated con-talk no avail,
For Murphy was the only nectarine.

This is a sample of the hand I get
When I am playing more than solitaire,
Showing how I become the slowest yet
When it's a case of razors in the air,
And competition knocks me off creation
Like a gin-fountain smashed by Carrie Nation.

VI

See how that Murphy cake-walks in his pride,
That brick-topped Murphy, fourteen-dollar jay;
You'd think he'd leased the sidewalk by the way
He takes up half a yard on either side!
I'm wise his diamond ring's a cut-glass snide,
His overcoat is rented by the day,
But still no kick is coming yet from Mae
When Murphy cuts the cake so very wide.

Rubber, thou scab! Don't throw on so much spaniel!
Say, are there any more at home like you?
You're not the only lion after Daniel,
You're not the only oyster in the stew.
Get next, you pawn-shop sport! Come off the fence
Before I make you look like thirty cents!

VII

Mayhap you think I cinched my little job
When I made meat of Mamie's dress-suit belle.
If that's your hunch you don't know how the swell
Can put it on the plain, unfinished slob
Who lacks the kiss-me war paint of the snob
And can't make good inside a giddy shell;
Wherefore the reason I am fain to tell
The slump that caused me this melodious sob.

For when I pushed Brick Murphy to the rope
Mame manned the ambulance and dragged him in,
Massaged his lamps with fragrant drug store dope
And coughed up loops of kindergarten chin;
She sprang a come back, piped for the patrol,
Then threw a glance that tommyhawked my soul.

IX

Last night I tumbled off the water cart—
It was a peacherino of a drunk
I put the cocktail market on the punk
And tore up all the sidewalks from the start.
The package that I carried was a tart
That beat Vesuvius out for sizz and spunk,
And when they put me in my little bunk
You couldn't tell my jag and me apart.

Oh! would I were the ice man for a space,
Then might I cool this red-hot cocoanut,

Corral the jim-jam bugs that madly race
Around the eaves that from my forehead jut—
Or will a carpenter please come instead
And build a picket fence around my head?

XI

O scaly Mame to give me such a deal,
To hand me such a bunch when I was true!
You played me double and you knew it, too,
Nor cared a wad of gum how I would feel.
Can you not see that Murphy's handy spiel
Is cheap balloon juice of a Blarney brew,
A phonograph where all he has to do
Is give the crank a twist and let 'er reel?

Nay, love has put your optics on the bum,
To you are Murphy's gold bricks all O.K.;
His talks go down however rank they come,
For he has got you going, fairy fay.
Ah, well! In that I'm in the box with you,
For love has got poor Willie groggy, too.

XVI

Oh, for a fist to push a fancy quill!
A Lover's Handy Letter Writer, too,
To help me polish off this billy doo
So it can jolly Mame and make a kill,
Coax her to think that I'm no gilded pill,
But rather the unadulterated goo.
Below I give a sample of the brew
I've manufactured in my thinking mill:

"Gum Drop:—Your tanglefoot has got my game,
I'm stuck so tight you cannot shake your catch;
It's cruelty to insects—honest, Mame,—
So won't you join me in a tie-up match?
If you'll talk business I'm your lemon pie.
Please answer and relieve

An Anxious Guy."

XVII

Woman, you are indeed a false alarm;
You offer trips to heaven at tourist's rates
And publish fairy tales about the dates
You're going to keep (not meaning any harm),
Then get some poor old Rube fresh from the farm,

As graceful as a kangaroo on skates,
Trying to transfer at the Pearly Gates—
For instance, note this jolt that smashed the charm:—
"P.S.—You are all right, but you won't do.
You may be up a hundred in the shade,
But there are cripples livelier than you,
And my man Murphy's strictly union-made.
You are a bargain, but it seems a shame
That you should drink so much.

Yours truly,
Mame."

XIX

A Pardon if too much I chew the rag,
But say, it's getting rubbed in good and deep,
And I have reached the limit where I weep
As easy as a sentimental jag.
My soul is quite a worn and frazzled rag,
My life is damaged goods, my price is cheap,
And I am such a snap I dare not peep
Lest some should read the price-mark on my tag.

The more my sourballed murmur, since I've seen
A Sunday picnic car on Market Street,
Full of assorted sports, each with his queen—
And chewing pepsin on the forninst seat
Were Mame and Murphy, diked to suit the part,
And clinching fins in public, heart-to-heart.

XXI

At noon today Murphy and Mame were tied.
A gospel huckster did the referee,
And all the Drug Clerks Union loped to see
The queen of Minnie Street become a bride,
And that bad actor, Murphy, by her side,
Standing where Yours Despondent ought to be.
I went to hang a smile in front of me,
But weeps were in my glimmers when I tried.

The pastor murmured, "Two and two make one,"
And slipped a sixteen K on Mamie's grab;
And when the game was tied and all was done
The guests shied footwear at the bridal cab,
And Murphy's little gilt-roofed brother Jim
Snickered, "She's left her happy home for him."

EPILOGUE

To just one girl I've tuned my sad bazoo,
Stringing my pipe-dream off as it occurred,
And as I've tipped the straight talk every word,
If you don't like it you know what to do.
Perhaps you think I've handed out to you
An idle jest, a touch-me-not, absurd
As any sky-blue-pink canary bird,
Billed for a record season at the Zoo.

If that's your guess you'll have to guess again,
For thus I fizzled in a burst of glory,
And this rhythmatic side-show doth contain
The sum and substance of my hard-luck story,
Showing how Vanity is still on deck
And Humble Virtue gets it in the neck.

Market Street at the turn of the century.

Three Pieces by Gelett Burgess

Short, bespectacled, brilliant, the very stereotype of an intellectual, Gelett Burgess was the self-proclaimed spokesman of *art nouveau* in San Francisco. After being fired from the University of California at Berkeley for overturning a statue in a fit of drunken caprice, he devoted himself to the life of a literary dilettante, modelling himself after the greatest dilettante of them all, Oscar Wilde. In 1895, Burgess began *The Lark* with his co-conspirator in the statue-razing incident. This little journal was, for its brief life, the voice of art nouveau in the City. It was started, said the editors, with "no more serious intention than to be gay."

For all his frivolity, Burgess was an acute observer of San Francisco life. He constantly nagged San Franciscans about the pretensions of their Victorian architecture (See "Architectural Shams") and their maladaptations to Grand Culture generally. But he could also appreciate the distinctive quality of life that grew on the slopes of the Golden Gate. "The Ballad of the Hyde Street Grip," with its profusion of exclamation points and galloping meter, effectively dramatizes the city from the moving viewpoint of a cable car. "The Bohemians," taken from his charming novel, *The Heart Line,* gives us a vivid picture of bohemian life at the turn of the century. The characters in "The Bohemians" are portraits of members of Burgess' circle of friends, called *Les Jeunes,* who gathered at Coppa's (Fulda's in our story) restaurant for evenings of badinage and literary conspiracies. The description of the poet Starr is Burgess' description of George Sterling; and other members of the Coppa circle undoubtedly recognized themselves in Burgess' story.

Ballad of the
Hyde Street Grip

Oh, the rain is slanting sharply, and the Norther's blowing cold,
When the cable strands are loosened she is nasty hard to hold;
There's little time for sitting down and little time for gab,
For the bumper guards the crossing, and you'd best be keeping tab!
Two-and-twenty "let-go's" every double trip—
It takes a bit of doing on the Hyde Street Grip!

Throw her off at Powell street, let her go at Post,
Watch her well at Geary and at Sutter, when you coast,

From *A Gage of Youth* by Frank Gelett Burgess. Boston: 1901.

259

Easy at the Power House, have a care at Clay,
Sacramento, Washington, Jackson, all the way!
Drop the rope at Union, never make a slip—
The lever keeps you busy on the Hyde Street Grip!

Foot-brake, wheel-brake, slot-brake and gong,
You've got to keep 'em working, or you'll be going wrong!
Rush her on the crossing, catch her on the rise,
Easy round the corners, when the dust is in your eyes!
And the bell will always stop you, if you hit her up a clip—
You are apt to earn your wages, on the Hyde Street Grip!

North Beach to Tenderloin, over Russian Hill,
The grades are something giddy and the curves are fit to kill!
All the way to Market Street, climbing up the slope,
Down upon the other side, hanging to the rope;
But the sight of San Francisco as you take the lurching dip!
There is plenty of excitement, on the Hyde Street Grip!

Oh, the lights are in the Mission and the ships are in the Bay;
And Tamalpais is looming from the Gate across the way;
The Presidio trees are waving and the hills are growing brown!
And the driving fog is harried from the Ocean to the town!
How the pulleys slap and rattle! How the cables hum and whip!
Oh, they sing a gallant chorus on the Hyde Street Grip!

When the Orpheum is closing and the crowd is on the way,
The conductor's punch is ringing and the dummy's light and gay;
But the wait upon the table by the Beach is dark and still—
Just the swashing of the surges on the shore below the mill;
And the flash of Angel Island breaks across the channel rip,
And the hush of midnight falls upon the Hyde Street Grip!

"The Bohemians"

"Say, Fancy, there's a gang of artist chaps and literary guys I'd like to put you up against," Gay said one afternoon. "I think you'd make a hit with the bunch, if you can stand a little jollying."

"You watch me!" Fancy became enthusiastically interested. "Where do they hang out?"

"They eat at a joint down on Montgomery Street. They're heavy joshers, though. They're too clever for me, mostly. It's the real-thing Bohemia down there, though."

From *The Heart Line* by Frank Gelett Burgess. New York: Bobbs-Merrill, 1907.

"Why didn't you tell me about it before?" she pouted. "I'm game! Let's float in there to-night and see the animals feed."

So they went down to the Latin Quarter together.

Bohemia has been variously described. Since Henri Murger's time, the definition has changed retrogressively, until now, what is commonly called Bohemia is a place where one is told, "This is Liberty Hall!"—and one is forced to drink beer whether one likes it or not, where not to like spaghetti is a crime. Not such was the little coterie of artists, writers and amateurs, who dined together every night at Fulda's restaurant.

In San Francisco is recruited a perennial crop of such petty soldiers of fortune. Here art receives scant recompense, and as soon as one gets one's head above water and begins to be recognized, existence is unendurable in a place where genius has no field for action. The artist, the writer or the musician must fly East to the great market-place, New York, or to the great forcing-bed, Paris, to bloom or fade, to live or die in competition with others in his field.

So the little artistic colonies shrink with defections or increase with the accession of hitherto unknown aspirants. Many go and never return. A few come back to breathe again the stimulating air of California, to see with new eyes its fresh, vivid color, its poetry, its romance. To have gone East and to have returned without abject failure is here, in the eyes of the vulgar, Art's patent of nobility. Of those who have been content to linger peaceably in the land of the lotus, some are earls without coronets, but one and all share a fierce, hot, passionate love of the soil. San Francisco has become a fetish, a cult. Under its blue skies and driving fogs is bred the most ardent loyalty in these United States. San Francisco is most magnificently herself of any American city, and San Franciscans, in consequence, are themselves with an abounding perfervid sincerity. Faults they have, lurid, pungent, staccato, but hypocrisy is not of them. That vice is never necessary.

The party that gathered nightly at Fulda's was as remote from the world as if it had been ensconced on a desert island. It was unconscious, unaffected, sufficient to itself. Men and girls had come and gone since it had formed, but the nucleal circle was always complete. Death and desertions were unacknowledged—else the gloom would have shut down and the wine, the red wine of the country, would have tasted salt with tears. There had been tragedies and comedies played out in that group, there were names spoken in whispers sometimes, there was silent toasts drunk; but if sentiment was there, it was disguised as folly. Life still thrilled in song. Youth was not yet dead. Art was long and exigent.

It was their custom, after dinner, to adjourn to Champoreau's for *cafe noir,* served in the French style. In this large, bare saloon, with sanded floor, with its bar and billiard table, foreign as France, almost always deserted at this hour save by their company, the genial *patron* smiled at their gaiety, as he prepared the long glasses of coffee. To-night, there were six at the round table.

Maxim, an artist unhailed as yet from the East, was, of all, the most obviously picturesque, with a fierce mustached face and a shock of black hair springing in a wild mass from his head to draggle in stringy locks below his eyes, or, with a sudden leonine shake, to be thrown back when he bellowed forth in song. He had been in Paris and knew the airs and argot of the most desperate studies. His laughter was like the roar of a convivial lion.

Dougal, with a dog-like face and tow hair, so ugly as to be refreshing, full of common sense and kindness, with a huge mouth full of little cramped teeth and a smile that drew and compelled and captured like a charm—he sat next. Good nature and loyalty dwelt in his narrow blue eyes. His slow, labored speech was seldom smothered, even in the wit that enveloped it.

Most masculine and imperative of all, was Benton, with his blur of blue-black hair, fine tangled threads, his melting, deep blue eyes, shadowy with fatigue, lighted with vagrant dreams or shot with brisk fires of passion. His hands were strong and he had an air of suppressed power.

The fourth man was Philip Starr, a poet not long for San Francisco, seeing that the Athanaeum had already placed the laurels upon his brow—he was as far from the conventional type of poet as is possible. He had a lean, eager, sharply cut face, shrewd, quick eye and sinewy, long fingers. His hair was close cropped, his mouth was tight and narrow. Electricity seemed to dart from him as from a dynamo. Just now he was teaching the company a new song—an old one, rather, for it was an ancient Anglo-Saxon drinking-song, whose uproarious refrain was well fitted to the temper of the assembly.

At one end of the table sat a young woman, *petite,* elf-like as a little girl, a brown, cunning, soft-haired creature, smiling, smiling, smiling, with eyes half closed, wrinkled in quiet mirth. This was Elsie Dougal.

Opposite her was a girl of twenty-seven, with a handsome, clear-cut, classic face, lighted with gray eyes, limpid and straightforward, making her seem the most ingenuous of all. Mabel's hair curled unmanageably, springy and dark. Her face was serious and intent till her smile broke and a little self-conscious laugh escaped.

Starr pounded with one fist upon the table, his thumb held stiffly upright:

> "Dance, Thumbakin, dance!"

he sang, and the chorus was repeated. Then with the heel of his palm and his fingers outstretched, pounding merrily in time:

> "Oh, dance ye merrymen, every one,"

then with his fist as before:

> "For Thumbakin, he can dance alone!"

and, raising his fists high over his head, coming down with a bang:

"*For*

"Thumbakin he can dance alone!"

They went through the song together, dancing Foreman, Middleman, and Littleman, ending in a pianissimo. Then over and over they sang that queer, ancient tune, till all knew it by heart.

Benton pulled his manuscript from his pocket and read it confidentially to Elsie, who smiled and smiled. Starr recited his last poem while Dougal made humorous comments. Maxim broke out into a French student's *chanson,* so wildly improper that it took two men to suppress him. Mabel giggled hysterically and began a long, dull story which, despite interruptions, ended so brilliantly and so unexpectedly, that every one wished he had listened.

Then Dougal called out:

"The cavalry charge! Ready! One finger!"

They tapped in unison, not too fast, each with a forefinger upon the table.

"Two fingers!"

The sound increased in volume.

"Three fingers, four fingers, five!"

The crescendo rose.

"Two hands! One foot! BOTH FEET!"

There was a hurricane of galloping fists and soles. Then, in diminuendo:

"One foot! One hand! Four fingers, three, two, one! Halt!"

The clatter grew softer and softer till at last all was still.

As Gay opened the door, Fancy heard a roar that increased steadily until it became a wild hullabaloo. Looking in, she saw the six seated about the table, the coffee glasses jumping madly with the percussion. The noise was like the multitudinous charge of troopers. Then the tumult died slowly away, the patter grew softer and softer, ending in a sudden hush as seven faces looked up at her. Gay P. Summer's advent was greeted with frowns, but Fancy gathered an instant acclaim from twelve critical eyes.

She stepped boldly into the room and shed the radiance of her smile upon the company.

"I guess this is where I live, all right!" she announced. "I've been gone a long time, haven't I? Never mind the introductions. I'm Fancy Gray, drifter; welcome to our fair city!"

They let loose a cry of welcome, and Dougal, rising, opened a place for her between his chair and Maxim's.

"I'm *for* her!" He hailed her with a good-natured grin. "She's the right shape. Come and have coffee!"

"I accept!" said Fancy Gray.

Gay's reception was by no means as cordial as hers, which had been immediate and spontaneous at the sound of her caressing, jovial voice and the sight of her genial smile, which seemed to embrace each separate member of the party. They made grudging room for him beside Elsie, who gave him a cold little hand. Mabel bowed politely.

"Where'd you get her, Gay?" said Starr. "You're improving. She looks like a pretty good imitation of the real thing."

"Oh, I'll wash, all right," said Fancy.

Gay P. proudly introduced her to the company. He played her as he might play a trump to win the seventh trick. Indeed, without Fancy's aid, he would have received scant welcome at that exclusive board. Many and loud were the jests at Summer's expense while he was away. Many and soft were the jests he had not wit enough to understand when he was present. Philip Starr had, at first sight of him, dubbed him "The Scroyle," and this sobriquet stuck. Gay P. Summer was ill versed in Elizabethan lore, but, had his wit been greater, his conceit would still have protected him.

He had already unloaded Fancy, though he was as yet unaware of it. She was taken up with enthusiasm by the men, whom she drew like a magnet. Mabel and Elsie watched her with the keenness of women who are jealous of any new element in their group. It was, perhaps, not so much rivalry they feared, for their place was to well established, as the admittance into that circle of one who would betray a tendency toward those petty feline amenities that only women can perceive and resent.

But Fancy Gray showed no such symptoms. She did not bid for the men's attention. She made a point of talking to Elsie, and she managed cleverly to include Mabel in the attention she received. Fancy, in her turn, scrutinized the two girls artfully and made her own instantaneous deductions. All of this by-play was, of course, quite lost upon the men.

The talk sprang into new life and Fancy's eye ran from one to another member of the group, dwelling longest upon Dougal. His ugliness seemed to fascinate her; and, as is often the case with ugly men, he inspired her instant confidence. She made up to him without embarrassment or concealment, taking his hairy hand and caressing it openly. At this, Elsie's eyelids half closed, but there was no sign of jealousy. Mabel noticed the act, too, and her manner suddenly became warmer toward the girl. By these two feminine reactions, Fancy saw that she had done well.

They sang, they pounded the table; and, as an initiation, every man saluted Fancy's cheek. She took it like an express. Then suddenly, Dougal held up two fingers. Every one's eyes were turned upon him.

"Piedra Pinta?" he cried, with a side glance at Fancy.

Every one voted. Mabel held up both her hands gleefully.

So was Fancy Gray, though she was not aware of the honor till afterward, admitted to the full comradeship of the Pintos. It was a victory. Many had, with the same ignorance as to what was happening, suffered an ignominious defeat. Fancy's election was unanimous.

And for this once, in gratitude for his discovery, Mr. Gay P. Summer, The Scroyle, was suffered to inflict himself upon the coterie of the Pintos.

There were other honors in store for Fancy Gray.

Piedra Pinta is two hours' journey from San Francisco to the north, in Marin County—a land of mountains, virgin redwood forests and trout-filled streams. One takes the ferry to Sausalito, crossing the northern bay, and rides for an hour or so up a little narrow-gage squirming railroad into the canyon of Paper Mill Creek; and, if one has discovered and appropriated the place, it is a mile walk up the track and a drop from the embankment down a gravelly, overgrown slope, into the camp-ground. Here a great crag rears its vertically split face, hidden in beeches and bay trees. At its foot a flattened fragment has fallen forward to do service as a fireplace. Beyond, there are more boulders in the stream, which here widens and deepens, overhung by clustering trees. Save when an occasional train rushes past overhead, or a fisherman comes by, wading up-stream, the place is secret and silent. Opposite, across the brook, an oat-field slopes upward to the country road and the smooth drumlins beyond. A not too noisy crowd can here lie hugger-mugger, hidden from the world.

To Piedra Pinta that next Saturday they came, bringing Fancy Gray, a smiling captive, with them. The men bore blankets and books; the women food and dishes enough for a picnic meal. They came singing, romping up the track, big Benton first with the heaviest load. In corduroys and jeans, in boots and flannel shirts they came. Little Elsie, like a girl scout, wore a rakish slouch hat trimmed with live carnations, a short skirt, leggings, a sheath knife swinging from her belt. Mabel had her own pearl-handled revolver. The rest looked like gipsies.

They slid down the bank and debouched with a shout into the little glade. Fancy entered with vim into the celebration. Not that she did any useful work, that was not her field; she was there chiefly as a decoration and an inspiration. She had dressed herself in khaki. Her boots were laced high, her sombrero permitted a shower of tinted tendrils to escape and wanton about her forehead. She found fragrant sprays of yerba buena and wreathed them about her neck.

It was all new and strange to her, all delightful. She had seen the artificial side of the town and knew the best and worst of its gaiety; but here, in the open for almost the first time, she breathed deeply of the primal joys of nature and was refreshed. Her curiosity was unlimited; she played with earth and water, fire and air. She unbuttoned the collar of her shirt-waist and turned it in, disclosing a delicious pink hollow at her throat. She rolled up her sleeves, displaying the dimples in her elbows. At the preparations for the dinner she was an eager spectator, and when the meal was served, smoked and sandy, and the bottles were opened, all traces of the fairy in her disappeared; she was simple girl. She ate like a cannibal and ate with glee.

The shadows fell. The nook became dusky, odorous, moist; the rivulet rippled pleasantly, the ferns moved lazily in the night airs. The moon arose and gave a mysterious argent illumination. The going and coming ceased, the shouting and lusty singing grew still. The blankets were opened and spread at the foot of the rock. Dougal and Elsie took their places in the center and, the men on one side and the girls on the other, they lay upon the ground and wrapped themselves against the cooling air. The fire was replenished and its glare lighted up the trees in planes of foliage, like painted sheets of scenery.

They lay down, but not to sleep. Dougal's coffee, black and strong, stimulated their brains. The talk ran on with an accompaniment of song and jest. One after another sprang up to sing some old-time tune or to recite a familiar, well-beloved poem; the dialogue jumped from one to the other. Some dozed and woke again at a chorus of laughter; some sat wide-eyed, staring into the fire, into the darkness, or into one another's eyes.

Maxim was prodigious. He blared forth rollicking airs, he did scenes from *La Boheme,* posturing picturesquely against the flame, his long black locks sweeping his face. Starr improvised while they listened, rapt. Benton climbed high into a beech tree and there, invisible, he recited *Cynara* and quoted *The Song of the Sword,* while Dougal jeered and fed the blaze. Mabel listened entranced and appreciative, and ventured occasionally on one more long, dull story—her tale always growing melodramatically exciting, as the attention of her listeners wandered. Elsie sat and smiled and smiled, wide awake till three.

Forgotten tales, snatches of song, jokes and verses surged into Fancy's head and one after another she shot them into the night. She, too, arose and sang, dancing. Not since her vaudeville days had she attempted it, but mounting to the spirit of the occasion, she thrilled and fascinated them with her drollery.

She and Dougal were the last ones awake. They spoke now in undertones. Maxim was snoring hideously, so was Benton. Starr lay with his mouth open, Mabel was curled into a cocoon of blankets, flushed Elsie was still smiling in her sleep.

At four the dawn appeared. They watched it spellbound, and as it turned from a glowing rose to straw color, the birds began to twitter in the boughs. Fancy shook off her lassitude.

"I'm going in swimming," she exclaimed, starting up. "Stay here, Dougal—I trust to your honor!"

"I'll not promise," he replied. "One doesn't often have a chance to see a nymph bathing in a fountain nowadays, but I have the artist's eye; it will only be for beauty's sake—go ahead!" He kept his place, nevertheless; the pool was invisible from the level of the camp-ground.

Fancy darted down the path to the wash of pebbles below. Dougal shook Elsie into a dazed wakefulness. Mabel's eyes opened sleepily.

"Fancy's gone in swimming," he whispered. "Don't wake up the boys."

Like shadows the two girls slid after her. Dougal lay down to sleep.

In half an hour he was awakened by their return, fresh, rosy, dewy and jubilant. Elsie crawled to his side under the blankets; Fancy and Mabel scrambled up the bank to greet the sun, chattering like sparrows. Maxim rolled over in his sleep. Benton and Starr, back to back, dreamed on. The sun rose higher and smote the languid group with a shaft of light. The men rose at last, and, dismissing Elsie from the camp, took their turns in the pool. At seven Dougal announced breakfast.

At high noon, after a climb up the hill and an hour of poetry, Fancy was crowned queen of Piedra Pinta, with pomp and circumstance. She was invested with a crown of bay leaves and, for a scepter, the camp poker was placed in her hand. Dougal, as her prime minister, waxed merry, while her loyal lieges passed before her to do her homage. She greeted them one by one: The Duke of Russian Hill, with his tribute of three square meals per week; Lord of the Barbary Coast; Elsie, Lady of Lime Point, Mistress of the Robes; Sir Maxim the Monster, Court Painter; Sir Starr of Tar Flat, Laureate; and Mabel the Fair, Marchioness of Mount Tamalpais, First Lady of the Bedchamber, to keep her warm.

Architectural Shams

The Efforts of San Francisco Architects to Achieve the Impossible

The untraveled Californian is usually very well satisfied with himself and his environment, full of boasts of the climate and resources of his city, complacent when it is praised, but surprised and hurt when it is criticized. Years of contact with the independent manners and methods of the West have obliterated most of the finer sentiments of civic pride, he sees the rights of the public sacrificed by the corporations calmly enough if he is undisturbed in his own smaller tyrannies, and he acquires by a long acquaintance with abuses a fatalistic creed that the city is doing as well as might be expected. He forgets that one of the most beautiful sites the continent affords has been butchered into streets out of all harmony with topographical conditions, proud of the fact that so many acres have been reclaimed from the sand dunes and so many from the harbor. Miles of treeless, narrow streets content his soul, and he accepts the wooden boxes of the town without a protest against their ugliness, and calls them houses.

It is not so, however, with the tourist, whose sarcastic comments upon Western provincialism are usually as incisive as they are merited. To the stranger, San Francisco is par excellence the city of extremes. Romantic in situation and in the complexity of its population—cosmopolitan, picturesque, radiant with local color—it has, besides, the unloveliness of youth and crudity with the sordid and dreary aspect of the Philistine as well. The intelligent tourist who has done the "sights" of the town, who has seen the Cliff, the Park, and Chinatown, does not rely upon these stock shows for his estimate of the character of the city. He carries away with him, and describes first to his friends, Kearny Street and the Western Addition—the painted faces of the women and the abominations of our so-called "architecture," and if a moralist as well as an observer, he sees a subtle analogy between the two which proves San Francisco to be a City of Shams. For as the women seek to counterfeit the charms denied them, by the use of rouge and enamel, so the men daub and spatter redwood to imitate marble and granite, copy wood-carving by machinery, and carry the deceptions of concrete and cement to indecent limits.

There is surely no better test of civilization and culture than the outward and visible signs afforded by architecture. A man's house is his castle, if you will: he may dwell in a wilderness of plush, onyx and "antique oak" furniture, but the outside of his dwelling is a part of the city itself, and within the province of criticism. His neighbors, indeed, are likely to see more of the outside of his residence than the owner himself, who turns his back to it as he goes down the steps to hail the street car, and who often returns too late at night to feel a shudder at its horrors.

But the citizen's quarrel is, after all, not with the owner or resident, for if one's wife fancies a bright sunny exposure, if there are closets enough, electric lights and bells that really work—if the drainage is all that is to be desired, and the kitchen attractive, the busy father has little time to waste in aesthetics or appreciation of the facade. It is the architect who should bear the brunt of the reviling contempt of the passer-by. He foists these edifices upon the ignorant tenant, and perpetuates the inartistic reign of terror, leagued with the Contractor upon the Installment Plan.

There are all grades of misdemeanors against Art, but the chiefest of them is dishonesty. An architect may fail in producing a beautiful building, but if he has had an idea in his head that he has tried to embody, an honest failure has a certain claim to the forbearance of the critic. There is this pathos about many San Francisco buildings—the architects have failed through ignorance and inexperience, but they themselves, no doubt, are often the first to profit by the lesson of their own dissatisfaction.

There are, however, thousands of houses erected without the professional advice of the architect, and the contractor and his foreman conspire together in the interests of discord. And here the result is usually an over-elaboration of ornament; many a simple and inoffensive one has been ruined by "mill-work." It is the turning-lathe and the band-saw that have made the "ginger-bread" house possible. The foreman has his stock brackets, borders, and panels at hand, and tentatively places one upon the first corner or unoccupied space he sees on the house-front. The contractor upon the opposite side of the street takes his cigar from his lips, yells "all right," and the ornament is nailed forth-with. The process is repeated until the front is covered, and the result is an "artistic home,"—to be reproduced in half-tone in the Christmas edition of a local weekly as the "Residence of one of our most able and popular mer-chants." Bad as is this tawdry and conspicuous pretense, there is ignorance to excuse the effort, and the time may come when the laughter of the citizens may shake off the superfluous trimmings. Good taste proselytizes very slowly, but one of its first lessons is that of simplicity; that useless and meaningless ornament has no place in art. The virtue of omission should be easy to acquire, but the sin of omission in architecture is seldom found in the category of the offenses of the craft.

But there is no pardon or justification for dishonest construction, and there is no new town that is not given over to deception. And most often it is "an attempt to imitate something, which, if genuine, would not be appropriate." There is more than one two-story wooden house in the Western Addition that pretends to be marble—they can hardly be called lies, because they could never have attempted to deceive; there are, on the other hand, houses that, from the trivialness of their design, should have been executed in cast iron, though the imitation was never intended. Between these extremes may be found parodies of every shade of deceit; wire nettings covered with cement that masquerade as solid masonry, red paint striped to pass for brick-work, and so on to the scene-painting that simulates vines and balustrades in the Italian quarter. So much for falsity in materials—cheats too artless to fool children. There are similar frauds in construction, that pass for design, of which the massive un-supported corner column of the semi-colonial styles is the type, the foot barely holding to the base with its toes. Arches supported from above may be seen in almost any house in process of erection—brackets neither useful nor or-namental, nailed on, as if only to spite the commonplace.

By the column one may identify the degree of debasement to which the whole house has fallen. In the early days the French influence was still felt, and the bay-window mansion of modest brown was treated with an innocent Corinthian charm. The portico was discreetly conventional, the formal ele-ments of the order were carefully preserved to the very module. Base, shaft and capital, moulding, arch and cornice were quite according to law, and the carving was all the hand work of the artisan. A few of these are still preserved, and shame the modern vogue. Notice the columns of later edifices, and one may see the decrescence of taste; they are shorter or longer, bellied or concave, encircled with rings capped with grotesque forms of infinite insanity; they become, in fact, "colyums," and the structure is distorted into a sort of appropriate ugliness. Bad design, dishonest construction, vicious in point of view of Art or Truth—such are three-quarters of the houses of San Francisco.

It would be hard to select the prize monstrosity. It should have the conical corner-tower, it should be built of at least three incongruous materias, or better, imitations thereof; it should have its window-openings absolutely haphazard; it should represent parts of every known and unknown order of architecture; it should be so plastered with ornament as to conceal the theory of its construction; it should be a restless, uncertain, frightful collection of details, giving the effect of a nightmare about to explode. It should be all this and more. Who shall choose amongst them? For there are a thousand such in San Francisco,— it is a city of wood, where all things are possible!

George Sterling.

 **X**

Two Poems by George Sterling

George Sterling was a complex man living in a complicated era of transition. He came to San Francisco in 1890, sent by his family after he had attempted to burn down a Presbyterian Church (George was a Catholic) in his home town of Sag Harbor, New York. Once in California, he went to work in his uncle's real estate office, married his secreaty, and seemed destined for the quiet life of a rising young executive. But during the 1890s, Sterling met three people who would decisively change his whole professional life. Joaquin Miller, the colorful poet and wild-man, encouraged him to write poetry. Ambrose Bierce, by this time the Grand Moghul of San Francisco's literary life, schooled him in the art of writing. Jack London introduced him to socialism and, more importantly, to the inspirational powers of hard drinking. Thus primed, George Sterling set out to become one of the outstanding lyricists on the West Coast.

Sterling's poetry may strike the modern reader as somewhat affected and old-fashioned. Certainly Ambrose Bierce was never able to teach him to sow with the hand instead of the whole sack. But underneath the profusion of all-too-lovely metaphors we can discern genuine passion. We can get a hint of the depth of his attachment to his adopted home in "Cool Grey City of Love"—perhaps the best poem ever written to San Francisco. "The Wine of Wizardry," though, shows Sterling in his more characteristic mood. Intoxication, beauty, and evil are brewed together in the manner of Tennyson's "Lucretius" and the French Symbolist and Decadent schools of writing. Surely written under the influence or recollection of wine and opium (see line seven), "The Wine of Wizardry" gives us the best of Sterling's consummate handling of rhyme and meter and his skill in conjuring up exotic fantasies from the semiconscious mind.

The Cool, Grey City of Love

Tho I die on a distant strand,
And they give me a grave in that land,
Yet carry me back to my own city!
Carry me back to her grace and pity!
For I think I could not rest
Afar from her mighty breast.

Sterling, George. "The Cool, Grey City of Love." San Francisco: 1920.

She is fairer than others are
Whom they sing the beauty of.
Her heart is a song and a star—
My cool, grey city of love.

Tho they tear the rose from her brow,
To her is ever my vow;
Ever to her I give my duty—
First in rapture and first in beauty,
Wayward, passionate, brave,
Glad of the life God gave.
The sea-winds are her kiss,
And the sea-gull is her dove;
Cleanly and strong she is—
My cool, grey city of love.

The winds of the Future wait
At the iron walls of her Gate,
And the western ocean breaks in thunder,
And the western stars go slowly under,
And her gaze is ever West
In the dream of her young unrest.
Her sea is a voice that calls,
And her star a voice above,
And her wind a voice on her walls—
My cool, grey city of love.

Tho they stay her feet at the dance,
In her is the far romance.
Under the rain of winter falling,
Vine and rose will await recalling.
Tho the dark be cold and blind,
Yet her sea-fog's touch is kind,
And her mightier caress
Is joy and the pain thereof;
And great is thy tenderness,
O cool, grey city of love!

A Wine of Wizardry

"When mountains were stained as with wine
By the dawning of Time, and as wine
Were the seas."

AMBROSE BIERCE

Sterling, George. "A Wine of Wizardry." San Francisco: 1909.

Without, the battlements of sunset shine,
'Mid domes the sea-winds rear and overwhelm.
Into a crystal cup the dusky wine
I pour, and, musing at so rich a shrine,
I watch the star that haunts its ruddy gloom.
Now Fancy, express of a purpled realm,
Awakes with brow caressed by poppy-bloom,
And wings in sudden dalliance her flight
To strands where opals of the shattered light
Gleam in the wind-strewn foam, and maidens flee
A little past the striving billows' reach,
Or seek the russet mosses of the sea,
And wrinkled shells that lure along the beach,
And please the heart of Fancy; yet she turns,
Tho trembling, to a grotto rosy-sparred,
Where wattled monsters redly gape, that guard
A cowled magician peering on the damned
Through vials in which a splendid poison burns,
Sifting Satanic gules athwart his brow.
So Fancy will not gaze with him, and now
She wanders to an iceberg oriflammed
With rayed, auroral guidons of the North—
Where artic elves have hidden wintry gems
And treasuries of frozen anadems,
Alight with timid sapphires of the snow.
But she would dream of warmer gems, and so
Ere long her eyes in fastnesses look forth
O'er blue profounds mysterious whence glow
The coals of Tartarus on the moonless air,
As Titans plan to storm Olympus' throne,
'Mid pulse of dungeoned forges down the stunned,
Undominated firmament, and glare
Of Cyclopean furnaces unsunned.
Then hastens she in refuge to a lone,
Immortal garden of the eastern hours,
Where Dawn upon a pansy's breast has laid
A single tear, and whence the wind has flown
And left a silence. Far on shadowy tow'rs
Droop blazoned banners, and the woodland shade,
With leafy flames and dyes autumnal hung,
Makes beautiful the twilight of the year.
For this the fays will dance, for elfin cheer,

Within a dell where some mad girl has flung
A bracelet that the painted lizards fear—
Red pyres of muffled light! Yet Fancy spurns
The revel, and to eastward hazard turns,
And glaring beacons of the Soldan's shores,
When in a Syrian treasure-house she pours,
From caskets rich and amethystine urns,
Dull fires of dusty jewels that have bound
The brows of naked Ashtaroth around.
Or hushed, at fall of some disastrous night,
When sunset, like a crimson throat to Hell,
Is cavernous, she marks the seaward flight
Of homing dragons dark upon the West;
Till, drawn by tales the winds of ocean tell,
And mute amid the splendors of her quest,
To some red city of the Djinns she flees
And, lost in palaces of silence, sees
Within a porphyry crypt the murderous light
Of garnet-crusted lamps whereunder sit
Perturbéd men that tremble at a sound,
And ponder words on ghastly vellum writ,
In vipers' blood, to whispers from the night—
Infernal rubrics, sung to Satan's might,
Or chaunted to the Dragon in his gyre.
But she would blot from memory the sight,
And seeks a stainéd twilight of the South,
Where crafty gnomes with scarlet eyes conspire
To quench Aldebaran's affronting fire,
Low sparkling just beyond their cavern's mouth,
Above a wicked queen's unhallowed tomb.
There lichens brown, incredulous of fame,
Whisper to veinéd flowers her body's shame,
'Mid stillness of all pageantries of bloom.
Within, lurk orbs that graven monsters clasp;
Red-embered rubies smolder in the gloom,
Betrayed by lamps that nurse a sullen flame,
And livid roots writhe in the marble's grasp,
As moaning airs invoke the conquered rust
Of lordly helms made equal in the dust.
Without, where baleful cypresses make rich
The bleeding sun's phantasmagoric gules,
Are fungus-tapers of the twilight witch
(Seen by the bat above unfathomed pools)

And tiger-lilies known to silent ghouls,
Whose king has digged a somber carcanet
And necklaces with fevered opals set.
But Fancy, well affrighted at his gaze,
Flies to a violet headland of the West,
About whose base the sun-lashed billows blaze,
Ending in precious foam their fatal quest,
As far below the deep-hued ocean molds,
With waters' toil and polished pebbles' fret,
The tiny twilight in the jacinth set,
The wintry orb the moonstone-crystal holds,
Snapt coral twigs and winy agates wet,
Translucencies of jasper, and the folds
Of banded onyx, and vermilion breast
Of Cinnabar. Anear on orange sands,
With prows of bronze the sea-stained galleys rest,
And swarthy mariners from alien strands
Stare at the red horizon, for their eyes
Behold a beacon burn on evening skies,
As fed with sanguine oils at touch of night.
Forth from that pharos-flame a radiance flies,
To spill in vinous gleams on ruddy decks;
And overside, when leap the startled waves
And crimson bubbles rise from battle-wrecks.
Unresting hydras wrought of bloody light
Dip to the ocean's phosphorescent caves.
So Fancy's carvel seeks an isle afar,
Led by the Scorpion's rubescent star,
Until in templed zones she smiles to see
Black incense glow, and scarlet-bellied snakes
Sway to the tawny flutes of sorcery.
There priestesses in purple robes hold each
A sultry garnet to the sea-linkt sun,
Or, just before the colored morning shakes
A splendor on the ruby-sanded beach,
Cry unto Betelgeuse a mystic word.
But Fancy, amorous of evening, takes
Her flight to groves whence lustrous rivers run,
Thro hyacinth, a minister wall to gird,
Where, in the hushed cathedral's jeweled gloom,
Ere Faith return, and azure censers fume,
She kneels, in solemn quietude, to mark
The suppliant day from gorgeous oriels float

And altar-lamps immure the deathless spark;
Till, all her dreams made rich with fervent hues,
She goes to watch, beside a lurid moat,
The kingdoms of the afterglow suffuse
A sentinel mountain stationed toward the night—
Whose broken tombs betray their ghastly trust,
Till bloodshot gems stare up like eyes of lust.
And now she knows, at agate portals bright,
How Circe and her poisons have a home,
Carved in one ruby that a Titan lost,
Where icy philters brim with scarlet foam,
'Mid hiss of oils in burnished caldrons tost,
While thickly from her prey his life-tide drips,
In turbid dyes that tinge her torture-dome,
As craftily she gleans her deadly dews,
With gyving spells not Pluto's queen can use,
Or listens to her victim's moan, and sips
Her darkest wine, and smiles with wicked lips.
Nor comes a god with any power to break
The red alembics whence her gleaming broths
Obscenely fume, as asp or adder froths,
To lethal mists whose writhing vapors make
Dim augury, till shapes of men that were
Point, weeping, at tremendous dooms to be,
When pillared pomps and thrones supreme shall stir,
Unstable as the foam-dreams of the sea.

But Fancy still is fugitive, and turns
To caverns where a demon altar burns,
And Satan, yawning on his brazen seat,
Fondles a screaming thing his fiends have flayed,
Ere Lilith come his indolence to greet,
Who leads from Hell his whitest queens, arrayed
In chains so heated at their master's fire
That one new-damned had thought their bright attire
Indeed were coral, till the dazzling dance
So terribly that brilliance shall enhance.
But Fancy is unsatisfied, and soon
She seeks the silence of a vaster night,
Where powers of wizardry, with faltering sight
(Whenas the hours creep farthest from the noon)

Genthe, Arnold, *As I Remember.* Copyright 1936 by The John Day Company.

Seek by the glow-worm's lantern cold and dull
A crimson spider hidden in a skull,
Or search for mottled vines with berries white,
Where waters mutter to the gibbous moon.
There, clothed in cerements of malignant light,
A sick enchantress scans the dark to curse,
Beside a caldron vext with harlot's blood,
The stars of that red Sign which spells her doom.

Then Fancy cleaves the palmy skies adverse
To sunset barriers. By the Ganges' flood,
She sees, in her dim temple, Siva loom
And, visioned with a monstrous ruby, glare
On distant twilight where the burning-ghaut
Is lit with glowering pyres that seem the eyes
Of her abhorrent dragon-worms that bear
The pestilence, by Death in darkness wrought.
So Fancy's wings forsake the Asian skies,
And now her heart is curious of halls
In which dead Merlin's prowling ape has spilt
A vial squat whose scarlet venom crawls
To ciphers bright and terrible, that tell
The sins of demons and the encharneled guilt
That breathes a phantom at whose cry the owl,
Malignly mute above the midnight well,
Is dolorous, and Hecate lifts her cowl
To mutter swift a minatory rune;
And, ere the tomb-thrown echoings have ceased,
The blue-eyed vampire, sated at her feast,
Smiles bloodily against the leprous moon.

But evening now is come, and Fancy folds
Her splendid plumes, nor any longer holds
Adventurous quest o'er stained lands and seas—
Fled to a star above the sunset lees,
O'er onyx waters stilled by gorgeous oils
That toward the twilight reach emblazoned coils.
And I, albeit Merlin-sage has said,
"A vyper lurketh in ye wine-cuppe redde,"
Gaze pensively upon the way she went,
Drink at her font, and smile as one content.

Bohemians and Writers: a group portrait at the Bohemian Club in the Redwood Grove. From the left, top row: Harry Wilson, Frank Pixley, Jack London, Edwin Markham. Second row: Charles K. Field, "Mr. Grovenor," Richard Lully, George Ade. Ernest Peixotto, Rufus Steele. Seated: George Sterling.

XI

Earthquake Writing

The lamented and celebrated fire and earthquake of 1906 drew forth some
of the most heartfelt writing of San Francisco's history. Because the disaster
was communal as well as personal, writers could expand the theme of their
own loss into a story of far greater proportions.

But, strange to say, most of the writing did not dwell exclusively on the
tragic aspects of the cataclysm. The famous poem by Lawrence Harris is
fiercely proud. He refuses to accept any manner of sympathy or offers of
assistance. Nothing can take his San Francisco from him—not earthquake
or Oakland.

The Field verse is proud, but in a different sense. The speaker is a lower-
class Irishwoman, sensible and strong. She exults in the new democracy
thrust upon the people by the common disaster. But she does not simply
glory in the fall of the rich; she realizes that the reacquaintance of rich and
poor is "doin' the both of us good." Not until the 1960s will San Francisco
again feel such bonds of brother- and sisterhood.

Arnold Genthe, the world-famous photographer, gives us a graphic narrative of one man's harrowing experiences and losses during those days. It is
to Genthe's credit, though, that he could see the humorous side to many of
the events, even while he himself had been utterly wiped out by the
catastrophe. An artist to the end, Genthe is partly reconciled to the calamity
by the sudden appearance of endless new subjects to photograph.

"The Damndest Finest Ruins"

Lawrence W. Harris

Put me somewhere west of East Street where there's nothin' left but dust,
Where the lads are all a'bustlin' and where everything's gone bust,
Where the buildings that are standin' sort of blink and blindly stare
At the damndest finest ruins ever gazed on anywhere.

Bully ruins—bricks and wall—through the night I've heard you call
Sort of sorry for each other 'cause you had to burn and fall,
From the Ferries of Van Ness you're a Godforsaken mess,
But the damndest finest ruins—nothin' more or nothin' less.

Harris, Lawrence. "The Damndest Finest Ruins." San Francisco: Ames Harris Neville Co.,
1906.

281

Ruins of a trolley car, Market Street, 1906.

The strangers who come rubberin' and a'huntin' souvenirs,
The fools, they try to tell us it will take a million years
Before we can get started, so why don't we come to live
And build our homes and factories upon land they've got to give.

"Got to give!" Why, on my soul, I would rather bore a hole
And live right in the ashes than ever more to Oakland's mole,
If they'd all give me my pick of their buildin's proud and slick
In the damndest finest ruins still I'd rather be a brick!

Barriers Burned
(A Rhyme of the San Francisco Breadline)
Charles K. Field

It ain't such a terrible long time ago
That Mrs. Van Bergen and me

I wish to thank the following publishers for permission to use the following material: Sunset Magazine: "Barriers Burned," by Charles Field.
Sunset Magazine. San Francisco: 1906.

Cable car tracks wrenched by the earthquake, 1906.

Though livin' near by to each other, y' know,
    Was strangers, for all ye could see,
For she had a grand house an' horses to drive,
    An' a wee rented cottage was mine,
But now we need rations to keep us alive
    An' we're standin' together in line.

An' Mrs. Van Bergen she greets me these days
    With a smile an' a nod of the head;
"Ah, Mrs. McGinnis, how are you?" she says,
    "An' do you like Government bread?"
She fetches a bag made of crockydile skin
    An' I've got a sack when we meet,
But the same kind of coffee an' crackers goes in,
    An' it's all of it cooked in the street.

Sure, Mrs. Van Bergen is takin' it fine,

Ye'd think she was used to the food;
We're gettin' acquainted, a-standin' in line,
An' it's doing' the both of us good.
An' Mr. Van Bergen and Michael, my man,
(They've always been friendly, the men)
They're gettin' together and layin' a plan
For buildin' the city again!

Earthquake and Fire by Arnold Genthe

One of the great social events of the opera season in the spring of 1906 was the joint appearance of Enrico Caruso and Olive Fremstand in *Carmen*. A large and enthusiastic audience filled the house for this gala occasion. It was the night of April 17th. After a quiet supper party with some friends, I walked home and went to bed with the music of *Carmen* still singing in my ears. It seemed as if I had scarcely been asleep when I was awakened by a terrifying sound—the Chinese porcelains that I had been collecting in the last years had crashed to the floor. (My interest in Chinese porcelains ever since then has been purely platonic.) The whole house was creaking and shaking, the chandelier was swinging like a pendulum, and I felt as if I were on a ship tossed about by a rough sea. "This can't go on much longer," I said to myself. "When a house shakes like this, the ceiling is bound to collapse. As soon as the plaster begins to fall, I'll cover my head and accept what comes."

An ominous quiet followed. I was about to get up when I found Hamada, my Japanese servant, standing beside me. An earthquake was, of course, no new experience for him, but now he looked thoroughly frightened and was as pale as a Japanese can be. "Master," he said, "very bad earthquake—many days nothing to eat—I go, yes." Before I could say anything he was on his way downstairs. I looked at the clock; the time was a quarter past five. I looked out of the window and saw a number of men and women, half-dressed, rushing to the middle of the street for safety. Pushing his way through them, with a sack of flour over his shoulder and carrying a basket of provisions, was Hamada.

I went to the top floor to see what had happened to my studio. The chimney had fallen through the roof, most of the book shelves had collapsed and the books were buried under mounds of plaster from the wall and ceiling. A sixteenth-century wood sculpture of Buddha had landed right side up and stood unharmed and inscrutable in the midst of the debris—"serene, indifferent of fate."

The earth continued to indulge in periodic tremors, though less violently. I started to get dressed and decided that the most suitable "earthquake attire" would be my khaki riding things—I was to live in them for weeks.

The streets presented a weird appearance, mothers and children in their nightgowns, men in pajamas and dinner coats, women scantily dressed with evening wraps hastily thrown over them. Many ludicrous sights met the eye: an old lady carrying a large bird cage with four kittens inside, while the original occupant, the parrot, perched on her hand; a man tenderly holding a pot of calla lilies, muttering to himself; a scrub woman, in one hand a new broom and in the other a large black hat with ostrich plumes; a man in an old-fashioned nightshirt and swallow tails, being startled when a friendly policeman spoke to him, "Say, Mister, I guess you better put on some pants." . . . But there was no hysteria, no signs of real terror or despair. Nor did buildings show an alarming evidence of destruction; here and there parts of damaged walls had fallen into the streets, and most chimneys had collapsed. At Delmonico's, the front of one of the rooms on the third floor had fallen into the street. A chair with some clothes had been carried with it. The distressed owner called out to a passing workman, "Do you want to make $20?" "Sure," he replied, "what is it?" "See that suit there? I want you to bring it up to me here." Just then another shock occurred. "Ah, you better come and get it yourself."

After wandering about for a while, I went to the house of some dear friends of mine, Milton and Mabel Bremer (she is now married to my old friend Bertram Alanson). I found them calmly sitting on the front steps. The one thing that Mabel was apparently most anxious to save was a pair of evening slippers—a purchase of the day before—which she thrust into my large coat pockets. But it did not save them. I left them at my studio when I returned there later and they were burned with all my possessions.

We decided that it would be a good idea to have some breakfast and went to the St. Francis Hotel which had not been damaged. When we arrived we saw that we were not the only ones who had had the brilliant idea of breakfasting there. The lobby and the dining room were crowded. Near the entrance we saw Enrico Caruso with a fur coat over his pajamas, smoking a cigarette and muttering, " 'Ell of a place! 'Ell of a place!" He had been through many earthquakes in his native Italy but this one was too much for him. It appeared that when he was awakened by the shock, he had tried his vocal cords without success. " 'Ell of a place! I never come back here." And he never did.

Inside the hotel, people in all kinds of attire from evening clothes to nightgowns went milling about. There was no gas or electricity, but somehow hot coffee was available which, with bread and butter and fruit, made a satisfying breakfast. When I asked the waiter for a check he announced with a wave of his hand, "No charge today, sir. Everyone is welcome as long as things hold out."

After seeing my friends home, I went back to my studio to get a camera. The one thought uppermost in my mind was not to bring some of my possessions to a place of safety but to make photographs of the scenes I had been witnessing, the effects of the earthquake and the beginning of the conflagration that had started in various parts of the city. I found that my hand cameras had been so damaged by the falling plaster as to be rendered useless. I went to Montgomery Street to the shop of George Kahn, my dealer, and asked him to lend me a camera. "Take anything you want. This place is going to burn up anyway." I selected the best small camera, a 3A Kodak Special. I stuffed my pockets with films and started out. It was only then that I began to realize the extent of the disaster which had befallen the city. The fire had started simultaneously in many different places when the housewives had attempted to get breakfast for their families, not realizing what menance the ruined chimneys were. All along the skyline as far as eye could see, clouds of smoke and flames were bursting forth. The work of the fire department was badly hampered, as the water mains had burst.

By this time the city had been put under martial law with General Funston in supreme command. He decided to check the progress of the conflagration by dynamiting a block in advance of the fire in order to create a breach over which the flames could not leap. All day and night the detonations resounded in one's ears and yet the fire continued to make headway. By noon the whole town was in flight. Thousands were moving toward the ferry hoping to get across the bay to Oakland or Alameda. On all streets leading to Golden Gate Park, there was a steady stream of men, women and children. Since all wagons or automobiles had been commandeered by the military authorities, only makeshift vehicles were available. Baby carriages and toy wagons, carts constructed out of boxes and wheels, were used to transport groceries, kitchen utensils, clothes and blankets; trunks mounted on roller skates or even without them were being dragged along by ropes. No one who witnessed these scenes can ever forget the rumbling noise of the trunks drawn along the sidewalks—a sound to which the detonations of the blasting furnished a fitting contrapuntal accompaniment.

Farther out on Geary and Sutter Streets, men and women cooked on improvised stoves on the sidewalks and as the crowds passed they called out invitations to stop for a rest and a cup of coffee. Up on the hill the wealthy were taking strangers into their homes, regardless of any risk they were running. I recall the picture of Henry J. Crocker laughing heartily as he carried the pails of water from the faucet to his garden to a little iron stove, probably one of his children's toys, set up by the curb in front of his red stone mansion.

I have often wondered, thinking back, what it is in the mind of the individual that so often makes him feel himself immune to the disaster that may be going on all around him. So many whom I met during the day seemed completely unconscious that the fire which was spreading through the city was bound to overtake their own homes and possessions. I know